Multihull Seamanship

Multihull Seamanship

Michael McMullen

David McKay Company, Inc.
New York

MULTIHULL SEAMANSHIP

First American Edition, 1976

Library of Congress Catalog Card Number: 75-37486
ISBN: 0-679-50622-5

MANUFACTURED IN THE UNITED STATES OF AMERICA

Foreword

By Robin Knox-Johnston, C.B.E.

Multihulls have begun only recently to establish themselves on the yachting scene, and the art of sailing them in the modern sense is only some thirty years old. The recent rapid expansion in the multihull fleets of Europe, North America and Australasia, has been due to a small band of adventurous enthusiasts, so there is no large core of experts with their experience for the newcomer to draw upon for guidance.

Many multihulls are still home built by people who have chosen this lighter form of boat, as it appears to present fewer problems for the amateur boat builder than a monohull. Many of these amateurs have little idea of the sort of stresses their boat will have to withstand in a sea, nor how to sail a craft whose sailing characteristics differ markedly from those of a monohull. This has lead, inevitably, to a number of well publicised accidents, due largely either to poor boat handling or to badly designed and constructed boats, which has reflected unfairly upon the multihull concept.

Until the day arrives when every yacht club has a small fleet of multihulls as a matter of course, the build up of experience and the increased safety that naturally goes with it, is bound to be a slow process.

Mike McMullen has done as much as anybody to show that a good multihull properly handled can make coastal and ocean voyages in perfect safety. He built up an enviable reputation in short-handed races in monohulls before transferring to multihulls in which he is now one of the acknowledged experts in offshore racing and cruising. In this book he is passing on his considerable experience, which will provide invaluable guidance to the veteran and novice alike. His comments upon seamanship and safety should be hung up in every multihull's cabin.

A book that covers the handling of a multihull by an experienced user has been long overdue, and will hopefully hasten the improvement in the standards of seamanship. I am particularly grateful to Mike for writing it, as it gives some idea of why he is so hard to beat!

Contents

Foreword by Robin Knox-Johnston, C.B.E.   5

Introduction   11

1. History   17
2. Design and Construction Comparisons   49
3. Basic Seamanship   77
4. Racing   100
5. Cruising   109
6. Accidents and Safety   125
7. Heavy Weather   162

Appendix I   Guide to International Offshore Multihull Rule
by Major-General R. H. Farrant, C.B. and V. Stern   182

Appendix II   Boundary of Short Handed Sailing Performances
by G. Boxall, M.A. (Cantab)   184

Index   198

List of Illustrations

1. A double canoe of 96 ft length   16
2. A schooner rigged double canoe   18
3. *Tongiaki*   19
4. Plan and bow view of the *Tongiaki*   20
5. Fijian single outriggers racing   21
6. Micronesian proa   22
7. Tacking a single outrigger   22
8. Indonesian double outrigger   23
9. Model of *Invention II*   25
10. Rig of *Invention II*   25
11. Was this how *Experiment* met her end?   27
12. John Mackenzie's 1868 catamaran   28
13. *Amaryllis*   29
14. Plans of a Herreshoff catamaran   28
15. The scow *Dominion*   30
16. *Kaimiloa*   32
17. Plans of *Kaimiloa*   33
18. *Manu Kai*   33
19. Views of *Manu Kai*   34
20. A Shearwater   35
21. *Ananda*   36
22. *Copula*   37
23. Don Robertson's *Fun*   38
24. *Toria*   39
25. Tabarlay on board *Toria*   41
26. *Pen Duick IV*   42
27. *Cheers*   43
28. *Yaksha*   44
29. *Koala III*   44
30. *Victress*   45
31. James Wharram's *Rongo*   46
32. *Rehu Moana*   47
33. Damage to *Tahiti Bill* after a collision   48
34. Beachability. *Three Cheers* on a Spanish beach   50
35. *Triptych*   51

36. *Crossbow* 52
37. *Snow Goose* 55
38. *Architeuthis* 55
39. Wave interaction 57
40. Hull sections 58
41. Long overhangs of *British Oxygen* 59
42. Sponsons fitted to *Manureva* to prevent pitchpoling 60
43. Plans of *Three Cheers* 61
44. Points in the outriggers of a trimaran 61
45. *British Oxygen*'s flexible connecting structure 62
46. If the bottom cross beam is too close to the sea 63
47. The advantages of a curved wing connecting structure 64
48. The outriggers of a trimaran should just 'kiss' the sea 65
49. The staying of a flexible structure such as *British Oxygen* 67
50. The staying of a trimaran's mast 69
51. Foam sandwich construction of *Three Legs of Man* 71
52. Large windows in an offshore yacht 75
53. Sailing stern first at 3 knots 80
54. The V-shaped hull without boards 81
55. The cutter headsail arrangement is very effective on a fast multihull 87
56. The low aspect rigs of *Three Cheers* and *Gulf Streamer* 88
57. *Sidewinder*'s masts were too close together 90
58. The high aspect rig of *British Oxygen* 91
59. Luff rope and slides 93
60. *Trifle*'s mainsail uses bamboo poles for battens 95
61. Using a spinnaker without a pole 96
62. Using the end of an outrigger to tack down a ghoster 99
63. Tacking downwind 101
64. Courses of *British Oxygen* and *Three Cheers* in the fourth leg of the Round Britain Race 1974 102
65. The deliberate use of leeway 105
66. Courses of *Three Cheers* and *Three Legs of Man* from the Lizard to Wolf Rock in the 1973 Crystal Trophy 107
67. Problems for a multihull at anchor in a tideway 111
68. The use of two anchors in a tideway 113
69. An offset outboard engine will effect turning circles 115
70. Drying out does not always go to plan 116
71. The Jumar 117
72. A single handed method of climbing a mast 118
73. A single handed method of climbing a mast 118
74. A single handed method of climbing a mast 119
75. Use of the Jumar in climbing a mast with hoop steps 121

76. Wind vanes are harder to use on fast multihulls   122
77. Solar cell panel   123
78. Auto pilot   123
79. Tom Corkill's capsize in *Clipper*   127
80. Nick Keig's *Tom Tom* ashore on the Isle of Man   129
81. Bill Howell's *Golden Cockerel*   132
82. *Golden Cockerel* overturned off the Isle of Wight   134
83. Howell and Hartman are picked up   135
84. *Triple Arrow*   138
85. *Triple Arrow* under tow after capsize   139
86. Hepplewhite automatic sheet release gear   141
87. The weight and windage of a masthead float   142
88. *Triple Arrow*'s capsize hatch   143
89. Quick release cleats   144
90. A spinnaker can cause a capsize if the yacht broaches   145
91. The capsize of *Apache Sundancer*   147
92. *Apache Sundancer*   149
93. *Triple Arrow* in the inverted position floated extremely high   151
94. Man overboard from *Three Cheers*   155
95. *Triple Arrow* under jury rig   158
96. Repairing an outrigger with the help of a dinghy   160
97. A chain lightning conductor   161
98. Use of a sea anchor from the quarter   167
99. *Gancia Girl* in an Atlantic storm   169
100. When a catamaran surfs sideways in a storm   173
101. Lying a-hull in a storm   175
102. Alain Colas   178
103. Storm seas   179
104. Storm seas   180

Graphs

          Boundary of shorthanded sailing performances   185
1–2   Round Britain Race 1974   187
3–4   Round Britain Race 1974   188
5–6   Round Britain Race 1974   189
7   OSTAR 1972   190
8–9   OSTAR 1972   191
10–11   Round Britain Race 1970   193
12–13   Round Britain Race 1970   194
14–15   Round Britain Race 1970   195
16   OSTAR 1968   196
17–18   OSTAR 1968   197

Introduction

My first yacht was a 25 ft. monohull sloop called *Binkie* and in 1970 I sailed her in the second *Observer* Round Britain Race. Ably crewed by Martin Read, we finished by winning the handicap prize. Neither of us then had a good word to say about multi-hulls and I remember pontificating at several bars to fellow sailors saying, 'you will never get me out in one of those machines . . . unsafe . . . unstable . . . held together by bits of string . . . unfit to cross the Thames and bloody ugly!' Like thousands of traditional monohull men, I was prepared to condemn without trial, a type of vessel about which I knew nothing and had never sailed. One of the factors that put me off was their bad 'track record', for in 1970 the history of their accidents was extensive. Many of the multihulls in the race had constant trouble and one catamaran capsized off the Isle of Wight in a force 8 gale. Several looked ugly and there is nothing more offensive to the eye than an ugly yacht. Like aeroplanes, unattractive yachts tend to be inefficient and sometimes dangerous.

Still without setting foot on one, my prejudice against multihulls continued unabated for the next year. By December 1971 *Binkie II*, my second boat, was launched. She was built for the purpose of winning the under 35 ft. prize in the 1972 *Observer* Singlehanded Trans-Atlantic Race. Needless to say she was a monohull, a sloop of the Contessa 32 class, very strong and quite heavy.

As the yachts for the 'Singlehanded' assembled in Plymouth it was quite obvious that there was going to be a large multihull entry, mainly of trimarans. I had to admit to a considerable latent curiosity about them and it was with alacrity that I accepted from Tom Follett the offer of a day sail on the American trimaran *Three Cheers*. I shall never forget the experience. We got up to a speed of eighteen knots in a fifteen knot wind. I simply could not comprehend how a yacht could travel so fast. She was skimming across the water like a beautiful yellow bird with a total lack of effort that left me breathless. Attractive to look at, obviously strongly built by her designer Dick Newick, she was a joy to sail. From that day onward my fascination with these unconventional yachts began.

After the 'Singlehanded', thanks to the kindness of my father's cousin Paul Mellon who bought *Three Cheers*, I sailed her back to England and from that day onwards have sailed entirely on multihulls.

This book is primarily about seamanship and is intended as a book of reference and practical advice for people who intend to put to sea in a multihull.

I have tried to be unbiased and I totally accept the fact that not all multihulls are as good as many of their designers and enthusiastic supporters claim. In my opinion many are badly designed, shoddily built, extremely ugly and in some cases dangerous. That is a condemning statement but, sadly, it is true. The poor building, in particular, of certain craft has done more to damage the multihull cause than anything. Because of this I have included a chapter on design and construction which will, I hope, give the potential multihull novice an idea of what to look for in a good yacht.

I could not have written the chapters on Accidents and Heavy Weather without the generous help of those people who sent me detailed descriptions of actual incidents that they had experienced and to them I am greatly indebted. I have in the last chapter put forward indications as to the correct course of action to follow in heavy weather as there is great danger in influencing the reader to follow a 'fixed line' course of action. The alternatives vary from situation to situation and he must decide for himself on the best tactic to follow in his particular craft.

There will always be a risk of turning a multihull over in much the same way as there is always the risk of crashing a motor car. In an offshore race when the blood runs quickly from the thrill of competition, this risk is increased and there is much truth in the old saying 'the nearer the bone, the sweeter the meat'. Skill is the key to success and that skill lies in going near the limit.

Because of this I believe that sailing a fast offshore multihull requires a higher standard of seamanship than a monohull. Everything happens faster and the crew's reactions have to be quicker. Moreover, there are many evolutions which, on the whole, require more skill than a monohull. As a result, I have included a chapter on Basic Seamanship and another one on Racing and Cruising.

The first chapter on history is included from an interest point of view, largely because the subject fascinated me and I wanted to write about it!

I must admit that my experience of sailing catamarans is not as great as sailing trimarans. I have not, I am ashamed to say, yet crossed an ocean in a catamaran or weathered a full Atlantic storm in one. Despite this, I feel I am qualified to write what I have written, particularly as I have been guided throughout by that extremely experienced catamaran sailor Don Robertson who has checked the manuscript and added invaluable advice and information throughout. Moreover, Bill Howell, another very experienced seaman and catamaran sailor, has given me extremely relevant information with regards to the last two chapters which filled the greatest practical gap in my knowledge.

I have frequently heard people compare the multihull's present stage of development to that of the aeroplane in the 1920s. I think that the comparison is a good one as, compared to the development of the single hulled yacht, these vessels are still in their infancy. Moreover, their future potential for speed increases annually as design improves and man discovers new and lighter methods of construction which retain a high level of strength.

For me, the beauty of the multihull lies in its speed and ease of motion—not in its cruising caravan capability where maximum use is made of available space and performance is similar to or in some cases worse than a monohull. This type of vessel, particularly the under 30 ft. size, does provide cheap floating accommodation but usually has a poor turn of speed and is so appalling to windward in anything over force 6 that it can become dangerous if it is caught on a lee shore in a seaway. So— 'you pays your money and takes your choice'—multihulls become safer as their size increases (provided that they are of good design) but, of course, they cost more.

Finally, it is worth remembering that these craft have been around for thousands of years and the Polynesians successfully colonised a large part of the Pacific Ocean with their use. They would not have been able to do this had they not been first class seamen and today's modern multihull sailor should heed their example. Sadly, too many multihulls come to grief because of the poor seamanship of their crews and every accident retards progress. So remember—however well designed or built any yacht is, the things that will ensure its safety—and more to the point, the safety of the crew—are **experience**, **understanding** and above all **GOOD SEAMANSHIP**.

Acknowledgements

Numerous people have helped me with this book which could not have been written without their assistance.

My thanks in particular go to Don Robertson and Dick Newick who read through the manuscript in whole or part and offered invaluable advice and comments. General Ralph Farrant and Gerry Boxall's respective appendices are extremely interesting and the result of much hard work which has produced two fascinating documents. Gerry Boxall's appendix should provide an intriguing 'measuring stick' for yachts, both monohulls and multihulls, in years to come.

The following people have all contributed to the content of the book in one way or another and I am much indebted to them for their time and kindness in so doing:

Colour Sergeant J. Allen, Royal Marines, Gerry Boxall, Mike Butterfield, Alain Colas, K. Adlard Coles, Ann Coles, Brian Cooke, Michael Ellison and the Amateur Yacht Research Society, General Ralph Farrant, Tom Follett, Colin Forbes, David Goddard, Bob Harris, Bill Howell, Nick Keig, Derek Kelsall, Major E. Kirby, M.C., curator of the regimental museum of the Royal Welch Fusiliers, Robin Knox-Johnston, C.B.E., David Lewis, Martin Minter-Kemp, Jean Luc de Moras, Président of the Association des Propriétaires de Catamarans et Trimarans (AS.CA.T.), Jim Morris, Dick Newick, Roland Prout, Martin Read, Don Robertson, Philip Weld, Paul Weychan, James Wharram.

I have had invaluable assistance with the thankless task of collecting photographs from Shirley Smith of *The Observer*, Bob Salmon, and the Royal Marine Commando News Team in Plymouth who have done everything in their power to help. My thanks are also due to the Royal Society for allowing me to research thoroughly Sir William Petty's catamarans and to photograph their unique model. Andrew Spedding and Paul Brookes have produced fine drawings and I am grateful for the trouble they took in getting them right. My thanks are due to *Yachting Monthly* for allowing me to reproduce part of Brian Cooke's article in their February 1975 issue.

Photograph and drawing credits are as follows:

Beken of Cowes, 56, 58, 60, 92, B. Boxall, 41, 49, The British Library, 1, The British Museum, 6, Paul Brookes, 2, 3, 4, 7, 12, (13, 14 15, Courtesy of AYRS), 17, 19, 21, 22, 93, B. Cooke, 95, C. Cove-Smith, MAIE, 84, Coral Print, 99, Captain E. De Lange, 103, 104,

Jean Luc de Moras, 16, 17, 19, 21, 22, Fiji Tourist Board, 5, R. Harris, 18, W. B. Howell, 81, N. Keig, 43 (insert), 51 A–F, D. Kelsall, 25, 35, 39, 70, M. McMullen, (9, 11, Courtesy of the Royal Society), 34, 52, 54, M. Montgomery, 36, J. R. Morris, 27, M. Muessel, 33, The National Maritime Museum London, 8, R. C. Newick, 43, *The Observer*, 42, 46, D. Robertson, 23, Royal Air Force, 24, 82, 83, The Royal Marine Commando News Team Plymouth, 48, 53, 55, 61, 62, 71–8, 86, 88, 89, 96, 97, author's photograph, Bob Salmon, 26, 28, 29, 30, 32, 37, G. Simpson, 57, Southern Television, 82, Andrew Spedding, (10, Courtesy of the Royal Society), 40, 44, 47, 50, 63, 64, 65, 66, 67, 68, 79, 90, 91, 94, 98, 100, 101, P. Weychan, 38, J. Wharram, 31.

Finally, I would like to thank Robin Knox-Johnston for writing the foreword, Martin Read for fishing me out of the North Sea, Ronnie and Rosemary Andrews for giving us the use of their lovely house in Cargreen where I found sufficient peace to write, Paul Mellon who has generously lent me his trimaran *Three Cheers*, and my wife, Lizzie, who typed the manuscript on a tiny typewriter.

1. *A double canoe of 96 ft overall length drawn by Webber, Captain Cook's artist.*

1 History

*Pacific Ocean Beginnings—The First Western
Multihulls—The Twentieth Century—The Part
Played by Racing—Acceptance as Cruising
Yachts.*

Pacific Ocean Beginnings

The sea has consistently provided man's enterprise and sense of adventure with a limit-less field for self expression. Discovery, colonisation, migration and history have all been possible because of it. Moreover, it has given him the opportunity for a necessary outlet of enjoyment: the pleasure of designing, building and sailing a sea going vessel.

Since our earliest beginnings when we noticed that certain materials floated, we have progressed from making primitive coracles and canoes to nuclear submarines and ice-breakers. It has taken a long time, and the means of propulsion for our craft have been many and varied; they have ranged from the paddle to the jet turbine, yet the most consistent means utilized has been the power of the wind. It is cheap, plentiful, generally reliable, and efficient. Furthermore, it has provided us with the power to settle success-fully on every corner of our planet's surface.

This colonisation, or in some cases, migration, was completed in an astonishing variety of vessels. No single race of mankind succeeded in producing identical craft, and the differences were as great as the languages that each race or tribe spoke. No-where, however, was the contrast in 'shipbuilding', so marked as in the Pacific Ocean. When Abel Tasman visited Tonga in 1642, European man saw with his own eyes the enormous ocean going double canoes of the South Sea Islands—the first multihulled sailing boats.

Why, and from where, Polynesian man colonised the mass of islands which cover a greater area than the continent of Africa is still controversial. Many theories have been advanced but it now seems fairly certain that colonisation was completed from the west—i.e., from south-east Asia and the offlying islands. Arguments still rage about whether or not this migration was deliberate or accidental and how the Polynesian was able to navigate. In Edward Dodd's *Polynesian Seafaring* (Nautical Publishing Company), the argument of systematic and deliberate settlement is forcibly put forward. Dodd con-vincingly discounts the 'accidental voyages' and 'drift' theories by examining in detail the ships and seafaring of the prehistoric islanders. He shows us how these magnificent multihulls of up to one hundred feet in length, were purposely designed for ocean voyaging and his disquisition on prehistoric celestial navigation reinforces his theory.

If we assume that Dodd is right, we are immediately faced with two remarkable facts. Firstly, colonisation took place to windward. This meant that these boats were able to sail close-hauled efficiently. Secondly, this colonisation took place many thousands of years ago and covered greater distances across open water than any other since. This proves that not only were their boats extremely safe but that multihulls, as developed by the islanders, were more sophisticated and seaworthy than any other sailing craft then built.

Three types of vessel were used by the Pacific islanders during their long migration from Asia. These were:

(a) The Double Canoe.
(b) The Single Outrigger.
(c) The Double Outrigger.

These compare roughly with today's catamarans, proas and trimarans. Let us examine each type of craft separately.

The Double Canoe

This was the main vessel of the islander's colonisation. It was the biggest of the vessels he built and Captain Cook's diagram of a Tahitian war canoe, the largest vessel recorded

2. *This reproduction from Webber's sketch of a double canoe shows it to have a schooner rig with a very small sail area and rather crude sails. It is doubtful that the vessel pointed very high. The bows are to the right.*

in early Polynesia, shows a ship one hundred and eight feet long. The double canoes were of two designs.

The first of these was a vessel with two hulls of equal size connected by a bridge deck on which the accommodation was situated in much the same way as the modern catamaran. It was designed to travel solely in one direction and was propelled by both sail and paddle. The mast was situated midway between the two hulls and the rig consisted of one, or possibly two masts with thin high 'sails' made of leaf matting. These sails, as can be seen from Webber's sketch, look highly inefficient and it is not clear precisely how they functioned. The straight edge is secured hard to the mast with stitching and the leech (or is it the luff?) consists of a long curved spar which starts as a boom and finishes higher than the top of the mast. It could not have been an efficient windward rig by any stretch of the imagination and it is likely that it was used only when the wind was on, or abaft the beam.

The second type of double canoe, however, was a far more sophisticated machine. This was the giant *tongiaki* of the Tongan islands. Here again, the two hulls were

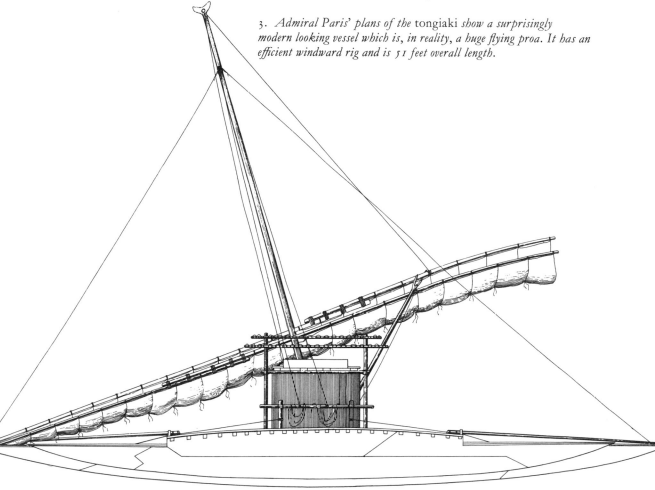

3. *Admiral Paris' plans of the* tongiaki *show a surprisingly modern looking vessel which is, in reality, a huge flying proa. It has an efficient windward rig and is 51 feet overall length.*

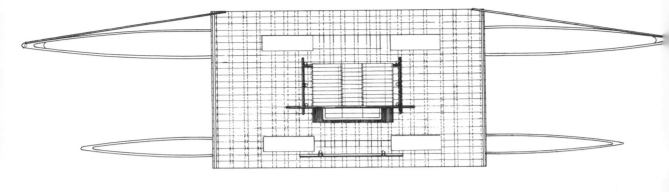

4. *Plan and bow views of the* tongiaki. *Leeway was minimised by the deep and narrow hulls.*

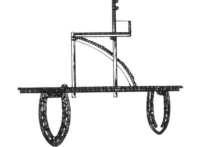

connected by a bridge structure but each hull was of a different shape and size. The vessel was in reality an enormous flying proa and the smaller hull formed the windward float. Both hulls were pointed at each end for the vessel 'tacked' by sailing backwards after the sail had been walked around the mast which was situated in the centre of the main, or leeward, hull. The sail was far more efficient than in the first type of double canoe. It was not unlike a lateen sail in appearance except that the foot, as well as the luff, was attached to a spar. This rig which was basically the same as is shown in the photograph of the Fijian single outriggers, was extremely efficient. It could be sheeted very flat and as can be seen from the Admiral Paris plan of the *tongiaki*, must have pushed the deep, leeway resisting main hull of the vessel efficaciously to windward. This type of ship was one of the most sophisticated multihulls of the Pacific and was probably responsible for much of the colonisation of Polynesia. The load carrying capacities of these two types of double canoes were considerable.

The Single Outrigger

These vessels differ from the double canoe in that the outrigger is usually a solid piece of wood as opposed to a large and hollow hull. Also, they tend to be considerably smaller and were used for shorter voyages. The principle of sailing them is, again, that of the flying proa. The outrigger is kept to windward and the weight of the crew is

5. *These Fijian single outriggers are extremely fast. They are exhausting vessels to sail as the outrigger must be balanced so that it is just skimming the sea.*

used to keep the vessel level. Single outriggers are extremely fast but tiring boats to sail on account of the gymnastics needed to keep level. The crew activity can be well seen in the photograph of the Fijian outriggers. They point well to windward and in some cases, notably those of the Micronesian vessels, were built with a one sided curve to the hull so as to offset leeway and the drag of the outrigger. The recognised way of going about was not to tack through the wind but simply to reverse direction by shifting the position of the sail in the same way as the Tongan *tongiaki*. Controlled drift, or leeway, was another evolution used with skill by the Polynesian. By altering the position of his sail angle, he could drift at controlled speeds in any direction downwind.

Steering was usually effected with a simple paddle but in some cases was managed

6. *The Micronesian proas were built with a one-sided curve to the hull so as to offset leeway and drag from the outrigger.*

7. *The single outrigger is tacked by shifting the tack of the spritsail from one end to the other and reversing direction.*

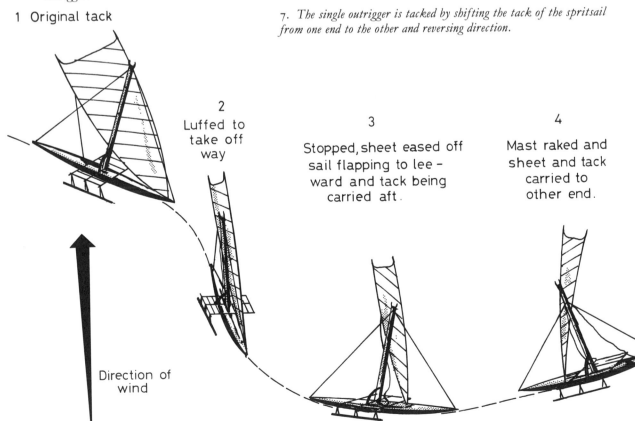

1 Original tack

2
Luffed to take off way

3
Stopped, sheet eased off sail flapping to lee-ward and tack being carried aft.

4
Mast raked and sheet and tack carried to other end.

Direction of wind

solely by weight distribution and sail adjustment. It is an important fact that the proa has proved, in modern times, to be one of the easiest multihulls to 'self steer' without vane gear.

The Double Outrigger

This craft, the forerunner to our modern trimaran, was, and still is, found only in the western part of the Pacific. In Indonesia it is prolific but, sadly, is almost unknown nowadays without an outboard engine driving it. Unlike the single outrigger, it is designed to be steered in one direction only and relies on an outrigger to leeward in addition to crew weight and a second outrigger to windward for stability. It has never been a sizeable vessel and, like the single outrigger, has been used largely for coastal voyaging.

Finally, the construction of these vessels is worthy of comment. When we think today of our plastic yachts and moulded hulls, it is astonishing to remember that these vessels were built before the advent of iron implements. The principal tool was the stone adze, and its importance was so great that it took on a religious significance. The keels of the vessels were made from hollowed out trees, usually breadfruit or tamanu and the planking was sewn together with natural fibres. Breadfruit gum was used as resin, coconut fibre was used for caulking, pandanus leaves were sewn into mats for sails, hibiscus and

8. *This Indonesian double outrigger as pictured by Webber is now almost unknown under sail.*

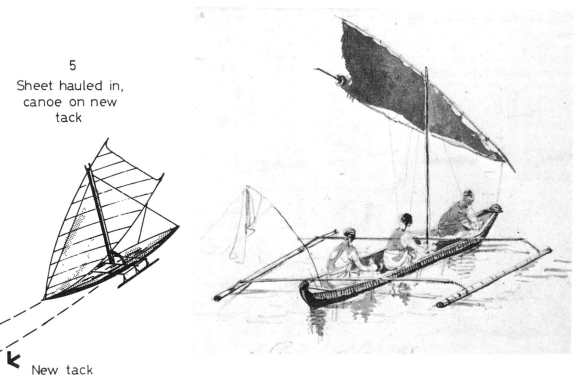

5

Sheet hauled in, canoe on new tack

New tack

coiar ropes were used in both standing and running rigging, and masts were usually made from the toa or ironwood tree. Unlike many builders of today, speed in building the vessel, was not important—but perfection unquestionably was. A giant double canoe might well take a decade to complete.

Sadly, the era of the sailing double canoes has long passed in Polynesia. It seems almost certain that these enormous craft were built purely for colonisation or war purposes originally, and it is only the single and double outriggers that remain in their original native form today.

The First 'Western' Multihulls

Although we know a considerable amount about the early Pacific multihulls as regards construction and design, our knowledge is limited about practical experience of sailing them. Both single and double outriggers have been sailed by Europeans but we know next to nothing of the performance of the huge double canoes. How fast were they? How close did they point? How much leeway did they make and were they safe in a storm? The *tongiaki* unquestionably appears to be extremely fast from her drawings and it would be an interesting enterprise to build a modern replica of her to compare with today's multihulls.

Apart from the Pacific Islanders, no other race of European origin perceived the possibilities of a multihulled design until a brief and amusing incident during the reign of the English king, Charles II.

In 1662 Sir William Petty, a distinguished economist, doctor and statistician, designed and built a twin-hulled vessel in Dublin. She was named the *Invention I* and although small (30 ft. LOA) proved successful enough to encourage him to build a larger version called the *Invention II*. *Invention II* was undoubtedly a success for we know that she won Sir William the princely sum of £50 by beating the Dublin packet boat to Holyhead with a clear three hours in hand. It would be interesting to know the weather conditions when she won this race, as it was the first multihull against monohull contest to be recorded. Although we have no evidence, it seems likely that Petty must have got the idea for the design from the knowledge, only recently available, that similar vessels existed on the other side of the world.

His third ship was partially financed by the king (probably the first and last multihull to be sponsored by such a distinguished patron!) and was named *The Experiment*. According to the *Diary of Samuel Pepys* she was 'Thirty ton in burden, capable of embarking thirty men in good accommodation and carrying ten guns of five tons weight'. Quite a ship by any standards but the weight of those guns and men could not have done much for her performance. She caused considerable controversy, even in those days. Volume 1 of *The Naval Chronicle* of 1799 is most complimentary and says of Sir William and his ships:

9. *This model of* Invention II *is held by the Royal Society in London. She was, on the whole, the most successful of Sir William Petty's catamarans.*

'Founder of the noble family of Shelburne, raised his reputation in 1663, by the invention of the double-bottomed ship, against the judgement of almost all mankind, to sail against wind and tide. When the ship first ventured from Dublin to Holyhead [*Invention II*], she stayed there many days before her return, which occasioned great exultation to its opposers; but her return in triumph, with such visible advantages above other vessels, checked their derision, the first point being clearly gained that she could bear the sea. She turned into that narrow harbour against wind and tide, among the rocks and ships, with such dexterity as many old seamen confessed they had never before seen. She appeared much to excel all other forms of ships, in sailing, carriage and security, but at length, in its return from a voyage, [*The Experiment*] was destroyed by a dreadful tempest which occasioned such havoc among the fleet, that the old system of ship-building had no reason to triumph over the new construction.'

10. *The rig of* Invention II *could hardly have given her a good windward performance. A reproduction from Sir William Petty's drawing in Royal Society letters.*

The bracketed names in the chronicle are mine as the writer has confused two of Sir William's Double Bottoms under one description. This was praise indeed from the navy.

The French however, were far less polite and the ambassador to Charles II, the Comte de Comminges, was outspoken in his dislike of *The Experiment*. In a letter to Louis XIV written in 1664 and recorded in *The Diary of Samuel Pepys* he ridicules the venture:

'This ship of Ireland which had made so much noise and which ought, in the future, to serve as a model for the building of ships is at last, after three months sailing, arrived at Woolwich near Greenwich. It really is the most ridiculous and useless machine that the spirit of man could conceive; the doctor who has invented it should return to his original profession and leave shipbuilding to those who are qualified.'

Obviously the Comte was a confirmed monohull man.

Three months from Dublin to Woolwich certainly sounds a long time but the month was January, and history does not tell us how many times *The Experiment* put into harbour on the way.

The gale in which she foundered occurred in the Bay of Biscay during her return voyage from Portugal. On the outward voyage she had been accompanied half way across the Channel where, again, she proved to be faster than any other vessel and good time was made to Oporto. It must have been a severe storm to sink her as she was not ballasted unlike the other fifteen ships which were lost in the same gale. Sadly, all hands perished and we shall never know whether she capsized or broke up.

The loss of *The Experiment* was a bitter blow to Sir William who was now Surveyor-General of Ireland and it was not until twenty years later that he tried again. This time the ship was far larger and proved so unmanageable that no crew could be found to take the ship to sea. *Saint Michael the Archangel*, as she was named, proved an expensive failure and was scrapped within a year of being completed.

It would appear from the results of Sir William's experiments that the most successful of the four ships was probably *Invention II*. This ties in with the various diagrams and papers lodged with the Royal Society where it can be seen that *Invention II* appears to be the lightest and handiest of the four craft. It is unlikely that Petty realised that one of the secrets of performance was light displacement.

Like many multihull enthusiasts, Sir William remained convinced of the future for his type of craft despite all the ridicule and discouragement he had suffered. It was an obsession with him for the rest of his life and on his death bed he stated clearly, only minutes before he died, that:

'The Devil can not long stifle what I have so amply demonstrated.'

Sir William Petty's efforts triggered off a series of twin hulled vessels throughout the next two centuries. The first of these was a sailing catamaran called *Double Bottom* built in Kerry in 1687 about which we know little save its existence. In the eighteenth century

11. *Was this how* Experiment *met her end, or did she break up?*

Captain de Germes built a catamaran at Brest which was a failure but the most notable experiments of this era were conducted by Patrick Miller between 1786 and 1788. Miller was one of the pioneers of steam navigation and built two large catamarans and a trimaran (the first recorded in the west) in this period. The largest of these was a 100 ft. catamaran with a 31 ft. beam built at Leith in Scotland. She had a colossal displacement of 235 tons and sported five masts with square sails and staysails and five paddle wheels on tandem between the hulls. Although she was described as 'a good seaboat' she was so strained on a voyage from Leith to St. Petersburg that she had to be abandoned in Russia.

In the nineteenth century several steam driven catamarans were built, the most notable of which was the *Calais Douvres*, a coal burning paddle steamer designed by Captain Dicey which was popular and successful for many years on the cross-Channel run. One of the most important innovations of this century came from John Mackenzie, who built in 1868 a 22 ft. LOA catamaran with 10 ft. beam which was designed purely for pleasure. It was gaff rigged, had asymmetrical hulls and was built in Belfast. As can be seen from the drawings this was really the first 'modern' catamaran design and despite its obvious faults, must have been fun to sail.

The next impetus which really put sailing catamarans on the map came in 1876 from the American yacht designer Nathaniel Herreshoff. 'The Wizard of Bristol', as he was known, built a 24 ft. catamaran called *Amaryllis* which trounced a fleet of thirty-three yachts in the New York Yacht Club's Centennial regatta. Several other designs followed and one of these the *Tarantella* was timed at 18 knots. Although their overall beam to length ratio was satisfactory, the hulls were narrow with too little buoyancy and liable to pitchpole over the lee bow. Each hull was well shaped with a minimum of wetted

27

12. *John Mackenzie's 1868 catamaran.*

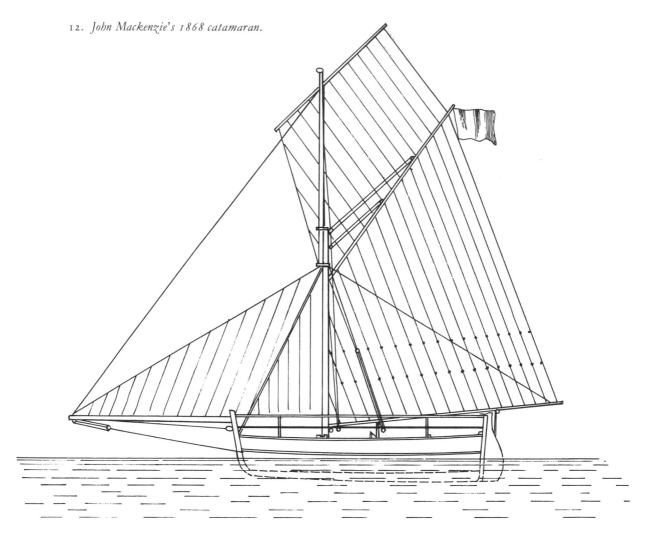

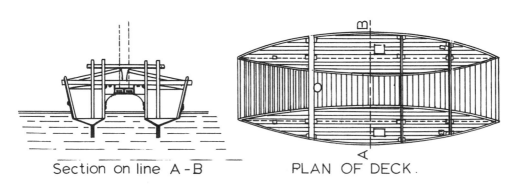

Section on line A - B   PLAN OF DECK.

surface and it was surprising that no further developments took place after the passing of Herreshoff's models. Perhaps the fact that the New York Yacht Club forbade them from ever racing again after the initial win of *Amaryllis* had something to do with it.

13. Amaryllis. *Nathaniel Herreshoff's catamaran of 1876.*

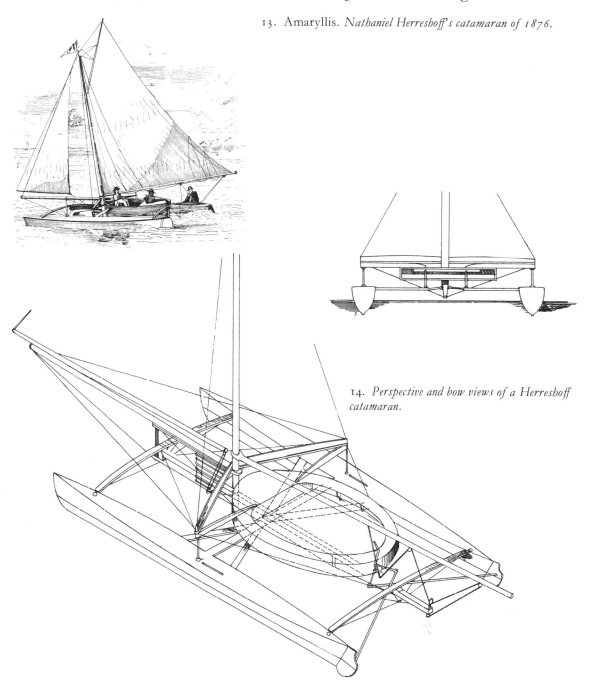

14. *Perspective and bow views of a Herreshoff catamaran.*

Herreshoff was followed by a builder called Fearon of New York who built similar catamarans but whose ideas were not enlarged upon either.

Finally, the only other development of note before the turn of the century was a 60 ft. schooner catamaran built in 1877 by Anson Stokes and the *Dominion* which was a scow with the bottom raised in the middle. She too was banned from racing after trouncing the field and history left the multihulled sailing boat alone for nearly forty years.

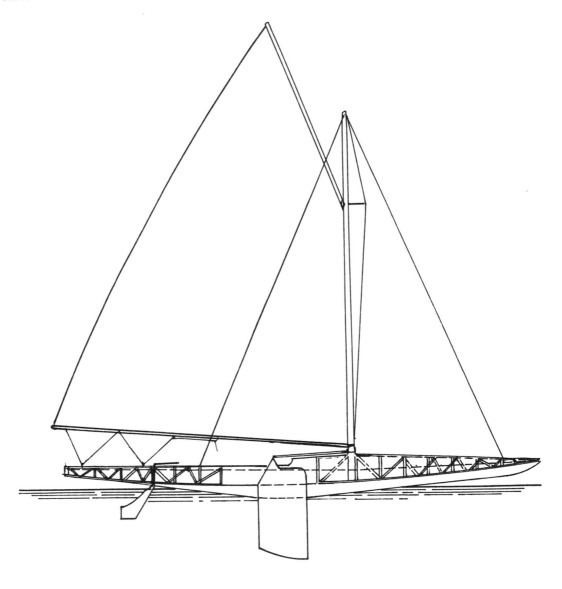

15. Dominion.

The Twentieth Century

After Herreshoff and Fearon there was little attempt to design or build sailing multihulls until after World War II. The reasons for this were numerous. Firstly, all catamarans built before 1900 had been banned from any type of racing. As we shall see later, racing plays an enormous part in the development of any yacht and there seemed scant point in building multihulls commercially. Secondly, construction methods provided considerable problems as it was difficult to reduce weight without the aid of modern resins and materials. Herreshoff was well aware of the fact that weight played a critical part in the speed of his boats and his catamarans were both difficult and expensive to build. They were also heavy by modern standards and required a good wind to push them along. Probably more important in this 'development gap' was the fact that from 1900 to the end of World War II, the world was going through a traumatic period socially, politically and economically. World War I, the Depression and then World War II slowed the development of sport and advances in the design of all sailing boats considerably.

Nevertheless, there were isolated instances during this period of multihulls cropping up and as long ago as 1908, Victor Tchetchet, a Russian who later emigrated to the U.S.A., was experimenting in his native Kiev. At the Spring Race of the Imperial Yacht Club of Kiev, he finished first in his home-made 18 foot catamaran.

As described in R. B. Harris' *Racing and Cruising Trimarans* (Nautical Publishing Company) 'I easily passed all types of small yachts of the Club and victoriously crossed the finish line. But instead of receiving first prize, I was told that my boat is not a boat, but none knew why, and it is disqualified—and for good!' How similar a fate to that of Herreshoff's craft thirty years previously. Tchetchet lived in the United States after the Revolution and pioneered small trimarans after World War II. The word 'trimaran' was his creation.

An important voyage prior to the end of World War II was that of Eric de Bisschop from Hawaii to Cannes, France, around the Cape of Good Hope in his catamaran, *Kaimiloa*. De Bisschop had been wrecked on the coast of Hawaii in his single hulled junk in 1936 and while recovering became interested in the models of Polynesian double canoes that were lodged in the Museum. After due consideration he and Joseph Tatibouet decided to build *Kaimiloa* on Waikiki beach. They completed her satisfactorily and set off from Honolulu on 7th March 1937 and arrived in France on 21st May 1938 after a voyage full of incident. *Kaimiloa* was 45 ft. long and proved that, without question, a modern catamaran could be made safe enough to cross oceans.

Several other incidents of multihulls, mainly catamarans, crop up before World War II but they were almost all power driven—the Mississippi ferries accounting for most.

World War II did more for multihulls than any other world event for it led to the discovery and extensive use of waterproofed sheet plywood and resin glues. Here at last was a method of building that was strong, and reasonably inexpensive. Moreover, it could be easily used by amateurs and was very suitable for lightweight construction, the essential factor which had been difficult to achieve before. This influenced the boat building trade enormously and has only fairly recently been caught up with by the use

(A)

(B)

(C)

(D)

(E)

(F)

16. Kaimiloa, *the first modern catamaran to complete an ocean voyage. (A) & (B) Construction of the yacht was completed on the beach at Honolulu. (C) The two hulls were connected by beams in a similar, though less sophisticated, way to James Wharram's modern designs. (D) Accommodation was in the hulls only. (E) Her junk rig proved effective, as shown on leaving Honolulu, while (F) records her arrival at Cannes to complete a courageous and remarkable voyage.*

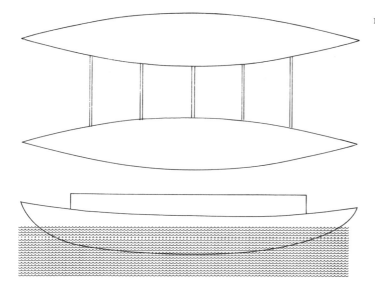

17. *Plan and side views of* Kaimiloa.

of fibreglass, foam sandwich and aluminium.

Manu Kai designed by Woodbridge Brown and built by Alfred Kumalai in 1946 was the catamaran that started the ball rolling. Brown, an American who was a glider pilot during the war lived in Hawaii. He had been stationed in the Micronesian islands and had been impressed by the flying proas and considered that two proa main hulls joined together would make a seaworthy vessel. His aim was to build a boat suitable for beach

18. Manu Kai.

day charter work and he therefore built *Manu Kai* without centreboards but deep as-symmetrical hulls. She was immediately a great success and proved to be extremely fast. She was 40 ft. long, 13 ft. wide and displaced only 3,000 pounds. This beam was narrow from a 'sailing capsize' viewpoint. Despite this, her speed astounded all who sailed in her and her reputation travelled rapidly to other parts of the world.

19. *Plan, side and bow views of* Manu Kai.

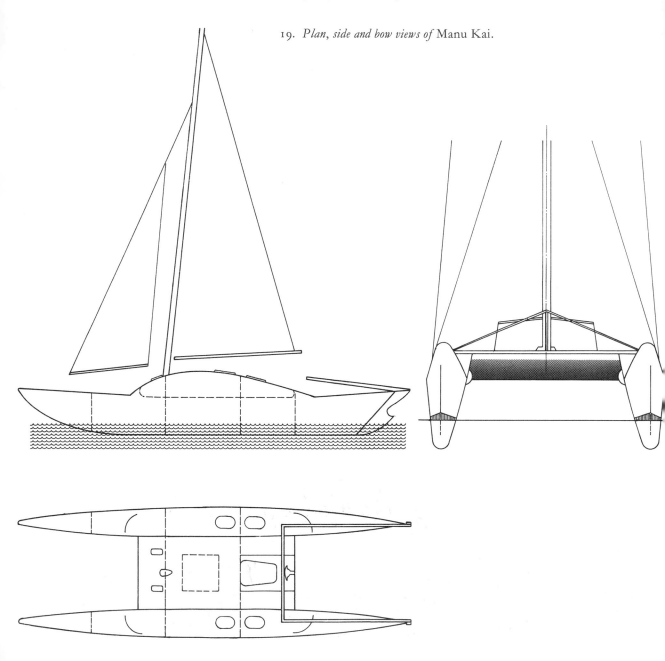

In England, Roland and Francis Prout, whose father ran a boatyard in Canvey Island, came out of the services at the end of the war. G. Prout and Sons were at that time building folding dinghies and kyak canoes. Considerably influenced by Brown, they experimented in lashing two kyaks together and came up with a surprisingly fast catamaran. One experiment led to another and *Shearwater I* evolved as the result of two racing kyaks being bridged together. Quite by chance the Prouts had stumbled on a most efficient hull form for catamaran speed—the semi-circular section which reduced the wetted surface area. The eventual development, the *Shearwater III*, became the first commercially successful multihull in the world and over 2,500 have now been built.

20.
A Shearwater.

At the same time as Brown was designing *Manu Kai* (1946) the North Atlantic was crossed for the first time by a multihull. Surprisingly, it was a trimaran that made the voyage called *Ananda* and she was skippered by a Frenchman, André Sadrin. *Ananda* was 42 ft. long and suffered from the basic design fault of having too short outriggers. She was well built of oak and mahogany in Sête on the Mediterranean coast. They sailed on 23rd September 1946 down the Trade Wind route to the West Indies. After a brief stop in the Cape Verde Islands, Sadrin sailed for Martinique and completed the 2,100 mile passage in twenty days. Half way across, they were caught in a violent storm which half filled one of the outriggers and proved her to have too little freeboard. She also suffered from a violent motion which made her uncomfortable to live in and difficult to steer. Humphrey Barton in his book *Atlantic Adventurers* (Adlard Coles Ltd.) describes her as an expensive experiment and states that her motion was so great that the crew suffered from eyesight trouble! He concludes that trimarans are highly unsuited for ocean crossing, and at that stage in their development, he was unquestionably right.

21. Ananda.

Still in 1946, Victor Tchetchet was sailing and for the first time, racing, a 24 ft. trimaran that he had completed the previous year in the United States. This was a successful boat and led to seven other trimarans being built and entered for various races over the next three years. They were all of similar size and it was not until an amateur designer from California, Arthur Piver, appeared that the first large 'commercial' trimarans started to be built in the early 1960s.

Meanwhile, interest in other parts of the world was beginning to increase. In Australia the Cunningham brothers began designing small catamarans at the end of the war using the Herreshoff design as a basis, and modern plywood for construction. The hulls were symmetrical, chined and canoe sterned. Their first boat, *Yvonne*, was an immediate success and paved the way to catamaran development in the Southern hemisphere.

In France, a further Atlantic crossing was made by Jean Filloux in a 49 ft. catamaran, *Copula* in 1949. *Copula* was steel, weighed 22 tons, and was not a success. She was

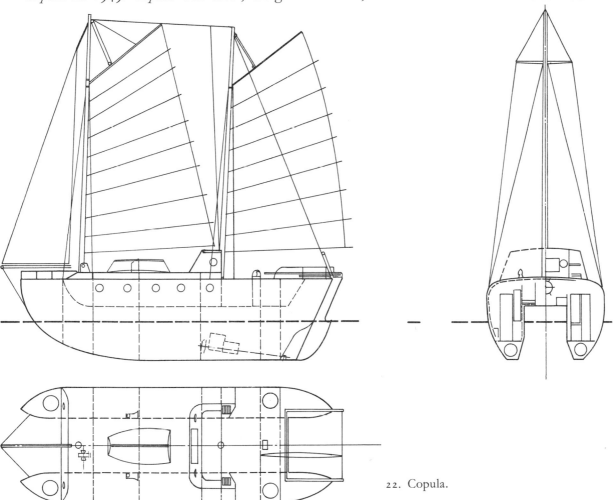

22. Copula.

abandoned in the West Indies. A German, Von Schwartzenberg, crossed the Atlantic with the north-east trades in a 30 ft. steel catamaran in 1950 which, like its French predecessor, was dangerously overweight and also abandoned. Undeterred, Von Schwartzenberg then built a trimaran which he attempted to sail to the West Indies in the mid 1950s. He capsized off the Azores and was lucky to escape with his life.

Modern catamaran design, therefore, advanced along three main lines. These were as follows:

(i) Brown in the United States, who was closely followed by Choy.

(ii) Prout in Britain who influenced O'Brien and MacAlpine-Downie in England, Harris in the United States, Young in New Zealand and Hooks in Australia.

(iii) The Cunningham brothers in Australia who laid the foundations for 'A' class catamarans in the Southern Hemisphere.

The trimaran was considerably slower to develop. The logical explanation of this probably being that two comes before three. In England, Don Robertson was the first person to experiment and he built his trimaran *Fun* in 1954. She had the centre hull of a racing canoe and incorporated a wing mast which was advanced thinking for that period. Robertson found her disappointingly slow due largely, as he discovered later, to the shortness of the floats. All he had done was to add drag and extra weight. Disappointed, he turned to catamarans and was later to become well known for his racing success in *Freedom* and *Snow Goose*, a Prout 36 footer.

23. *(left) Don Robertson's* Fun.

24. *(right)* Toria, *winner of the 1966 Round Britain Race.*

Arthur Piver popularised his trimaran designs of the early sixties by considerable advertising of the fact that they could be easily and cheaply built by amateurs. This had two results. The first was to encourage many people who had little knowledge of seamanship or construction to build inadequate boats too cheaply for strength.

The second was a great splurge in trimaran development throughout the world.

Unfortunately, the combination of these two factors had severe detrimental results. There were numerous cases of accidents due to construction failures caused by shoddy building and multihulls started to develop a bad name. Several capsizes occurred, for many of the designs were dangerously narrow and little more than a catamaran with a third hull dropped in the centre.

Nonetheless, Piver's designs began to be built throughout the world and improved upon. In Australia Hedley Nicol, a policeman, took the basic design, improved it, and increased the sail area. Tragically, he lost his life in the 36 ft. *Privateer* which capsized in a typhoon 400 miles north-east of Sydney. Piver himself also perished at sea in March 1968 while sailing a 25 ft. trimaran of his own design, off the coast of California. During his life he completed two Atlantic and one Pacific crossing in boats to his designs.

Derek Kelsall, an English yachtsman, became the first man to sail a trimaran across the Atlantic from east to west single handed in the 1964 *Observer* Singlehanded Trans-Atlantic Race. This was a Piver design built by Kelsall called *Folatre*. As a result, Kelsall turned designer and pioneered offshore racing trimarans in England. He broke completely from Piver's V shaped hulls and narrow overall beams. Instead he built wider, making his outriggers and main hull with semicircular sections. His designs had centreboards and their increased speed was shown by the performance of *Toria* in the 1966 Round Britain Race. She completed the 2,000 mile course in a staggering eleven sailing days.

Back in America, other trimaran designers were following lines independent from Piver. The most notable of these was Dick Newick, a Virgin Islander who lived in St. Croix. From the beginning in the early sixties, Newick was designing and building wider and more stable craft than Piver. His trimarans had no accommodation in the outriggers and were built mainly for charter. His sections were more of a rounded V than Piver's and his aim was speed. In this he was a disciple of L. Francis Herreshoff (the 'Wizard of Bristol's son) who once wrote:

'To me, the pleasure of sailing is almost in direct proportion to the speed.'

Newick's designs were neither lavishly advertised nor well known until his successes with *Cheers* and *Three Cheers*.

It is not the aim of this book to discuss in detail every catamaran or trimaran designer throughout the world. Suffice to say that the multihull became established as a viable yacht after World War II. The catamaran came first in the late 1940s and was followed by the trimaran in the 1960s.

Finally, this section would be incomplete without mentioning the Amateur Yacht Research Society. This international society was founded in 1955 by Dr. John Morwood, a keen multihull sailor. Within a very short time it became a world authority and discussion media through its booklets and meetings, for all types of yacht research. Designers, builders and sailors were all given an excellent forum to aim their views, and because multihulls were going through the initial stages of development at this time, the society did a considerable though unassessable amount to further their future.

The Part Played by Racing

As we have seen, every effort to sail a multihull in races before World War II ended in ridicule and ostracism. Herreshoff, Tchetchet and even Sir William Petty suffered, like most inventors, from the prejudices of people who were not prepared to listen, let alone see, whether or not a multihulled craft made sense.

Racing enhances design for only by comparing the speeds of similar craft can performance be evaluated and satisfactory hull forms and other factors be achieved.

When Tchetchet produced his day sailing trimaran, he was allowed to enter for the 1946 handicap race of the Corinthian Yacht Club at Marblehead Race Week. This was the first race that any multihull entered and it proved the potential of Tchetchet's designs. He then founded the International Multihull Boat Racing Association, also in 1946 which ran regattas each year. This was later taken over by the American Multihull Sailing Association in 1962.

In England, multihull racing began with the advent of the Shearwater and races for dinghy catamarans caught on fairly fast. In 1963 the Royal Yachting Association formed a committee to help multihulls. P. V. MacKinnan (later to be R.Y.A. chairman) presided, while most of the active catamaran open boat sailors were members or came to advise. The outcome was the establishment of the A, B and C classes based on length and sail area. Later this committee helped to organise and start offshore racing and in 1967 the first Crystal Trophy Race was held with the sponsorship of British Petroleum.

The R.Y.A. was of very great help and influence in getting multihulls accepted for racing in Britain and its efforts advanced development enormously.

Reaction to the advent of multihulls from the yachting world in general was extremely reserved and in many cases, distinctly hostile. Britain's Royal Ocean Racing Club stated from the beginning that it had no intention of allowing multihulls to enter any of its races as, apart from their 'obvious unseaworthiness', they could not be handicapped.

The same sentiments were aired by many other influential race organisations throughout the world and it seemed that the multihull was doomed for ever to race against itself.

However, in 1960 a retired Royal Marine, Colonel 'Blondie' Haslar, had invented a trans-Atlantic race without rules, open to any craft provided it was only crewed by one man. This race from Plymouth, England to Newport, Rhode Island was to establish the multihull more firmly in yachting history than any other event. Sponsored by the *Observer* the Singlehanded Trans-Atlantic Race (OSTAR) quickly became a world classic. Chichester, Tabarly and many others made their names as a result of it, while the enormous publicity that it generated quickly publicised multihulls as they came to be entered. In the 1964 race, two catamarans, *Rehu Moana* and *Misty Miller*, with one trimaran *Folatre*, successfully completed the course. *Folatre* in particular, made a good time of 35 days despite having to turn back initially, while all three entrants showed that, length for length, their boats were as fast and as weatherly, as monohulls of equivalent size.

Haslar's inventive genius for organising first class races did not stop at the OSTAR. In 1966 came his next brain child, the two-handed *Observer* Round Britain Race which produced Kelsall's revolutionary *Toria*. Kelsall's performance in this trimaran so impressed Eric Tabarly, who had won the 1964 OSTAR, that he asked Kelsall to take him for a sail in her. Colin Forbes, a film maker who was later to sail the trimaran

25. *Eric Tabarly on board* Toria.

Startled Fawn to America in the 1968 single handed race said of the sail:

'Tabarly showed no special enthusiasm and remained quiet and observant throughout. We sailed from Padstow, Cornwall, to the Thames Estuary and had a strong fair wind the whole way. After a rapid reach to Land's End we surfed up the Channel with the speedometer touching 20 knots at times and Tabarly closely observed everything that went on. He was obviously impressed by her speed but said at the time that he thought a traditional yacht would be a better proposition for singlehanded ocean sailing.'

Nevertheless, Tabarly was so amazed by *Toria*'s speed that he approached the French designer André Allegre and asked him to design a trimaran for the 1968 Singlehanded race. The result, *Pen Duick IV*, was remarkable. She was a massive 70 ft. long with a beam of 34 ft. and incorporated pivoting wing masts and fully battened sails. Unfortunately, however, delays were so numerous that her teething problems were not

26. Pen Duick IV, *the result of Tabarly's reasoned approach to winning the 1960 Singlehanded Trans-Atlantic Race. Note the original wing masts and the damaged starboard outrigger caused by a collision.*

fully overcome by the time the race started. In addition, Tabarly had a collision and was forced to retire. After that *Pen Duick IV*'s famous career really started; she broke a series of records for crossing oceans and was eventually acquired by Alain Colas who raced her to victory in the 1972 OSTAR, beating the massive 128 ft. monohull, *Vendredi Treize*. Colas then changed her name to *Manureva* sailed her singlehanded around the world with the Whitbread Round The World Race fleet in 1973. In 1974 he entered the third Round Britain Race but was beaten into fourth place, largely on account of the considerable weight that he had added to her for his circumnavigation.

To return to the 1968 OSTAR, multihulls produced some very mixed results. On the credit side, the brilliant performance of Newick's proa *Cheers* amazed the sailing world by finishing third. Superbly sailed by Tom Follett, *Cheers* showed that a well designed and built multihull, however unconventional, will easily outsail a monohull of the same size. Also, Bill Howell, an Australian dentist, sailed his catamaran *Golden*

27. Cheers, *the only successful racing proa to date, was sailed to third place in the 1968 Observer Singlehanded Race by Tom Follett.*

Cockerel to a good fifth place and weathered a force 11 storm by lying a-hull. To my mind *Golden Cockerel* (now *Tahiti Bill*) could be made safer with a few more feet of beam and Howell had already capsized her in the first Crystal Trophy. It was, therefore, extremely relevant that the boat had weathered the storm safely; this aspect of heavy weather will be discussed in detail in Chapter 6.

On the debit side, there were a number of dramatic, highly publicised and predictable disasters. The first of these came from the trimaran *Yaksha* designed and sailed by an ebullient but eccentric Frenchman, Joan de Kat. *Yaksha* was possibly the best example of how not to build a multihull. She was a poorly engineered spidery contraption loosely connected with bits of wire, odd rope and hollow tube. As confidently predicted by many of the 'goofers' in Millbay docks, she broke up on the high northern route. An efficient air-sea rescue operation was put into force and luckily de Kat was found alive. The other trimaran to break up was sailed by an inexperienced German lady, Edith Baumann. *Koala III* was unimpressive, and Baumann was rescued near the Azores. These two near tragedies made headline news in the European press and did considerable harm to the development of multihulls.

28. Yaksha, *with her skipper Joan de Kat, who was rescued 20 days after the start of the 1968 Singlehanded Trans-Atlantic Race, when his boat had broken up.*

29. Koala III *was another construction disaster in the same race. She proved too weak and broke up.*

In the same year a British newspaper, the *Sunday Times*, sponsored a singlehanded non-stop Around the World Race. There was only one finisher, Robin Knox-Johnston, who completed the course in his ketch *Suhaili*. Nigel Tetley, a retired naval officer did, however, complete the first non-stop multihull circumnavigation in that he crossed his outward track in his trimaran *Victress*. Sadly, his Piver designed yacht broke up only a thousand miles from England so he did not win the race. His achievement was, however, quite outstanding.

30. Victress *completed a remarkable voyage around the world, the first to be made by a trimaran, but broke up off the Azores before reaching harbour.*

By now, offshore multihull only races were becoming popular. In England the Crystal Trophy, in America the Trans-Pac and Newport–Bermuda races, while in Australia the Sydney–Hobart and Brisbane–Gladstone, all contributed to development.

In the 1972 OSTAR multihulls took four of the first six places, then in the 1974 Round Britain Race, they took the first five places.

Rodney Marsh's *Tornado* became well established in the late sixties as the B class catamaran selected by the R.Y.A. for national and international events including the Olympic Games. Other ocean races popularised the craft further and the International Offshore Multihull Rule was produced by the American Vic Stern to give some semblance of logic to the previous rating attempts. All in all, racing for multihulls had become accepted and well established by the 1970s.

Construction and capsize failures did, however, continue and it slowly came to be realised that three factors which are essential to any sailing craft applied with even more relevance to multihulls:

(i)   Good design.
(ii) Good construction.
(iii) Good seamanship.

Acceptance as Cruising Yachts

The cruising multihull has always had certain advantages over the monohull, providing of course, that the basic structure is safe and the boat inherently seaworthy. These advantages, which will be discussed in Chapter 2, led to various people, many of them amateurs, building and sailing both catamarans and trimarans over long distances.

As we have seen, *Kamiloa* and *Ananda* were among the first of these craft but two interesting voyages which led eventually to a popular design of cheap cruising catamaran were undertaken by an Englishman, James Wharram. Wharram, with almost no experience of sailing at all, built a 23 ft. Polynesian style catamaran, *Tangaroa*, which he sailed from England to the West Indies in 1955. Wharram's crew consisted of two young German girls and after a fairly fraught voyage, they reached Trinidad in one piece although they nearly had to abandon the voyage with rudder trouble. While in Trinidad, they built another catamaran, the 40 ft. *Rongo*, which they sailed home to

31. *James Wharram's* Rongo *made the first west to east crossing of the Atlantic by a multihull.*

England via New York, encountering a tropical cyclone on the way. This voyage was made in 1959 and was the first multihull crossing of the Atlantic from west to east. Wharram, and his ideas, were not taken seriously for some considerable time and it is only recently that he has received some of the recognition he deserves. The plans of his boats, which have a good safety record, are now sold extensively over the world.

Other designers carried their experience into cruising boats. In England the Prouts built their first cruiser in 1958 which soon led to Don Robertson's *Snow Goose*. Six other 35 footers followed and became popular, which led to the Ranger and modified Snowgoose classes.

In America, Rudy Choy elaborated on Brown's designs establishing offshore cruising catamarans, but he continued to build relatively narrow vessels with asymmetrical hulls which slowly evolved as design progress was made elsewhere.

Rehu Moana, a Prout-built Colin Mudie design, was sailed round the world by David

32. Rehu Moana, *the first multihull to complete a circumnavigation.*

Lewis after the 1964 OSTAR. Lewis was accompanied by his wife and two young daughters and rode out two force 10 gales in the open sea. This was the first ever multihull circumnavigation, and although only 40 ft. long and 17 ft. wide, *Rehu Moana* gave Lewis, an experienced seaman, no cause for concern with regards to her stability.

Numerous other long distance cruises of note then took place, mostly by catamarans, and the multihull became rapidly established as a cruising yacht. The Pacific, in particular, proved to be a fine cruising ground for multihulls due to its regular winds and often shallow water; so the islanders were soon to gaze with interest at the new double canoes.

In the West Indies, charter operators soon discovered that large catamarans provided good value for money as far as space and accommodation was concerned, while all over the rest of the world the appeal of the stable platform persuaded many to try this new type of vessel. By the 1970s, the good multihulls had become generally accepted as cruising boats.

33. *Bill Howell's catamaran* Tahiti Bill *holed after a collision with a Russian trawler in the 1972 Singlehanded Trans-Atlantic Race. See 'Unsinkability' opposite.*

2 Design and Construction Comparisons

Why a Multihull?—Catamaran and
Trimaran—Design—Construction

Why a Multihull?

Before studying the advantages and drawbacks of the three types of multihull, we should first ask ourselves 'Why a multihull anyway?' and 'What advantages, if any, have boats with more than one hull over the conventional monohull?'

To answer the first question, possibly the greatest reason for the advent of the modern multihull is man's wish to experiment. Man inevitably tries anything once, and if it is successful to any degree he experiments further; moreover, if his inventions prove commercially saleable, they will no longer be inventions but will soon become facts of life. In the case of the multihull, all these things happened. Two factors more than any other have ensured development, performance and stability. It was found at the end of World War II, and indeed before this, that an unballasted yacht, which is all that a multihull is, was astonishingly fast—particularly on a reach. Speed under sail has always been a driving force in yacht development and led straightaway to a rapid increase in interest. The second factor, stability, is a thing that many cruising people have sought for years. Because of its beam, the multihull does not heel to anything like the same extent as a monohull and this makes life more comfortable on board.

Its advantages over a monohull are:

(a) *Unsinkability*. Almost all multihulls are positively buoyant; there are exceptions but they are being actively discouraged at present. This is an enormous advantage for it means that in the event of collision people have a better chance of escape with their lives than in a monohull. Examples are legion of deaths from collisions when people have drowned because their craft sank in a terrifyingly short space of time. This is unlikely to happen with a multihull, even when inverted.

(b) *Speed*. There is now little doubt that a well designed racing multihull will easily outpace its monohull equivalent on all points of sailing. However, it must be emphasised that this is by no means true of all multihulls. It is distressing to see the vast numbers of ugly, wind resistant, commercial catamarans in existence today which have a very poor performance, particularly to windward in a seaway. One of the main reasons for this is that designers and builders have pushed the commercial advantages of space and accommodation to sell more boats with the result that the extra weight and windage impairs performance. An unballasted yacht will not retain her speed advantages if she is loaded down with extra ballast in the form of all the commercial trimmings. Nevertheless, it is surprising to see how fast most well designed multihulls will sail in comparison to an equivalent monohull, even when heavily laden.

(c) *Stability*. It is definitely more comfortable to sail upright than over on one's ear. This also tends to give an easier motion in a well designed multihull and lessens sea-sickness. A catamaran remains almost horizontal under a good blow of wind whereas a trimaran is often designed to heel up to as much as $10°$, which is not excessive when compared to a monohull. Cooking, sailing and general living are all simpler on an even keel.

(d) *Space and Accommodation*. Almost all catamarans have more room inside than the equivalent sized monohull. This, however, is not necessarily always an advantage for an ocean-going yacht when that extra space has been achieved by dangerously high bridge decks with enormous windage. Trimarans, on the other hand, unless of ugly and dangerous design or very large, do not normally have accommodation in the outriggers. This means that they usually have similar accommodation to a monohull of equivalent length. There are wide variations on both sides of the scale so these are fairly broad generalisations; for instance *British Oxygen*, at 70 ft. the largest purely racing catamaran in the world, is not designed at present for more than two people while *Manureva*, Colas' 70 ft. trimaran, is only designed for one. Deck space, particularly in hot weather, is important and it is a great advantage for sunbathing and crew morale to have the large deck area of a multihull.

(e) *Shallow draft and beachability*. This is a very distinct advantage over the monohull. The cruising multihull can visit shallow water anchorages and dry out without problem, provided of course, that it is designed to do so. This is not always the case with some racing multihulls which may have a skeg that cannot be sat on; but generally speaking, once centreboards are up, most multihulls can take the bottom. This has mooring

34. *Beachability is a great advantage to a multihull.* Three Cheers *on a Spanish beach.*

advantages in that tidal estuaries which dry out can be used. A monohull has to use legs and this is always a worry to the owner. Anti-fouling and scrubbing become far less of a problem if it is possible to dry out simply at any time and place.

(f) *Heavy weather performance*. This will be discussed in detail later on, but the well designed multihull has certain advantages over the deep displacement monohull in gale to hurricane conditions.

On the other side of the coin, the multihull unquestionably has certain disadvantages. These are:

(a) *Capsize danger*. All multihulls can be capsized if the people who design, build and sail them make certain mistakes. Anyone who puts to sea in a multihull must realise from the outset that there is no such thing as a catamaran or trimaran that cannot be capsized; furthermore, the chances of righting a capsize are negligible. In a monohull, however, even if you are rolled over or pitchpoled, the boat will roll upright, again often without its rig, **provided** of course that she has not filled up and sunk.

(b) *Construction*. Because of the increase in various forces on a multihull, construction has to be excellent. This is often difficult to achieve, particularly with amateur building and mass production, and there have been a distressing number of failures. Construction in a monohull is no longer an experimental area and the problems are correspondingly less.

(c) *Large Beam*. The large beam of the multihull has manoeuvrability and parking disadvantages in certain circumstances. It can be costly in marina fees as owners are usually charged length and a half or more and it is frequently disliked by harbour authorities due to the space taken up and the difficulties of mooring in crowded ports.

(d) *Ugliness*. A large proportion of multihulls are staggeringly ugly. Not only does this

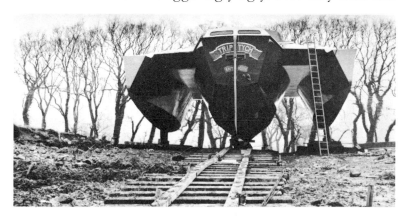

35. *Many people find so many multihulls lack beauty to their eyes.*

offend the eye but it also gives the multihull a poor reputation. There is truth in the saying that if a thing looks good it will usually perform well. This is certainly true of aeroplanes and also of multihulls. A classic example of ugliness is the catamaran with excessively high raised accommodation in between the hulls. This is both unsightly and potentially dangerous. The danger lies in a high centre of gravity combined with considerable windage that together can help cause a capsize. Certain trimarans, particularly some of the smaller ones which utilise all three hulls for accommodation, are hideous and often dangerously narrow. On the other hand the trend today is to more efficient and handsome catamarans or trimarans.

Of the three types of multihull, the proa has not yet reached a state of development where it can be described as an ocean going vessel for the cruising man. In its racing form, only the Atlantic Proa, which keeps the outrigger to leeward, has had any success and only Newick's *Cheers* has achieved anything of note. The Pacific Proa (the flying proa with outrigger to windward) has not yet been developed for ocean voyaging despite attempts by several designers. Having said that, it must be made clear that the

36. Crossbow, *the world speed record holder (1975) over half a kilometre.*

Pacific Proa unquestionably has the greatest potential for speed for the obvious reason that it has far less wetted surface area than any other configuration when the outrigger is flying. *Crossbow* holds the world speed record with a staggeringly fast 29.3 knots over half a kilometre, but she cannot turn, tack or sail in any sort of seaway whatsoever. One day, someone may develop fast flying proas for ocean voyaging but at the present, they have little relevance.

Catamaran and Trimaran

Of the two remaining types of multihull, the catamaran and the trimaran, both have their advantages and disadvantages when compared against each other. We will discuss these briefly and it must be remembered that they are compared size for size (including sail area, displacement etc) throughout.

(a) *Speed*. In theory, a catamaran should be faster than a trimaran. This is because a catamaran can lift its windward hull with ease and reduce the wetted surface considerably. A trimaran, however, will always have its centre hull in the water, unless something is wrong. This sounds splendid in theory but in practice it is obviously risky for an offshore catamaran to fly a hull. It is however acceptable in dinghy catamarans and this is the reason why they have developed and dinghy trimarans have not. Therefore, on the assumption that both a trimaran and catamaran will always have two hulls in the water, there should be no difference in speed provided that the wetted surface area, waterline length, displacement and sail area are the same. It is not, of course, as simple as this for inevitably numerous other factors such as hull profile, length of trimaran outrigger, angle of heel when sailing, rig and a host of other design features all enter into it. Consequently, it is extremely difficult to say which configuration is faster. Trimarans, on the whole, have taken the lead at present as fast offshore racers and one only has to look at General Farrant's *Trifle*, which has finished first home in the Crystal Trophy six times running, to find an excellent example. Most well known fast offshore racers have been trimarans—for instance *Toria*, *Trifle*, *Manureva*, *Three Cheers*, *Gulf Streamer*, *Three Legs of Man*, *Triple Arrow*, and now *Great Britain III*. On the catamaran side, the massive *British Oxygen*, which narrowly won the 1974 Round Britain Race from *Three Cheers*, proved fairly slow compared to size with her trimaran rivals.

This is not to say that a catamaran is slower than a trimaran, but it is definitely harder and more worrying to drive as fast because it gives less warning of when it is going to capsize. As a result, most leading offshore multihull sailors have gone for the trimaran. Nevertheless, there are many good examples of fast catamarans other than *British Oxygen*. Don Robertson's *Snow Goose* held the Round the Island Race record for many years. Gerry Boxall's *Minnetaree* and the American *Seabird* are all extremely fast boats.

On the west coast of the USA the offshore multihull racing scene was dominated by the big catamarans during the sixties, but they now share the honours with some fast trimarans.

(b) *Safety*. The trimaran has the advantage on the capsize problem. This is because it heels like a monohull, though to nothing like the same extent, and it is far easier to tell when the vessel is overpressed. A catamaran, on the other hand, hardly heels at all and gives little warning of decreasing stability. The trimaran is usually a beamier boat, length for length, and this increases safety. A catamaran, on the other hand, is generally narrower in overall beam because of the stressing problems, and in addition tends to have more windage with its high flat sides and cabin top. Another danger is that the centre of gravity is almost always higher than that of a trimaran because the accommodation is frequently between the two hulls and built up above deck level. There are exceptions to this but for the most part, the catamaran is more easily capsized while sailing than a trimaran.

Most catamaran designers consider that a two to one length to beam ratio, or thereabouts, is desirable and the lesser the beam the lesser the safety margin. This ratio is even more important in smaller multihulls and certain modern catamarans are dangerously narrow. It must be realised that the smaller the boat, the more prominent the capsize problem becomes. I have not yet seen a catamaran below 30 ft. in length that I would like to sail across an ocean.

(c) *Ease of Sailing*. Because a trimaran heels it is easy to tell when to change sail. The warning signs are obvious—the leeward outrigger submerges, the angle of heel increases and often speed will reduce if the boat heels too far. This means that it can be sailed off the seat of one's pants without recourse to instruments. The case with a catamaran is exactly the opposite. There is hardly any heel and very few signs to indicate when to change down. As a result, the wind speed indicator and sail shapes are often the sole means of deciding when sail should be changed. This makes offshore catamaran sailing more difficult for the novice and also explains to some extent why many leading monohull sailors have turned to trimarans and not catamarans.

(d) *Accommodation*. Here the catamaran scores as both hulls can be used without problem and even small catamarans have considerably more accommodation than monohulls. The trimaran does not, generally, have accommodation in its outriggers and so is little better than a monohull for internal accommodation; there are exceptions and large trimarans such as the *Trimar 52*, designed by the trimaran pioneer Louis Macouillard, are laid out with accommodation in all three hulls. This type of trimaran is not designed for racing but proved itself surprisingly fast in the 1972 OSTAR when Gerard Pesty sailed *Architeuthis* to sixth place. Designers have tried to use trimaran outriggers for accommodation in smaller craft but the result is usually unsatisfactory as the extra size and depth of the outriggers weigh and drag.

37. *Don Robertson's* Snow Goose.

38. Architeuthis *has accommodation in all three hulls.*

Design

This subject is extremely complex and it is not necessary for the newcomer to multihulls
to have a detailed knowledge of it. What is important however, is for people to have
sufficient knowledge to prevent them from buying or building potentially hazardous
craft. Various boats are designed for different purposes and there is a world of difference
between the cruising and racing multihull. Certain principles do apply to all craft and
it is these that concern us.

(a) *WEIGHT*

To me, a slow multihull loses its reason for being, as there is no point in joining two or
three hulls together if the end result cannot perform well. Cheap seaworthy floating
space can be equally well achieved by a fat ballasted monohull without going to the
extent of building extra hulls. This means that it is vital to build and design light multihulls should one agree with the concept that they lose their point if they cannot perform
considerably better than their monohull equivalents. If the reader does disagree with
such a viewpoint, this book will have little relevance to him as he wallows round the
coast in his unsightly multihulled floating caravan. Happily, however, most multihulls
and even some of the heavier cruising ones can out-perform their single hulled equivalents.

The secret to speed is, without doubt, heavily dependent on the multihull being built
as lightly as possible. This is hard to achieve if the owner's specification is for a luxury
cruising yacht.

The American designer, Dick Newick, tells his prospective design clients that they
can have two only of the three major design attributes:

(i)   High Performance.
(ii) Fine Accommodation.
(iii) Low Cost.

If they choose (i) and (ii) they get a very large (over 60 ft.) and expensive yacht; (i) and
(iii) gets a stripped out racing machine while (ii) and (iii) gets a slower and heavier boat
which will not be as attractive or as seaworthy as the first two combinations. Newick
is being extremely honest and it is a pity that more designers do not follow his example.
Far too many make enthusiastic claims for their vessels which actual sea going experience
cannot justify.

(b) *OVERALL BEAM*

The capsize danger is greater, the narrower the beam. This is particularly the case if the
rig is extremely high. On the other hand, an excessive beam is little use if the outriggers
of a trimaran, for instance, have too little buoyancy. As a general rule, the 2 to 1 length/
beam ratio is desirable for a catamaran and greater beam is necessary for a trimaran.
This is not always found, especially with certain catamarans, and some vessels go down
to as little as a 3 to 1 length/beam ratio. This can be unsafe, particularly in a light racing
boat, although the danger will decrease if a narrow boat is extremely heavy or has a

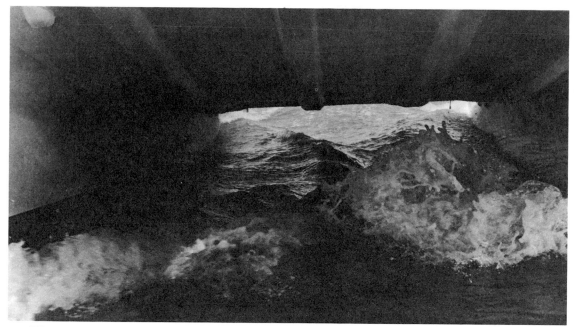

39. *Wave interaction will build up the sea in the middle and perhaps damage the bridge deck, if the hulls are too close together.*

very low rig. Another problem with narrow beam on a catamaran is wave interaction between the hulls where the inner bow waves cross and mount up to smash against the bottom of the bridge deck. The main reason that catamarans tend to be narrower than trimarans is the stressing problems involved when the mast has to be supported over space. Also, their hulls are more buoyant than a trimaran's outriggers.

In a small multihull of under 30 ft., it is even more important to have a relatively greater beam. One reason for this is because the chances of a sailing capsize increase as wave heights are relatively larger to a smaller vessel and craft are usually lighter. Another reason is that stability goes up more quickly than heeling moment as size increases.

(c) HULL FORM

The shape of the main hull, outriggers, or hulls in a catamaran, is a very complex subject and wide differences of opinion exist among designers as to the best shape for speed, safety when surfing, and sea kindliness. With a catamaran, certain factors are relevant:

(i) *Hulls should be symmetrical.* There was a school of thought, started by Brown and Choy in the United States, that the asymmetrical hull helped a catamaran sail to windward. This theory was based on the fact that when the windward hull was nearly out of the water, the aerofoil effect of the leeward hull helped the boat claw to windward. In practice, however, this is rarely the case because it is unsafe to sail an offshore cruising

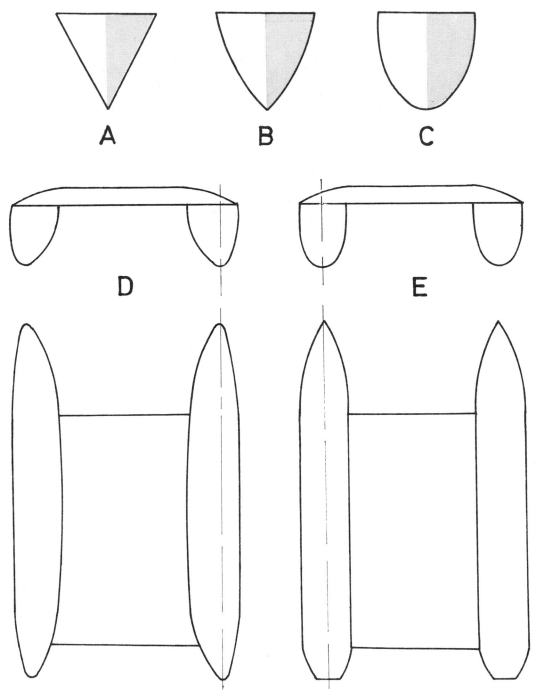

40. *Hull sections. The three principal sections now used are (A) V-shaped, (B) rounded-V, (C) U-shaped. There are numerous permutations. The asymmetrical hull configuration (D) is now considered less preferable to (E) the symmetrical configuration.*

or racing catamaran with one float almost flying. Therefore if asymmetry is effective, the two hulls, almost equally immersed, cancel each others lift.

(ii) *Hulls should not be too narrow*. If they are, there is a tendency for the centre of buoyancy to come close under the centre of gravity earlier as the boat heels with resultant loss of stability, which could lead to a capsize. There is far greater stability in a wider hull as it will be more buoyant and better able to support the weight of the whole boat should she fly a hull. A narrower hull is more likely to dig its lee bow in earlier and to trip, which could then lead to pitch-poling. To avoid this, a narrow hull should be longer for a given weight.

(iii) *Hull Shape*. Hulls should have a fine entry and gradually flatten out as they come aft. The flat semi-circular bottom surfs well but will pound going to windward in a seaway. It is, therefore, Hobson's choice and the resulting compromise is usually a V-shape in the first third of the hull which flattens and rounds out as it comes aft. However, the rounded V-shaped hull has been found to be as fast as a flatter section. Directional stability is maintained by use of centreboards, skegs, low aspect keels or rudders. Fine hulls that are symmetrical fore and aft about the centre line tend to pitch considerably.

(iv) *Forward Lift and Buoyancy*. This is most important, particularly when surfing, for if there is insufficient forward lift and buoyancy, the catamaran will tend to trip over her lee bow or dig in. In most catamarans, this is achieved by long overhangs or by 'dynamic lift' from a knuckle. It is not necessary, as I believe it is with the outriggers of a trimaran, for catamaran hulls to have an upward sheer at the bow on account of the great height of the deck above the water when compared to the floats of a trimaran.

41. *Long overhangs, such as those in* British Oxygen, *help to prevent 'digging in' while surfing. Note also the knuckle which gives dynamic lift and buoyancy.*

In a trimaran, the same comments on hull form are similar in many ways but certain differences apply:

(v) *Length of outriggers and positioning of them relative to main hull.* The outriggers on a trimaran should be positioned well forward so that buoyancy is kept forward and they should not be shorter than four-fifths of the length of the main hull. If they are, a loss in speed will result.

(vi) *Buoyancy of outriggers.* Some designers produce racing trimarans with submersible outriggers. There is a danger that this may result in the outrigger becoming **too** submersible with insufficient buoyancy to stop the boat capsizing quickly in a gust. This is not to say that they are undesirable, but they must have good buoyancy and large overall beam will not compensate for lack of it. Buoyant cross beams or wings will assist with a reserve of buoyancy.

(vii) *Outrigger Shape.* As with catamaran hulls, the outriggers should have a fine entry. I believe that they should have more of a rounded V-shaped section rather than a semi-circular one from half way back, as this reduces pounding and gives more lateral resistance. Because the outriggers are well forward relative to the main hull, any flatish or semi-circular section is bound to pound going to windward. Trimarans which have rounded V sections in all three hulls, do not pound when hard on the wind, whereas others with flatter sections do pound, with resultant loss of speed and extra strain on the structure.

(viii) *Forward buoyancy and sheer.* The trimaran's small, low outriggers have obvious potential for digging in particularly when surfing. This means that they must be buoyant up forward and also have an upward sheer. *Three Cheers* is a fine example of a trimaran with upward sheer in all hulls and there was no tendency to dig in when surfing at 18 knots under bare poles in a North Atlantic gale. Alain Colas was so worried by *Manureva*'s tripping potential that he fitted sponsons to all three hulls to give her lift and forward

42. *Sponsons on all three hulls of* Manureva *were fitted to give her lift when surfing in the Southern Ocean during Alain Colas' singlehanded voyage round the world in 1973. Colas considers lift more important than buoyancy.*

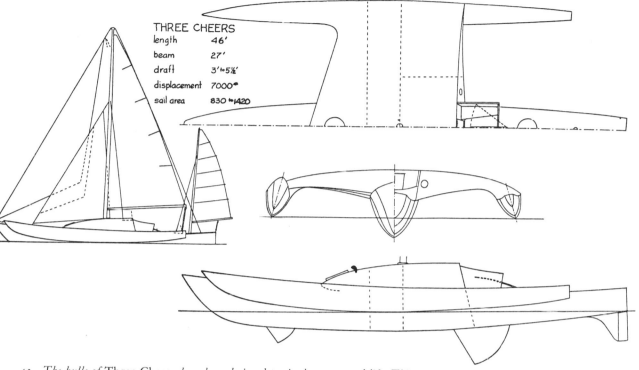

THREE CHEERS
length   46'
beam   27'
draft   3' to 5½'
displacement 7000#
sail area   830 to 1420

43. *The hulls of* Three Cheers *have been designed to give buoyancy and lift. This prevents any tendency to dig into the sea when surfing. Note also the rounded V-sections of the outriggers which prevent pounding to windward.*

buoyancy before tackling the Southern Ocean.

Some trimarans, on the debit side, have a reverse sheer on the bows of the outriggers with the result that there may be a tendency to dig in when surfing if the bows of the

44. *Points to look for in the outriggers of a trimaran. The shaped area represents an outrigger that is wrong in all respects—reverse sheer (a) may dig in, the shortness (b) encourages digging in as there is too little buoyancy forward, while the lack of height and lift (c) encourages a nose dive even further. A correctly shaped outrigger should have more lift and buoyancy forward (a), besides being higher and longer (e).*

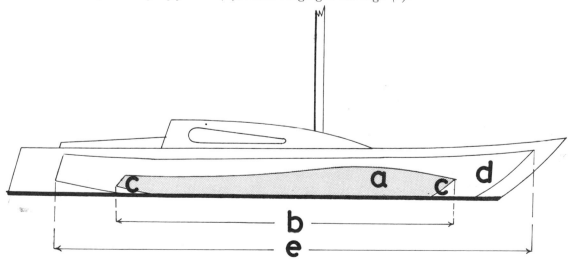

outriggers are too low. This is obviously extremely dangerous and may lead to a capsize or break-up.

(d) *OVERALL CONFIGURATION*

(i) *Structure*. The designer's problem in how he sticks the two or three hulls together is only equalled by that of the builder, or if neither of them do a good job, that of the owner. In the case of the catamaran, the central structure or bridge deck is usually solid so that accommodation can be used in between the hulls. This is satisfactory provided it does not put too much weight and windage high up. It is vital with this type of bridge deck that the bottom of it is well off the sea to avoid wave damage. There have been several cases where bridge decks have been split by wave action. Certain catamarans have a dropped centre in the bridge deck in order to get more standing room. I do not think that this is a wise idea as inevitably it will take a pounding from the sea in rough weather even if it has a good hydrodynamic shape. With a solid structure, the whole catamaran will tend to be rigid, or at least more so than one which has accommodation in the outer hulls only and is joined solely by cross-beams. Such examples of the latter structure are Wharram's catamarans and Macalpine-Downie's *Mirrocat* and *British Oxygen*. In all these examples, there is considerable working as the two hulls have slightly independent motions. This is acceptable in the Wharram cruising catamarans which are not designed for high performance, but it takes more sophisticated engineering to produce a flexible structure that can be driven hard in a race. *British Oxygen* is brilliantly engineered to accept these strains and has proved that it can be done. Generally speaking,

45. *The flexible connecting structure of* British Oxygen *was brilliantly engineered.*

however, a more rigid structure will take less punishment and is far easier to rig.

A trimaran can also be too flexible—particularly if the mast is stayed from the outriggers. The more flexible the attachment of the outriggers is to the main hull, the more likely will working cause damage. Examples of this are numerous—*Yaksha* which sank, *Pen Duick IV* (now *Manureva*), which had to be made more rigid and many others besides. In addition to being rigid, the cross beams or transverse method of connecting outriggers to hull should go right through or across the main hull to ensure strength of attachment at the 'armpits'. The method of joining the outriggers to the cross beams or other types of transverse structure should obviously be extremely strong and can be helped by angling the bottom of the outrigger outwards. This will have the effect of making the outrigger enter the sea symmetrically when the trimaran is heeled which will mean that there is a pushing strain along the cross beam or wing as opposed to a purely snapping strain. It also has the desirable effect of reducing leeway, particularly with a rounded V-sectioned outrigger. A buoyant wing connecting structure will give a tremendous reserve of buoyancy as heel increases.

A solid wing trimaran can be badly designed particularly if too much area between outriggers and main hull is decked in. This also applies to a catamaran up forward where solid structures will be pounded when going to windward. The other danger in

46. *If the bottom crossbeam is too close to the sea, speed may be reduced when pounding to windward and structural damage could be caused by a flat forward surface.*

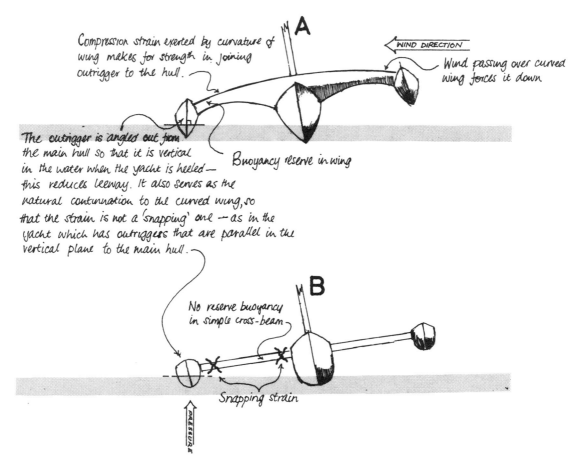

47. *The advantages of the curved wing connecting structure for a trimaran (A) are greater than the configuration of straight cross beams (B). A curved wing is less easy to snap, and the wing contains a good reserve of buoyancy. Also the curved wing deck allows the wind to press down on it, while a flat wing may catch the wind underneath.*

a trimaran is excessive windage **under** the wing when heeled. This can be avoided by keeping the wing area small and by curving the upper deck so that there is in fact, a downward pressure on it even when the windward outrigger is out of the water. The outrigger itself, if angled outwards, will deflect air over the deck and cause a lee underneath it. *Three Cheers'* wing area is under a third in length of the main hull and very curved to give this effect.

Crossbeams do not have the problem of windage under them. They should, however, not present flat surfaces forward and should be as high off the water as possible to reduce slamming. Certain designs exist with two or more crossbeams, one above

48. *The outriggers of a trimaran should just 'kiss' the sea when the yacht is on an even keel in calm water.*

the other, supporting the outrigger in one place, say forward, and the same arrangement aft. This can be satisfactory provided the bottom beam does not come out of the main hull too low down.

The outriggers should be supported in such a way that when the trimaran is on an even keel in calm water, the bottom of each outrigger just kisses the water. This should be the case when the boat is loaded to the designer's specification for the weight in people, stores and equipment that she is designed to carry. If both outriggers are well down in the water, there will be a considerable amount of extra wetted surface area and drag, particularly down wind when the trimaran will not be heeling at all.

Certain types of trimaran have been designed to fold their outriggers alongside the main hull to make them trailable and less expensive when berthing in marinas. This is still an experimental area but no well proven offshore trimaran of this type has yet been produced. The problems of making the joints and hinges strong enough is immense.

(ii) *Centreboards, skegs and rudders.* With some exceptions, most multihulls rely for their lateral resistance on centreboards. There are certain cruising catamarans which do not—notably, Prout's *Snow Goose*, or *Solaris* and Wharram's designs. In the case of Wharram's catamarans, their deep V-section gives them their lateral resistance and the *Snow Goose* and *Solaris* designs depend on low aspect keels. Although these three types will go to windward they are not as close winded as multihulls with a centreboard, particularly in rough offshore conditions. They also make more leeway.

From the design viewpoint, the centreboard has certain problems. Firstly, it takes up accommodation space. In a catamaran, there must be two boards—one in each hull. Obviously, the casing has to be extremely strong and in a small catamaran, especially, this take space. Some designers have attempted to place a board between the two hulls but this has not proved satisfactory and is not recommended. In a trimaran, it is usual to have the board in the main hull which again takes up a lot of space. There are exceptions and General Farrant's *Trifle* has proved extremely weatherly with a plate in each float, each one slightly angled to give her more lift to windward. Some trimarans have two centreboards (one forward, one aft) in the main hull to assist balance, notably Newick's designs. On the whole, it is preferable to have the centreboard(s) in the main hull of a trimaran as the boat is more manoeuvrable with it down and it is easier to get at the board(s).

There are two basic types of centreboard, the dagger board and the pivot board. The dagger board is self explanatory, it is pushed or pulled up and down a casing like a dagger and is usually fairly short in section. Consequently, its casing takes up relatively little room compared with the pivot board. It does, however, have the disadvantage that should one hit the bottom, or anything else for that matter, it cannot hinge up like a pivot board and will either break or damage the hull. There are certain ways of designing these boards so that there is a collision space in the casing which will take up the initial impact but it does not help if you hit something high and steep like a rock, as opposed to just touching the sea bed. The pivot board on the other hand, swivels round a bolt at its head and will come up into its casing immediately anything is hit. The casing, however, has to be as long as the board is deep and will therefore, take up a large amount of room in the centre hull of a trimaran or the hulls of a catamaran. Once again, it is a compromise and most multihulls go for the daggerboard due to its space advantages. Personally, I think the pivot board is more seamanlike as, however good a sailor one is, there are very few people who have never at some time run hard aground.

Rudders have to be exceptionally strong on a multihull because the stress on them is considerably greater than with a monohull. This is because speeds are generally higher and considerable force may have to be applied to keep the boat on a straight course when she is surfing. There is also another factor why they must be strong, and this is that if the craft is caught in irons in a seaway, because of her light displacement she may well sail backwards quickly. This has been the cause of several accidents, when rudders have been torn off completely, so they should be designed in such a way that the yacht can be sailed safely backwards. Apart from anything else, the ability to sail backwards, when leaving a mooring or manoeuvring under sail in a crowded anchorage, is essential. Rudders tend to be smaller on multihulls because less surface area is needed when moving fast. Obviously, they must not be too small to prevent the boat being

66

operated at slow speeds. Many designs use a skeg to strengthen the attachment of the rudder to the boat by means of additional pintles. This is an excellent idea, but the skeg must be strong enough to dry out on. It also has the advantage of giving good directional stability when surfing. All catamarans should have twin rudders and these should be deep enough not to come out of the water when the yacht is pitching. In both cases, the rudders are usually best situated right aft to ease the problem of drying out and to give the greatest turning movement. Fold up or slide up rudders are satisfactory but make sure that they have a good track record of strength before going for this type.

(e) *STANDING RIGGING*

There are two basic ways of rigging a multihull. They are:

   (i) making use of total beam,
  (ii) using only a small proportion of the total beam.

The whole question of rigging depends on the boat's rigidity. If possible, it is advisable to use the total beam of a multihull because the compression load on the mast will be considerably reduced if the angle subtended by the shrouds and the mast is as large as possible. Because a monohull heels, the heeling movement spills wind and to a certain extent reduces the strain on the athwartship's rigging. A multihull, however, will hardly heel at all and there may therefore be considerable strain on the mast and rigging in a gust. This is particularly true of a catamaran which does not heel as much as a trimaran. However, if the rigging is stayed right out to the maximum beam possible, strains caused by the stability of the boat are more than compensated for. This can only be done if the structure is reasonably rigid. The moment it becomes too flexible, there will be alternative tightening and slacking of the rigging which will lead to whip

49. *The staying of a flexible structure such as* British Oxygen. *Note that the cap shrouds do not go right outboard; however the backstay goes to the bridle.*

67

in the mast and a possible break from metal fatigue. With a flexible structure, the shrouds should lead down further inboard, but not necessarily as close to the centre as with a monohull. A good example of this is the catamaran *British Oxygen*. Because of her wide beam (32 ft.) and lack of rigid central cabin structure, the two hulls are designed to move independently. As a result, her mast is stayed well inside the hulls so that all the shrouds are chainplated athwartships to the main crossbeam and the forces of the backstay and forestay are taken out directly fore and aft. This is done by leading the forestay directly to the forward crossbeam which is stressed by an 'upside down' dolphin striker exerting a downward force to offset the upward pull of the stay. The backstay, on the other hand, goes to a bridle, each end of which is chainplated to the transom of each hull. This has the effect of producing a fore and aft tension line and allows the hulls their independent movement without adverse affects on the rigging or mast. It must be emphasised that this method of rigging a flexible structure is highly sophisticated and that the engineering acumen involved is considerable.

It is far simpler to rig a rigid structure because the shrouds can be carried to the extremities of the vessel without any problems. It is also possible in a catamaran to have twin backstays rather than a bridle provided the boat is not too large or flexible. An advantage of twin backstays is that when the weather hull is nearly out of the water, say going to windward, there is a downward strain on the weather backstay which has the effect of tightening the forestay. This is fine in a very rigid catamaran but will cause whip in a large flexible boat. It is also possible, particularly with the normally wider beam of a trimaran, to stay the whole mast without spreaders. This cuts down on expense and windage and means that direct compression loads on the mast are extremely low. *Trifle*, for instance, General Farrant's well known 42 ft. LOA and 27 ft. beam trimaran has a staying angle of 40° between the outer shrouds and the mast. Because of this, the shrouds only have to take a 3 ton load and will break at 5 tons. There is no need to increase the size because the load cannot be more than the force required to capsize the boat and she will go over before 5 tons is reached.

It is sometimes necessary to have a diamond shroud with a small spreader, even when rigging is taken to extreme beam. This is because, to take the case of a trimaran which is not completely rigid, the weather hull may be slightly bent upwards on, say a stiff reach, causing the top of the mast to sag to leeward with resultant bowing of the mast to windward in the centre. A diamond shroud will overcome this. This is fairly usual with trimarans that are connected together with crossbeams. With a rigid structure, such as Newick's designs, a diamond shroud is not needed because the curved wing section prevents the weather outrigger being bent upwards. The inner shrouds with this type of design should, however, be looser than the outer shrouds to compensate for the lack of a diamond shroud.

Generally, all rigging on multihulls which are stayed to their extremities should be reasonably tight but nothing like so tight as on a monohull. This is because there is no need to build in such additional forces on account of the wide angles and low compression loads. If rigging is set up bar taut it will only have the effect of putting far

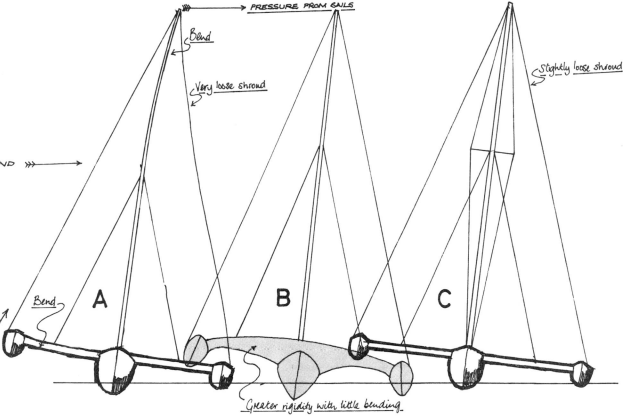

50. *The difference in staying a flexible crossbeam structure (A) and a more rigid curved wing structure (B). In the case of the former a diamond shroud will be needed (C) to prevent the mast bending unnecessarily to leeward. If this diamond shroud is not put in, the bend in the crossbeam (A), which is exaggerated for diagrammatic purposes, will allow the mast to bend considerably.*

greater strains on the overall structure when the craft is sailing. Many people tension multihull forestays too much to try and get a straight luff when beating to windward. This can be damaging to the craft because it will put an unnecessarily large compression load on the mast and bend the hulls like a banana. Both a catamaran and a trimaran have far narrower hulls than a monohull and any attempt to tighten the forestay too far will bend the structure upwards at both ends. Moreover, the boat will still have a slack forestay when sailing because the weight of the sails will bend the hulls even more. This is not always true of a solid cruising multihull which is very rigid, wide of hulls, and not designed for speed; but it is true of any craft which has pretensions to good performance. Headsails **must** be designed to set on a slack forestay.

On a flexible craft like *British Oxygen*, athwartship's rigging has to be as taut as a monohull because of the narrowness of the staying platform. Spreaders must be used extensively and rigging wire must be extremely strong to take the loads. The same rule about headsails still applies, however, as it is unadvisable to put too much strain on a single crossbeam—however well supported.

It is a sensible idea to have stainless steel toggles between the chainplates and bottle screws to give flexibility and prevent metal fatigue. I prefer two so that the rigging can breathe in any direction.

(f) SPARS

Almost all yacht spars are now manufactured from aluminium alloy and this has generally proved to be strong and weight saving. The masts on multihulls do not, on average, have to take similar compression loads as monohulls because of the wide staying angle. However, due to their lack of heel, a compression strain can be induced very rapidly by a strong squall. This, combined with rigging that is too tight, can lead to a mast breakage. It is more common with a catamaran because of the lack of heel when hit by a gust. Masts should therefore be greater in diameter than on a monohull.

Booms should also be stronger because they will take far greater loads, particularly on a fast reach when the kicking strap may be used to get a better sailshape by pulling the boom down, as well as in.

Spinnaker poles, if used, will be similar in every way to a monohull except that they may be longer because of the ship's central mast and large beam. If this is the case, they must be well stressed in the middle to take any sudden loads.

Construction

There are numerous methods of building a multihull and I do not intend to describe them in great detail. They all incorporate the use of three main materials:

   (i)   Wood.
   (ii) Glass fibre and associated products.
   (iii) Metal.

Most methods use either glues or resins for bonding purposes. The missing link, ferro cement, has not yet been proved efficient in multihull construction and seems unlikely to do so for some time on account of its weight strength ratio when used for light displacement craft. It is more viable when used with a heavy displacement monohull where it works out to be reasonably cost effective.

The designer's and builder's problem when deciding on a method of construction for a multihull results, as usual, in a compromise. In this case, cheapness, strength and weight have to be balanced one against the other.

It is debatable whether it is even worth discussing material expenses in these rapidly changing times. At one stage, wood was unquestionably the cheapest way to build any boat. Now there is very little between wood and fibreglass and the race to top the bill

(A)

(D)

(B)

(E)

(C)

(F)

51. *Stages in the foam construction of the trimaran racer* Three Legs of Man. *A male mould is built over which the panels of P.V.C. are laid (A). The gaps between the sandwich panels are filled with stopper (B). The hull is glassed on the outside (C) and the mould removed (D). The inside is then glassed and the cabin top put on (E). The final result (F) was economical and proved to be a fast and successful yacht.*

is fought between the scarcity of timber and the scarcity of oil. Aluminium is still pro-hibitively expensive and also extremely difficult to build with, but this difference is less in the larger sizes where the light metal's advantages become more apparent. Glues and resins increase in price almost daily.

There are three types of construction that I favour to give a good strength and light-weight combination. These are:

(a) Foam sandwich.
(b) Cold moulded veneer sheathed in polypropelene or some good glass fibre cloth.
(c) Moulded fibreglass for the smaller multihull.

These three types may be combined in that the hull may be of one construction and the deck of another. Used purely for hull construction some points are considered.

(a) *FOAM SANDWICH*

Foam sandwich is used mainly in large 'one off' boats and is an excellent method of light-weight construction. Initially, a male mould or framework is built and the foam is tacked to it. The outside is glassed over, the mould removed and the inside is then glassed. The best type of foam in existence at present is the rigid polyvinyl chloride (PVC). This comes in sheets of varying size and density and is of uni-cell construction, i.e. should water come into contact with it, it will not absorb it like a sponge. PVC foam is also the strongest and most flexible type available and there is no tendency for the fibreglass 'bread' to de-laminate from the filling of the sandwich. Other types of foam include polyurethane which is much weaker and another 'core' is balsa wood which can absorb water like a sponge should the outer skin be punctured.

The main advantages of foam sandwich construction using a good filler are:

(i) *Positive buoyancy.* Sandwich foam is highly buoyant. In the event of the ship becoming totally waterlogged, the structure will float in the water. No additional buoyancy is required.

(ii) *Strength and lightness.* Hull structure will be more resistant to side pressure and vibra-tion as the 'strength faces' are spread apart by the foam resulting in more strength with less weight per square foot. Stiffness is therefore enhanced as large unsupported panels will 'pant' or 'oil can' less.

(iii) *Insulation.* A sandwich hull is far warmer in cold climates as it works on the 'string vest' principle. It also provides excellent insulation from noise and is cooler in hot climates. Because foam is a good insulator, condensation is not a problem.

(iv) *Collision penetration.* A blow which would pierce a thin skin of straight fibreglass will not necessarily go right through a sandwich hull. This is because there is a greater overall thickness, there is a compression 'give' in the foam which will dampen the blow, and the force will be distributed over a wider area. Repair will also prove to be easier as the foam provides an excellent 'base' for glass fibre to set on.

The disadvantages of foam sandwich construction are:

(i) *Stress points.* Where, for instance, a cross beam in the case of a trimaran, goes through the hull of a sandwich construction, the hull must be strengthened by removing the foam and filling the gap with resin and glass. If it is not, the constant stresses on the edges of the sandwich will cause wear and disintegration. This reinforcement can be quite difficult to do and there have been cases where air bubbles have caused failures.

(ii) *Bolting.* A similar disadvantage is apparent if it is necessary to bolt or screw a fixture to the hull. The sandwich core must be drilled out and filled with resin and glass before the bolt or screw can be placed.

(b) *COLD MOULDED WOOD VENEER SHEATHED IN CLOTH*

For strength, resilience and light weight it is very difficult to beat a construction of good cold moulded wood veneer. As with foam sandwich, a male mould is constructed and the veneer, usually no thicker than $\frac{1}{8}$ in., is stapled to it. Normally, three layers are used, glued together and the resultant hull is sheathed in some form of polypropelene or glass cloth to provide additional strength. The result is an exceptionally strong and light hull. However, it is now an expensive method of construction and needs experienced and precise workmanship to produce a good finished product.

Advantages:

(i) *Positive buoyancy.* The material is positively buoyant but not quite to the same extent as foam sandwich. This depends on the amount of glue or resin used.

(ii) *Strength and lightness.* A cold moulded veneer hull is the strongest and lightest method of construction available at present. It has colossal resilience and no amount of pounding will cause fatigue provided the structure is well built and sheathed.

(iii) *Attachment of fixtures.* Almost anything can be used, glass, glue, screws or bolts though it is preferable to use the first two for small fixtures. No internal reinforcement is needed at stress points and additional strength can be added by fibreglassing straight on top of the construction.

Disadvantages:

(i) *Insulation.* The hull skin is unlikely to be much thicker than $\frac{1}{2}$ in. and cold is easily conducted. Similarly, the noise level will be higher than with a foam sandwich vessel.

73

(ii) *Internal longitudinal stringers.* These are occasionally necessary to strengthen the hull and are usually glassed and screwed to it. They give a slightly unfinished look and tend to collect dirt.

(c) *MOULDED GLASS FIBRE*
This is normal with mass production multihulls as it provides a reasonably cheap and simple method of construction once the initial mould has been built. It is not, however, particularly suitable for larger vessels as in order to get sufficient stiffness, the glass must be fairly thick with a result that the overall hull may prove too heavy.

Advantages:

(i) *Simplicity.* An easy method of building which is highly suitable for commercial multihulls. Most production catamarans and trimarans are built of straight fibreglass. The two or three hulls are usually moulded independently and the deck is also made in a separate mould.

(ii) *Strength and lightness.* In the smaller multihull, moulded glass fibre construction produces a good lightweight construction. This is not so true above 35 feet overall length.

Disadvantages:

(i) *Negative buoyancy.* This is true of all 'straight' fibreglass boats. It can be overcome in a multihull by building water tight compartments and this is usual to most glass moulded production yachts.

(ii) *Insulation.* Hull thickness is unlikely to be as great as with a cold moulded veneer craft and as a result, cold and noise may be a problem at speed.

(iii) *Initial expense.* The cost of the mould will be considerable compared to the mould for a foam sandwich or wood veneer construction because it must be flat and perfect in shape. This is difficult to build initially. With the other two types of construction, a good framework will suffice.

There are, of course, numerous other methods of construction which are used all over the world other than the three which have been described. The most common is straight plywood which is used by most amateurs and fixed directly on to a frame. It is not so strong as the other methods or so weight saving and it is harder to build with on curved surfaces. It is, however, excellent for decks, bulkheads and areas where flat surfaces are the order of the day. Aluminium is light and strong and *Pen Duick IV* (now *Manureva*) is a fine example. It is an expensive and extremely difficult metal to work and welding it is a job for a specialist. The end product is fast and seaworthy.

Steel and ferro cement have yet to have any great success on account of their weight.

CONSTRUCTION WEAK SPOTS

(i) *Rudders.* The twin rudders of a catamaran and the single rudder of a trimaran **must** be well secured to the main hull, preferably with a minimum of three pintles. There is a far greater strain on multihull rudders due to the reasons already discussed, than there is on a monohull.

(ii) *Centreboards.* A multihull's centreboard will take considerable lateral strains when the boat is beating into a heavy sea. It is essential that the board is solidly built and that the grain, if wood, runs vertically up and down the centreboard. There have been cases where boards have broken because the grain was fore and aft (with the board down). A sheathed board will be stronger but the sheathing must be well finished so that no air or water bubbles can get between the sheathing and the board. If this happens, there is a good chance of the board breaking. Fibreglass boards must be of sufficient thickness to take a heavy lateral load.

(iii) *Centreboard casings.* It is vital that where the casing joins the hull there is sufficient strength to prevent a leak occurring after a period of time during which heavy side loads have been placed on the board. This area should be *strongly* reinforced and the casing itself should have additional lateral stressing further up it, i.e. it should not be entirely supported where it joins the hull. If it is, there is an open invitation to trouble for the joint becomes a potential pivot point when the plate is down.

(iv) *Windows.* Although this is common sense to most competent seamen, it is still frightening to see the number of multihulls built with vast windows which positively cry 'break me, break me' to the sea. Obviously, small windows or portholes are far less likely to be damaged.

52. *Windows as large as these are unwise in an offshore yacht. Note also the windage of the superstructure which will increase leeway.*

(v) *Flush decks.* Similarly, it is undesirable to have any flat vertical surfaces on the upper deck where possible. There is no reason why cabin tops should not slope gently forward rather than vertically downwards and this is more shapely and seaworthy, particularly if your decks are swept by that 'won't ever happen' freak wave.

(vi) *Armpits*. The armpits of a trimaran are where the wings or crossbeams join the main hull. There is an obvious stress point here and the whole of this area must be reinforced. If crossbeams are used, the area of the main hull where they enter must be strengthened. A reinforcing sleeve on the beam itself at this point will help strengthen the structure. The beam should be carried right across the main hull or if this is not possible, some other stressing method should be used.

A catamaran's armpits are where the bridge deck joins each hull. Here again, the same stressing points apply and the area must be strongly reinforced. How this is done is, in both cases, principally a design problem.

On a trimaran, the attachment of the wing or crossbeams to the outriggers is a weak spot and must be well reinforced. For preference, extra strength can be frequently gained by making the crossbeam or wing extend into the basic shape of the outrigger. This makes the whole thing one reasonably rigid structure and avoids the dangers of bolted joints and hinges.

(vii) *Hatches*. Deck hatches on the hulls of a catamaran are obviously acceptable because the hulls are high off the water. Even so, they must be as watertight as possible as there is bound to be high speed water over the deck at some stage. Obviously, the method of securing them must be excellent.

On a trimaran, however, it is a different matter and there are few high performance trimarans that I have come across that have completely successful watertight hatches in their outriggers. Inevitably, the constant passing of water over them will almost certainly cause a leak however well secured they are. It is far better to have no hatch at all but a small screw opening for the bilge pump or permanently fixed hoses which lead through the beams or wings to the main hull where pumping can take place. This has the obvious disadvantage that one cannot look inside the outriggers or feel around for damage etc. However, if there is a leak in the outrigger, the chances are pretty high that it will have to be cut open to make the repair anyway.

3 Basic Seamanship

Sailing Differences in Multihulls—Sails and
Sail Trimming

A seaman is defined by the Concise Oxford Dictionary as a 'person expert in the practice of nautical matters'. Similarly, the dictionary defines seaworthy as 'in fit state to put to sea'.

If we accept these two definitions, we soon realise that anybody who puts to sea, rather than goes out on river or lake, must do so in a seaworthy vessel and should be a seaman. This all sounds very obvious but it is relevant to sailing all boats, and in particular multihulls. A seaman should be capable of taking almost any vessel to sea and may even get away with skippering an unseaworthy craft. Numerous successful voyages have been completed in dangerously unseaworthy yachts, but they were achieved because of the competence of the skipper and crew; on the other side of the coin, perfectly seaworthy vessels have been wrecked because of bad seamanship.

With a multihull, it is even more important for the skipper to be a seaman and for the boat to be seaworthy because, compared with a monohull, everything happens faster and there are more stress points. The boat sails faster (assuming she is not a floating caravan) so navigation and pilotage need to be faster, the ship's movement in a seaway is quicker, anticipation must be earlier, reactions faster and it should always be remembered that a capsize can happen faster. Because of all this, more basic skill is required to sail a multihull.

What, therefore, constitutes a seaworthy multihull? Obviously a Tornado catamaran is not designed for crossing the English Channel and a 23 ft. Hirondelle is not designed to sail across the Atlantic Ocean. This is not to say that, well sailed by a seaman, they will not succeed in doing either. It is a question of knowing the limitation of each vessel, and these will only be known by a seaman with multihull experience. It is easy to sit back and say 'Every cruising yacht should be capable of crossing oceans in safety', but people with limited cash may not be able to afford such a craft. It is therefore better, from their point of view, that they own a small boat which may not be ocean-going rather than no boat at all. The danger comes when they get caught out by adverse conditions in the open sea, or attempt something which would be unseamanlike because of their lack of knowledge or experience of that particular vessel. Many of the accidents that happen in sailing boats occur because people do not know their own or their yacht's limitations. The solution is education and experience.

However, much can be done by designers and builders to improve the overall seaworthiness of their craft. I believe that all multihulls that purport to be seaworthy cruising yachts should be capable of making long open sea passages and weathering storm conditions. This is not always the case and I hope that the reader can judge from this book the points which make a multihull seaworthy for such voyaging.

Sailing Differences in Multihulls

(i) *Apparent Wind*. Perhaps the most obvious difference to the monohull sailor who sails on a multihull for the first time is that a large percentage of one's time is taken up by sailing with the apparent wind forward of the beam. The reason for this is speed. The faster that any moving vehicle goes, the further ahead will the wind be felt. For instance, if you put your hand out of a car window when it is travelling at eighty miles per hour, your hand will feel a very strong wind coming from directly in front; this will happen whether or not there is a strong side wind or tail wind, provided it does not exceed eighty miles per hour, and your motorcar invariably appears to travel 'hard on the wind'.

Because a multihull has such a high potential for speed, it also will appear to be sailing close-hauled for long periods when the true wind is on or even abaft the beam. This will not happen if the multihull is a slow vessel although, like a monohull, there will be a slight difference between the true and apparent wind. The faster the boat goes, the further ahead will the wind be felt; this is self limiting with our present fore-and-aft rig because there will come a stage where the boat goes so fast that the wind will come from directly ahead. This cannot happen at present because no sailing boat can yet travel that fast, but if it could do so all the sails would flap uselessly, however flat they were cut. Thus a speed limit is imposed by the vessel's design and rig, but this has not yet been reached. What it does mean, however, is that fast multihull sails must be cut far flatter than those of a monohull to allow for the increase in wind speed and the narrow angle caused by the vessel sailing very close to the apparent wind. This point is seldom appreciated by sailmakers who insist on cutting full sails as they would do for a monohull.

When the wind is way aft of the beam and the yacht is running, the situation is reversed and the wind speed over the deck may be almost zero. Even in a strong blow of twenty knots or so, the wind speed over the deck may be negligible if the yacht is surfing at up to twenty knots. Because of this it may be difficult to tell if the yacht is running by the lee, particularly at night.

(ii) *Acceleration*. Because a multihull has a negligible angle of heel, when it is struck by a gust there is only one way for it to go, assuming it does not capsize, and that is forwards. With a monohull however, the force of the gust is taken out initially by the boat heeling and the sails slipping the wind. This cannot happen in the same way on a multihull because of the boat's considerable beam and stability; however it does happen slightly more on a trimaran than a catamaran because a trimaran is designed to heel a little;

in both cases there will be a very rapid forward acceleration which will call for an instant hardening of all sheets as speed increases and the apparent wind draws forward. The lighter the boat the more rapid this acceleration will become, and it is quite possible to go from a broad reach to apparent close-hauled sailing in the space of seconds due to a relatively small increase in wind. This calls for constant alertness on the part of the crew and very fine sail trimming; frequently sheets will have to be hardened and eased continuously to get the best out of the boat in gusty conditions.

(iii) *Slowness in stays*. Because a multihull is light, she will be far slower to tack than a monohull. This is because the moment she comes head to wind there is very little forward momentum as the boat is so light that she almost stops dead when put head to wind. The extent to which this happens is dependent on the weight of the individual boat and the sea state; in a rough sea a very light multihull will be harder to tack than a heavier vessel. Sometimes it may be necessary to back the headsail to windward while going about in order to get her round; this is quite normal and is not the sign of a bad design. Moreover, in the case of a yawl or ketch, it may even require an easing of the mainsail or the mizzen after the boat has been through the eye of the wind to prevent her coming back up again. In the trimaran schooner *Manureva*, Alain Colas hauls the mizzen to windward before tacking so that it pushes the boat through the eye of the wind during the evolution and once she is round, the slack sail allows her to pay off rather than push her back up into the wind.

While the manoeuvre of tacking is being carried out, a constant eye must be kept on the sea immediately beside the helmsman to check whether the boat is moving forwards or backwards. If she starts to move backwards, reverse helm should be applied immediately to get her round and the main sheet, with the mizzen sheet too when the sail is set, let out. This will have the effect of allowing her to pay off and sailing may be resumed on the other tack. It is vital to stress that the spot where the helmsman decides to tack should be pre-selected, and the golden rule is **always give yourself plenty of room**. I have seen certain multihulls which do not come about easily, drift downwind in irons for a hundred yards or so; this can be dangerous and worrying, particularly for anyone who is in the way! However, if the multihull is well designed, little problem will normally be experienced with tacking, and it is purely a matter of getting used to a slightly different technique.

(iv) *Gybing*. Gybing a multihull is far easier than a monohull because there is usually very little weight in the mainsail when running dead before the wind. This is because the extra speed of the boat takes the strain off the sail as the speed through the water will be closer to the wind speed than with a monohull. As a result, the boom, more often than not, can be flicked across easily and there will be no immediate change in the angle of heel to accelerate the process like on a monohull. In really strong conditions, it is wise to sheet the mainsail amidships and as flat as possible before gybing, then to let it out quickly after the evolution is completed. The main point to watch in strong conditions is the helmsman's steering; as with any boat there will be a tendency to come up to wind immediately after a gybe and this will lead to acceleration and a possible broach. A good helmsman will be able to correct this without trouble.

(v) *Sailing stern first*. It is frequently necessary and desirable to sail stern first in a multihull for a variety of reasons. The most common of these is close quarter manoeuvring under sail. Very frequently, when anchor is weighed or mooring let go, it may be necessary to lose a short amount of ground downwind in order to go off on the right tack. It may also be necessary to do this after getting caught in irons in the open sea or to pick up a man who has gone overboard. Thus it is essential that rudders are strongly attached.

It is possible to sail stern first quite fast in a light multihull and this may put a specially large strain on the rudder. Indeed I have sailed backwards at about four knots in *Three Cheers* in strong conditions and it was amazing how easily she could be manoeuvred provided the right sails were backed. A good tip when leaving a mooring or weighing anchor is physically to hold the main boom forwards so the mainsail pushes her back. If the tiller is over the same side, the boat will back very quickly into a close-hauled sailing position and allow one to sail off with the greatest of ease on the desired tack without having to adjust the mainsail too much. While doing this, the headsail should be backed on the opposite side to give an even greater turning moment. These techniques were once used with great success by square riggers making a stern board.

53. *Sailing stern first at about three knots in* Three Cheers.

(vi) *Leeway.* Because multihulls are light and of shallow displacement, they tend to make more leeway than a monohull when hard on the wind. This is reduced by using centreboards or low aspect keels but the tendency to make leeway will always be there. It is most noticeable when the boat is hard on the wind and many skippers will allow between two and five degrees of leeway over any distance when close-hauled; however the tendency to make leeway persists when forereaching because the apparent wind is often well forward. Some vessels will make far more leeway than others, particularly in a rough sea. Any multihull which relies on V-shaped hulls or low aspect keels for its weatherliness is bound to make considerably more leeway than a craft with deep centreboards; this is partly because the top portion of the sea is likely to be moving slowly to leeward in a blow and the vessel has nothing which can dig deep into the 'solid' water below, but also the V-shaped hull has no flat, vertical surface to present resistance to the sea. The more windage a vessel has, particularly high up, the greater will be the tendency to make leeway; thus the steep, slab-sided cruising catamaran with a large high square deckhouse will make more leeway when compared with the lower profile of the racing trimaran.

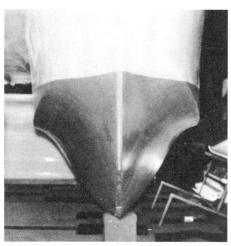

54. *The V-shaped hull without boards will make more leeway than one with boards.*

(vii) *Close hauled ability.* There is an enormous amount of difference from boat to boat when it comes to pointing hard on the wind. The more surface area of yacht that is presented to the wind the worse the boat will point and the more leeway she will make; also if the sails are badly cut she will naturally be less close-winded. Almost all multihulls point further off as the sea and wind worsen because they are so light that there is a tendency to be thrown off. However, the good racing catamaran or trimaran will point almost as close as the most close-winded of monohulls. In the 1974 Round Britain Race, the catamaran *British Oxygen* and the trimarans *Three Cheers, Gulf Streamer* and *Triple Arrow* were all pointing as high at the start as the 80 ft. lightweight monohull *Burton Cutter* and were going quicker. On the other hand, the Admiral's Cupper *Quailo III* was out-pointing every boat but was still beaten to windward by the multihulls as they were going so much faster. Most racing multihulls will point at 45–47° to the true wind which is extremely good, but generally speaking, they have a justifiably bad reputation for close-hauled ability which is caused by the large numbers of poor performance cruising vessels. On this score, the cruising monohull will often beat a cruising multihull to windward in bad weather unless the latter is a high performance cruising yacht such as *Gulf Streamer*. A multihull is more difficult to steer well to windward than a monohull because the 'feel' is far less as the boat will remain close-hauled if you bear away a little when the apparent wind is still just as far forward. Some boats are easier to feel than others and the best key to success is constant practice. At night it is even harder to steer well to windward and many multihull sailors put heavy reliance on instruments to help them. Personally, I do not think that this is always a good thing as reliance on any instrument dulls human awareness and if you have to do without them your feel for the boat will soon materialise.

(viii) *Turning circles*. A multihull has a larger turning circle than a monohull of the same length. This is due to a number of reasons, the most important of which is beam, because it takes longer to drag an extra hull round a corner when it is in itself providing resistance to the turning moment. Another reason may be the rudder size, frequently small on racing multihulls; other causes can be lowered centreboards in the outriggers of trimarans; two centreboards down in a fore-and-aft direction, one of which is bound to create lateral resistance; bad weight distribution, for instance too much weight forward will cause the head of the vessel to go down and create resistance.

A large turning circle is not necessarily a great disadvantage, but it does take a little bit of getting used to and some practice is required. It has obvious disadvantages in a tight situation where a high degree of manoeuvrability is needed and the skipper may have to use cunning and anticipation before he succeeds in whatever he is trying to do in these circumstances. It is, in a way, the difference between driving a large lorry and a small car, daunting at first but no problem when you become used to it.

(ix) *Use of centreboards*. The majority of multihulls use centreboards to give them their lateral resistance and weatherliness. A catamaran has a board or two in each hull and a trimaran usually has a board or two in her main hull. Anybody who has sailed a dinghy will soon appreciate that their use is much the same in a multihull; when the ship is going hard to windward she will need all the lateral resistance she can get and the board(s) should be fully down. However, the moment she comes off the wind, speed will increase enormously and the tendency to make leeway will decrease. The board(s) should therefore be partially raised to give less drag and to take the strain off them. There have been several cases of centreboards breaking due to being fully down when screaming along on a broad reach, which is both stupid and unnecessary.

On a run, the boat will normally go faster with the board(s) up. However, certain vessels may need a bit of plate down to give them directional stability, particularly if they have no skeg at the stern. This can only be discovered by trial and error in individual craft; a multihull with a flattened rounded bottom, will need the directional stability of a vertical board when running much more than a craft with a V-cross-section.

The reason that some multihulls have two centreboards in a fore-and-aft line is to provide the ability to balance the boat on any point of sailing, and is particularly relevant to boats designed for short handed sailing. With two centreboards, an excellent degree of balance can be achieved under any rig; with only one, there is bound to be some point of sailing where the boat will carry either lee or weather helm under various sail conditions. Because a multihull goes so much faster than a monohull, it is vital that she should balance well, as if she does not the helm which must be applied to correct her will slow the boat's speed, besides causing undue strain on the helmsman. This may not be so important on a cruising multihull which will always be fully crewed, but it is vital on a racing yacht where it can cut down speed by as much as a knot. Balance is vital to performance.

There is a capsize danger through tripping over the leeward centreboard in a catamaran, and this will be examined closely in the chapter on accidents.

(x) *Weight distribution.* The distribution of weight on a multihull is important both to its safety and performance.

On any point of sailing, the force of the sails will be forward and to leeward because:

(a) The push of all sails is forward.
(b) The heeling moment (prevented by outrigger or hull) is to leeward.

The result of this force is that all multihulls usually have a downward pressure on the lee bow when sailing. If the boat is on a dead run without a spinnaker, the pressure will be directly forward over the bows, but still downwards; however a spinnaker will create a lift and counter this.

It is important that weight is distributed in a correct way, and the two golden rules are:

(a) Keep the weight out of the bows.
(b) Keep the weight low.

Generally speaking, weight should be kept as much amidships as possible in both a catamaran or a trimaran, particularly when going to windward or reaching. If there is equipment far aft when close-hauled in a rough sea, it may well be thrown all over the place because of the quick motion. On a fast reach, the downward pressure on the lee bow is at its greatest because the sails are pulling with their maximum driving force and the heeling moment is at its maximum. It is therefore particularly important that crew members should not walk out to the lee bow as even this weight can be hazardous, particularly in the smaller vessel.

There are occasions, particularly in catamarans with flattened rounded stern sections, when it helps the performance of the craft to bring weight into the sterns if she is surfing fast down large seas. This is because any flat surface will surf far better than a V-section and by putting the weight on the flat surfaces aft, the boat has more flat area on the water and emulates a surf board.

Similarly, performance and safety can also be helped by weighting the windward side of a multihull on a long passage. This will keep her more upright and will decrease the capsize possibilities. However, it must not be done on a run as it could encourage a broach.

In a multihull it is important to keep the weight as low down as possible to maintain a low centre of gravity as the higher the boat's centre of gravity the more easily she can be capsized. Weights such as anchors, water tanks or containers, chain, outboard engines, deflated dinghies (but not self-inflating life-rafts) must all be kept in the bilges for preference.

(xi) *Motion*. In general, the motion on board a multihull is far kinder than on a monohull, because the boat is upright and more stable in all weathers. There is practically no rolling whatsoever even when running before the worst of seas, and in an anchorage where a monohull may roll considerably, the multihull will be a level and stable platform. Certain multihulls do, however, have a tendency to pitch rather heavily and this is normally more common in a catamaran which is fine of section at both ends and has considerable top weight; this is a design problem and vessels which tend to flatten out as they come aft will pitch less. A well designed multihull will not pound at all going to windward, particularly if she is fine of entry and fine of section from amidships forward; there are exceptions and many heavy cruising vessels will pound considerably, particularly if overloaded.

Probably the most noticeable difference in motion is that the multihulls have a quicker movement than monohulls, because they are lighter. This gives force to the rule 'one hand for yourself and one for the ship'; in particular, there is definite bounce motion on both bow and stern when boating to windward in a seaway, and anybody who goes forward or aft under these circumstances should do so with extreme care. Similarly when moving over exposed points, like getting out of the cockpit, care must be taken. Many people consider that bunk leeboards are unnecessary on multihulls; this is not the case, particularly on a trimaran, and a number of people have been injured by being thrown out of their bunks in gale conditions.

Off the wind, both types of multihull have a delightfully steady motion and when surfing fast in near gale conditions.

(xii) *Anticipation, preparation and alertness*. In any sailing boat, anticipation and preparation is required before undertaking any evolution, while alertness is vital at all times. In a multihull, particularly a fast one, these requirements become even more imperative because everything happens faster.

Anticipation of sailing manoeuvres must be that much sooner, particularly in crowded waters, and the skipper must think several hundred yards ahead. He must pre-select the place where he tacks with a view to other boats, sea state, tactics when racing, closeness of lee shore and 'fall back' area in case the ship does not come around. He must select the spot where he changes sail if, for instance, he knows that his vessel is not so easily handled under mainsail alone and makes leeway. When approaching an anchorage or picking up a mooring, the skipper should be working out the problems of preparation at least half a mile or more before the evolution takes place and he should reduce in good time to the rig under which he intends to manoeuvre. Navigation and pilotage must be precise, especially in a really fast racing yacht which may be averaging twelve or thirteen knots; at such speeds one is travelling faster than many coasters and the land goes by with frightening rapidity; buoys, rocks, sand banks and headlands all become harder to identify at speed and an accurate dead reckoning should always be kept.

Finally, and most important, alertness is absolutely essential on a fast multihull. Because of the sheer speeds possible it is vital to **keep a good look out** at all times. It frequently happens that a merchant ship and a multihull may be on a collision course at a combined speed of well over thirty knots, so that on a clear night, if the other craft's masthead lights first become visible seven miles away, you could be on each other in only fourteen minutes, which gives little time for avoiding action if you do not anticipate fast enough. It is also worth remembering that in daylight it is equally important to keep a good look out. Merchant ships on seeing a sail will assume it is a monohull and will assume a monohull's speed; it is only when close that the exceptional closing speed becomes apparent and by then a collision is imminent. So it is up to the multihull sailor to keep clear in those circumstances; always go astern of another vessel if there is the slightest doubt; remember the wind can ease! Imagine also the effect on your boat if you smash into a floating log during an eighteen knot burst of speed.

Alertness in sail handling is just as important and will be discussed fully in the chapter on accidents. In squally weather the crew must be exceptionally alert to the possibility of a gust capsizing the vessel and they must be ready to ease sheets or bear away.

All this leads me to state that sailing a multihull, particularly a fast one (and all multihulls should be fast or they lose their point), needs more skill than sailing a monohull. Any reasonable seaman should have no difficulty in getting used to the technique, but it does require practice, and most important, experience.

Sails and Sail Trimming

(1) RIG

A multihull's speed and lack of heel present certain immediate differences from the monohull. The first of these is that the slot effect of the sails takes on far more significance, so that most fast and large multihulls go for the cutter rig, which has the advantage of increasing the number of slots in the rig and thus gives definite increases in speed. To give an example, it is very noticeable in *Three Cheers* that if sailing under full main and staysail only, speed can be increased by reefing the main fairly heavily and adding the No. 2 jib; this does not increase or reduce the sail area but just distributes it over three sails and adds one more slot. It also brings the centre of heeling moment lower, which reduces the risk of capsize in strong weather.

This last point leads us on to the advantages and disadvantages of high or low aspect rigs on multihulls. A high aspect rig incorporating a tall mast and short boom will often be sloop rigged because of a smaller fore triangle and will seldom, if ever, be part of a two masted rig. A low aspect rig will usually have a mast that is about the same length or less than the overall length of the yacht and may well be part of a cutter rigged ketch or yawl.

The main advantages of a high aspect rig area are:

(a) Good light weather performance, because sail can be set high up, including large light wind genoas and drifters that will catch the air high above sea level where it is stronger. This also gives an advantage when running dead before the wind under spinnaker as more lift can be generated in light weather.

(b) There is no need to make up for lack of sail area by going to a ketch or yawl rig, which entails another mast and is not usually so efficient to windward because backwinding from the mainsail counters the power of the mizzen, although this is by no means always true. Nevertheless wind tunnel tests show that a high aspect rig reduces drag when full sail can be set.

The disadvantages of a high aspect rig to my mind outweigh the advantages. They are:

(a) Capsize danger from the height of rig. Obviously, the higher a multihull's rig, the more top weight it has; this means that the inertia is greater even when well reefed, and in heavy weather this can help towards a capsize. Also inertia will tend to increase the boat's pitching motion, which is one of the reasons why the Americans reduced top weight by using titanium for the top twenty feet of mast on 12-metres for the *America*'s Cup.

With a high rig in squally weather when the average wind speed may not call for a reefed mainsail the crew will have to be very alert either to ease sheets or pay off to avoid a capsize from a sudden puff. The alternative is to sail under-canvassed, which is fine when cruising but not so good in a race.

Many capsizes of catamarans have occurred because they have been over-rigged, and it is rather tempting providence to sail a cruiser/racer with such a tall rig that it tempts an inexperienced crew to hang onto full sail until the last moment. Obviously, this does not apply to the same extent in out and out 'one off' racers such as *British Oxygen*, which have very high aspect rigs but are designed to be sailed by very experienced seamen.

(b) A low aspect rig is far more efficient in heavy weather, because sail can be carried low down in a variety of places which will maintain good slot effects; also there is not the extra drag and heeling moment of a high mast, part of which is useless when it cannot carry full sail because of high wind strength. On a reach, in particular, a low aspect cutter rigged ketch will be extremely fast in heavy weather as it will be able to carry four sails low down with good slots and little heeling moment; it will also be more easily handled and balanced.

55. (Right) The cutter headsail arrangement is very effective on a fast multihull as it increases the number of slots.

(c) Rigging problems. The higher the mast the more difficult it becomes to stay, which adds both weight and windage. Compression strains also increase and a high aspect mast will almost certainly need spreaders. The strains on deck fittings will be increased and the overall structure may be pulled out of shape more easily. The forestay will have more sag in it because it is longer and there will be greater strains on halyards, particularly the main halyard, if a fully battened mainsail is used.

To sum up, there is very little difference in efficiency between high and low aspect

56. Three Cheers *and* Gulf Streamer *sailing together in the Solent. Note the low aspect rig, particularly of* Three Cheers *which enables her to carry several sails low down in strong weather. Neither yacht has a fully battened mainsail.*

rigs but a considerable difference in safety. As one should always err on the side of safety, I believe that a low aspect rig is more suited to multihulls.

Although the basic sloop and cutter rigs are the most common on multihull boats, ketch, yawl and schooner rigs are frequent on larger yachts. A two-masted rig of any type is less efficient on a catamaran than on a trimaran, because there is no angle of heel on a catamaran which results in the wind from the forward mast spilling directly backwards onto the mizzen; this is especially true at speed and when the vessel is close

57. The *Atlantic* proa Sidewinder *had to retire from the 1970 Round Britain Race because her masts were too close together. This resulted in such wind interference on the aft sail that her efficiency suffered.*

58. *(Opposite) The high aspect ratio of* British Oxygen *is less of an advantage in rough weather when the top of the mast is of no use, and is extra weight in the wrong place. In light weather, however, her rig is hard to beat.*

hauled. On a trimaran however, there is a fair degree of heel, and this spills the wind to leeward, so the mizzen is not so useless, provided that it is set well back; inevitably, it will not be 100% efficient but it should give at least some drive in a well designed rig. Off the wind, it is a different matter and the mizzen becomes a good working sail. One of the factors to bear in mind with any two-masted rig is that the mizzen should be further aft of the main mast than on a monohull, because a multihull is faster and wind speeds over the sails will be greater so there will be more back draught to interfere with the mizzen. Certain designs have failed because their designers did not appreciate this. One of the great advantages of a two-masted rig on a multihull is that it is possible to tack more easily, sail backwards with simplicity, and balance the boat better by slight adjustment of headsail and mizzen sheets. This latter point is important as far as performance goes because any lee or weather helm will slow down a fast multihull.

A further advantage of a mizzen is that it will serve to keep the head of the ship up into the wind if she is hove-to in a gale. This can prove a great asset and will be discussed later.

(2) SAIL SHAPES

(a) *Headsails.* As we have seen already, it is extremely important that all sails are cut flatter than on a monohull because multihulls are generally faster. It is easy for a sail maker to do this but not always so easy to convince him that multihulls' sails require this! They must also be cut to allow for a sagging forestay, which is a little harder for a sailmaker to do but provided that he knows how much sag to allow for, should not present any great problem. It is more important to allow for this sag on large sails such as genoas than small, hard weather sails which will be used when the vessel will not be able to point so high anyway. It is amazing how many people still believe that a bar tight forestay is essential to good windward performance; it is not, provided that the headsails are cut to allow for it.

All headsails except ghosters and light genoas should be treble stitched, as there is far more strain on a multihull's sails than a monohull, and the apparent wind will be crossing the sails faster, with that much more chance of them blowing out.

As well as treble stitching, it is essential that the three corners of each sail are adequately strengthened. It is remarkably easy to pull a clew out at high speed by simply letting the sheet out and allowing the sail to flap itself to death; when the sail starts to flap violently the sheets inevitably 'ball up' in a knot just aft of the clew, and become impossible to unravel without lowering the sail; if the knot is left flapping the weight of it will pull out the clew and the sail will be ruined. Thus it is important when changing sail at speed to ensure that the crew sheet in the new headsail quickly once raised to avoid a 'ball up'. If one is shorthanded, it is advisable to have the sheet of the new headsail partially sheeted in and secured before hoisting sail to avoid the problem.

An interesting observation of fast multihulls is that the cutter rig with a high cut yankee jib and staysail is faster than using a large genoa with enormous overlaps. This is a generalisation and it should be realised that in light weather large genoas have obvious advantages; however, there is little doubt that most racing multihulls reach their maximum speeds under the cutter rig with a high cut jib set, because the aerofoil is far better with such a combination than with one large genoa, and the slot effect that can be produced by a high cut jib which has its clew midway and at right angles to the centre of the luff, gives an extremely efficient wing type of aerofoil section, provided that the jib is cut flat enough. This is one of the hardest sails for a sailmaker to cut well and it may need much adjusting to get right.

All cutter rigged multihulls should have a storm jib and a No. 2 jib. The latter should be cut similar to the high cut No. 1 jib, but should have a luff of only approximately two-thirds the length of the forestay; this gives the vessel the capability to sail hard on a reach or to windward in heavy weather by enabling her to use a low aspect ratio fore-triangle without losing the advantage of the extra slot given by a cutter rig. There should be a wire strop, not a rope strop, from the head of the No. 2 jib to the snap shackle of the halyard. If rope is used, the stretch in the luff can cause the top of the halyard to belly to leeward, where it may fray against the side of the halyard block at the masthead and part.

The staysail in a cutter rigged multihull is the sail that usually suffers more wear and tear than any other sail; it is usually the last sail to be taken down in a blow before the storm jib is set, and it is also the centre foil of the two slots. It must, therefore, be extremely robustly constructed of good strong material.

(b) *Mainsail.* It is important that the mainsail of a multihull is cut extremely flat, is treble stitched and has good, well attached corners. There have been several cases of mainsail headboards pulling out, particularly with heavy, fully battened sails, so sailmakers must take particular care in making this part of the sail as strong as possible. There is more strain on the luff than in a monohull and the strongest form of joining the sail to the mast is recommended; a good combination is a luff rope which goes up a slide in the mast and hanks which go up a further slide in addition. This gives a strong means of attachment.

59. Luff rope and slides provide a strong and non wind resistant method of attaching the luff of the mainsail to the mast.

93

The main points in favour of a fully battened sail are:

(i) It is extremely well mannered and never flaps or flogs whatever the wind strength, even if it is feathering head to wind.

(ii) It is possible to increase sail area by using battens to give extra roach.

(iii) It is safer when released in a gust as it does not flog, which could capsize a small multihull.

The arguments against a fully battened mainsail are:

(i) It puts considerable weight in the wrong place, i.e. up the mast which can aid the capsize moment. It also means extra all up weight.

(ii) It puts a greater strain on the main halyard, and all fittings. The battens can also damage the cloth of the mainsail if the sail rubs against shrouds or other rigging.

(iii) Probably only slab reefing is possible. Roller reefing is largely excluded because it is best not to roll extremely long battens onto the boom as they usually twist over it and break, which can at times be avoided by having battens parallel to the boom.

(iv) A fully battened mainsail is more expensive.

(v) A fully battened sail is difficult to lower on a run as the battens push against the luff groove, which can be dangerous.

The theory that a fully battened mainsail will improve performance is not sufficiently proven. Those who support the fully battened school say that additional stiffness from long battens gives more drive, particularly to windward. This may be true if the battens can be made stiff enough, but in more than moderate winds the battens will usually bend along the natural curve of the sail giving no advantage. However, the only case I know where the battens do not curve is General Farrant's trimaran, *Trifle*, in which bamboo poles give extreme rigidity and an exceptionally flat windward sail; the sail is extremely stiff and heavy, so in light airs it is necessary to tauten lines which put an artificial bend in the battens, but they add weight and windage besides being inconvenient to use. The flat batten cannot be made stiff enough to give any real advantage over the soft mainsail in a vessel of any size; however in a small dinghy catamaran it needs to retain stiffness over a much smaller length and will therefore be more rigid and efficient. A fine example of this is the Olympic Tornado class which would be slower with a soft mainsail.

What is not often realised is that a fully battened mainsail on a large multihull needs exceptionally careful tuning to be at all effective. The battens themselves, must be very carefully measured and of the right thickness. It is advisable to have battens thicker and stiffer nearer the foot and lighter towards the head of the sail. Tuning lines such as on *Trifle* may be needed in light weather, and particular care must be taken to see that no areas of the sail are liable to chafe from the corners or ends of the battens. A good supply of spare battens should be carried because breakages can occur fairly frequently.

To my mind, the real advantage of a fully battened mainsail is its potential to increase sail area and its excellent manners when hoisted. These good points, however, are offset by the weight and strain disadvantages, particularly in a large multihull.

60. Trifle's *mainsail uses bamboo poles for battens. Note the flat reaching spinnaker.*

(c) *Mizzen*. Strangely enough, there is more of an argument for a fully battened mizzen than a fully battened mainsail:

(i) The battens will be more effective and give a flatter sail if the sail is smaller.

(ii) Extreme flatness is necessary if there is any danger of backwinding from the mainsail.

(iii) The mizzen is often totally slackened off when manoeuvring and it is therefore advantageous to have a well mannered sail.

(iv) The extra roach moves the centre of effort of the sail slightly aft and lessens the risk of backwinding from the mainsail.

(d) *Spinnakers*. When the fast multihull first appeared many designers and sailors discounted the use of the spinnaker, because it was thought that the high speed of the craft would make tacking down wind without one more profitable, as the apparent wind could be brought forward to increase speed. To some extent this was true, but only so in the case of an extremely fast multihull; even the very fast boats need a spinnaker on certain points of sailing—mainly dead down wind or just off it. The slower multihulls certainly must have spinnakers for all down wind sailing and many of them carry spinnakers with the wind forward of the beam. This will not be possible in a high performance boat other than in extremely light weather with a very flat sail. It is impossible to lay down any fixed rules about when or when not to fly a spinnaker; it depends entirely on the type of craft and its speed potential.

There are two basic ways of flying a spinnaker on a multihull:

(i) With a pole, which may have its base on the mast or the forecastle.

(ii) Without a pole and using eyes fixed on the forward end of the outriggers for windward sheets.

Both methods are practical on all multihulls but the poleless method is far easier on a trimaran than a catamaran because a trimaran normally has greater overall beam.

In both cases, it is necessary for the spinnaker to be much flatter than on a monohull, because the apparent wind will still move forward, unless the boat is absolutely dead before, and a full spinnaker will simply collapse. On *Three Cheers* a spinnaker pole is

61. Three Cheers *does not use a spinnaker pole, but makes use of her beam instead.*

not used and the sail is best set when the true wind is 10° from right astern in a force five. If the wind increases the angle of use decreases, while if the wind decreases, the spinnaker can be used harder on the wind. A slower boat would be able to carry a spinnaker much closer to the apparent wind angle, but it is not possible to stipulate rules and every boat must experiment to find which course of action gives the fastest speed.

Only when dead downwind is it possible to fly a full, conventional spinnaker. This has a big advantage over twin headsails or goose-winged sails in that a spinnaker gives lift forward; this serves to increase speed and to cut down the risk of digging in. A very light multihull should be able to carry a spinnaker dead downwind for some time as the wind increases because the boat will be travelling nearer the wind speed than a monohull and the chance of blowing the sail out is therefore less.

One very real hazard with a spinnaker on a multihull is the risk of it wrapping around the forestay in a strong wind. If it does this a multihull, because of its lightness, will only be able to travel in one direction, and that is dead downwind, which can be inconvenient, at least, if there are obstacles such as the coast in the way. It must be remembered that more alertness is required when flying spinnakers.

(3) SAIL TRIMMING

One of the joys of a multihull is that it has a wide sheeting platform, which means that sails can be trimmed with greater flexibility than on a monohull.

(a) *Sailing close hauled.* Generally speaking, there is little benefit from sailing faster off the wind to make a better speed when beating to windward. However this is a grey area and it may not necessarily be the case in an extremely lengthy passage with a liability to major fluctuations in wind direction. On windward legs of under 200 miles or so when there is unlikely to be a wind shift, it is usually better to be as close winded as possible without pinching the yacht. We have already seen that the apparent wind draws ahead very considerably in a fast multihull and it is quite usual for a racing yacht to be averaging nine knots and sailing only 17° or 18° to the apparent wind. She may still be sailing 45° to the true wind but because the apparent wind is so far forward, sheets must be absolutely bar tight so that the sails are as flat as possible; otherwise efficiency will be greatly reduced and the boat will not point so high.

In a cruising catamaran which relies on low aspect keels or V-sections to reduce leeway, this will not necessarily apply and it may be better to sail faster further off the wind.

In very light winds it is not advisable to have the sheets so tight and it will pay to ease them slightly and bear away a little to increase speed. Similarly, in squalls, it is usually possible to claw a bit more to windward by luffing the boat. In heavy squalls the golden rule of multihull sailing is to bear away from the wind to avoid the capsize moment of centrifugal force caused by luffing as this may tip the boat. However, in a severe squall when hard on the wind, it is quite safe to feather the sails by luffing. This does NOT apply on any other point of sailing.

(b) *Reaching*. As with most yachts, the reach is the fastest point of sailing for a multihull. A reach is usually defined as when the true wind is dead on the beam; a close reach is when the wind is slightly forward and a broad reach is when the wind is slightly aft of the beam. Any of these points of sailing may be fastest for a given yacht, depending on the wind conditions. In light airs, a close reach will be very much faster than a broad reach and the reverse will apply in stronger weather when it will be necessary to reduce sail if the wind is forward of the beam. It is very important, and especially to the racing man, that the multihull skipper should know how his boat's speed can be improved on a reach by only a small alteration of course. Instruments are of value here as the apparent wind can be rapidly moved by small changes of direction which may give a speed boost.

The actual trimming of the sails on a reach makes a significant difference to speed. It is here that the beam of the multihull offers an advantage as it allows the sheets to lead further outboard than would be possible on a monohull; thus much better sail shapes can be obtained and therefore higher speeds. Obviously, the sheet lead positions on a reach will not be the same as when close hauled so sheets may have to be changed to new leads when reaching or a track may need to be used.

With the mainsail, greater speed can often be achieved by using a kicking strap to pull the boom vertically downwards; this has the effect of flattening the sail which will increase speed in strong winds. It will also help to increase sail area when running and may prevent standing gybes. On most multihulls there is no kicking strap as such because the main sheet track allows the main sheet to be used for both purposes by sliding the bottom block of the main sheet out along the semi-circular track to the position in which the sheet pulls the boom and sail vertically downwards.

The reach is the point of sailing on which there is the highest danger of capsize because the boat is sailing at her highest speed and the capsizing moment is at its maximum, i.e. a right angle to the course. This will be dealt with later.

(c) *Running free*. We have seen how advantageous the spinnaker can be on a run, but there are other ways of trimming headsails used to good effect on a multihull. One of these is to tack the foresail down to the end of the windward hull or outrigger when the wind is on the quarter. This exposes more headsail area to the wind and can be particularly useful in light weather when a large ghoster is used. The sail has to be set flying so this is usually not a suitable evolution to carry out in strong weather.

Twin headsails for cruising are extremely efficient on a multihull because of the high stability of the craft and lack of roll.

(d) *Reefing*. Reefing on a multihull is usually easier than on a monohull because of its stability and the level platform that it provides. Every vessel needs to be reefed at differing times and experience must tell when this is. As with all yachts, slab reefing usually gives a better sail shape but it is often not as quick nor as convenient as roller reefing.

62. *Tacking a ghoster to the end of an outrigger may give better exposure of sail area to the wind.*

One point that needs to be watched in a multihull is reefing when travelling directly down wind. The stability and ease with which a multihull can run before the wind may allow reefing to be left a little too late, with the result that the sail is extremely hard to pull down because of the weight of wind in it; yet the helmsman is loath to put her head to wind because of the centrifugal force in the sails and the fact that he is carrying too much sail anyway. If this situation does arise, and it shouldn't, there are two ways out; the first is to lower the headsails and then put her head to wind for reefing, while the second is to sheet the main absolutely flat and attempt to reef while still running. This second alternative is more difficult, but it may be possible.

99

4 Racing

Racing Tactics

In all multihull racing, one of the first facts for the novice to realize is that although the distance between competing yachts may be quite large during the course of a race, the time gap may still be quite small. This applies only to the fast multihulls and there will be little difference from single hulled racing for slower yachts with a performance that equates to a monohull.

A multihull's fastest point of sailing is a reach, so the leading boat will always draw rapidly ahead once a mark is rounded from say, a close-hauled to a reaching leg; this distance gap may be significant to strategy with particular view to tides and impending wind shifts.

(i) *Speed made good (VMG)*. It is vital that the skipper has a good idea of the boat's best points of sailing to get the maximum VMG out of his yacht for any given leg.

As we have already discussed, it does not usually pay on a short windward leg to sacrifice close-winded ability by bearing away slightly to increase speed; however, on a leg of anything over 200 miles or thereabouts, it may well pay to do this. A classic example of this was presented by the courses followed by *British Oxygen* and *Three Cheers* in the North Sea leg of the 1974 Round Britain Race.

The leg of 470 miles from Lerwick to Lowestoft was sailed in approximately 43 hours by *British Oxygen* and in $53\frac{1}{2}$ hours by *Three Cheers*. Until this leg, the two boats had proved very similar in speed, as *British Oxygen* had won the first two legs to Crosshaven and Barra by an hour and eleven minutes each, but *Three Cheers* had taken the lead on the third leg by just over an hour. On leaving Lerwick, the wind was from the west, force 3–4; the forecast predicted that the wind would increase and back to the S.W. and then veer to the N.W. once a frontal trough had gone through. The rhumb line course for Lowestoft is 180° magnetic from Lerwick and within six hours of leaving Shetland the wind had backed to the S.W. so both yachts were close-hauled on the starboard tack. *Three Cheers* decided to remain as close-hauled as possible on the rhumb line, whereas *British Oxygen* headed further east at a higher speed making good progress in the increased wind of force 6–7, but to leeward of the direct track. This tactic paid off in a very definite way as the wind veered to N.W. and dropped to force 3–4 when *British Oxygen* was well out to sea and *Three Cheers* was still on the rhumb line course. As a result *British Oxygen* managed to finished the leg on a fast reach whereas *Three Cheers* came in on an insipid run, which left her ten hours behind *British Oxygen* at Lowestoft.

The risk of such strategy is obvious. If the wind had remained in the S.W. *British Oxygen* would have had to beat the last bit home; however the forecast correctly predicted the wind shift and her tactics paid off.

Thus in a long windward race such as the *Observer* Singlehanded Trans-Atlantic, when one knows that the wind may frequently vary from S.W. to N.W., it may be advantageous to steer further off the wind to increase speed. (See figure 64.)

The decision whether or not to aim off the rhumb line course on other points of sailing is equally important. In lightish airs a multihull will always go appreciably faster if the apparent wind can be brought forward of the beam; so it may pay on a broad reach to alter course slightly to bring the wind forward, particularly if the wind is fluky and variable.

63. *Diagrams show the profitability or otherwise of tacking downwind in* Three Cheers. *In Force 2–3 it does not pay, but in Force 4 it pays if a 10° 'aim off' is made. As the wind increases this angle decreases and at Force 5 she will sail fastest with the wind 5° off the stern, while at Force 6 it is best to steer directly downwind again. Above this strength the spinnaker has to come down and in Force 7 the best course is 10° off the wind's direction under fore and aft sails. As the wind increases past gale force the direct course downwind becomes more desirable.*

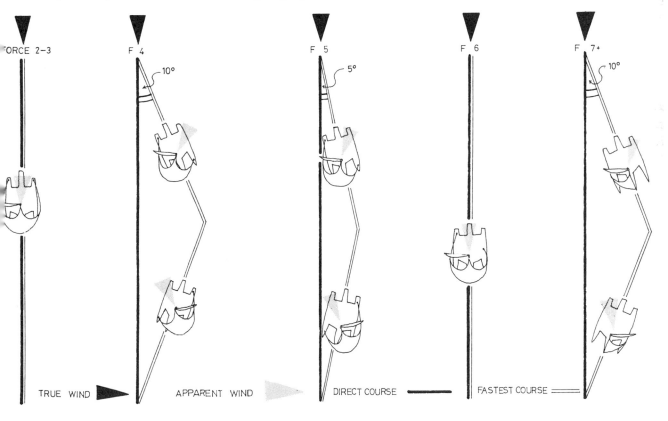

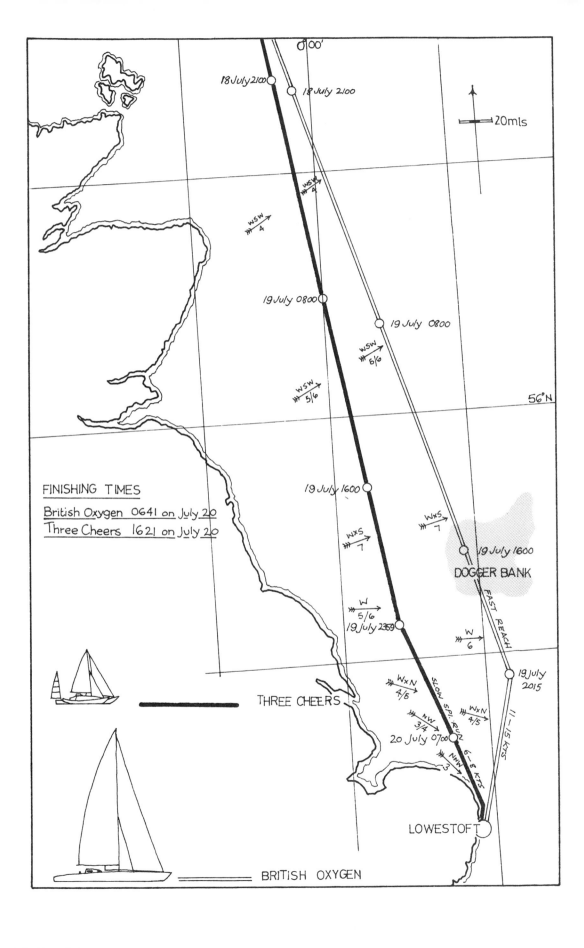

0°00'

18 July 2100

18 July 2100

WSW
4

WSW
4

19 July 0800

19 July 0800

WSW
5/6

WSW
5/6

56°N

20mls

19 July 1600

WxS
7

WxS
7

19 July 1600

DOGGER BANK

FAST REACH

FINISHING TIMES

British Oxygen 0641 on July 20
Three Cheers 1621 on July 20

W
5/6

19 July 2359

W
6

19 July 2015

WxN
4/5

SLOW SPI. RUN

WxN
4/5

11–15 KTS

THREE CHEERS

NW
3/4

20 July 0700

6–8 KTS

NNW
3

LOWESTOFT

BRITISH OXYGEN

When running it may pay to tack downwind using a spinnaker. In *Three Cheers* it is definitely profitable to do this in winds above force 4 as it is only necessary to be five to ten degrees off the true downwind track to get a reasonable speed increase. On the other hand it does not pay to tack downwind in lighter airs because one has to aim too far off to make it worthwhile. It is also unprofitable to tack downwind without a spinnaker in any wind strength. Ways to discover whether or not aiming off pays for a particular boat are either by using some form of performance computer or by simple trial and error. In the latter case, it will be necessary to sail a short downwind track both direct and tacking downwind; alternatively one can race against a yacht of comparable speed, each using the different tactics.

It is important so far as possible to cover one's nearest rival in a short race, but obviously in a longer ocean race this is not always possible.

(ii) *Use of Instruments*. It is now generally accepted modern ocean racing practice to use whatever instruments the rules allow as an aid to beating the opposition. These instruments usually consist of:

Log/speed indicator.
Radio direction finding set.
Wind speed and direction indicator superimposed over the ship's head.
Echo sounder.

Personally, I dislike putting reliance on a large cluster of instruments. A log/speedo, echo sounder and a DF set are essentials, but the others are definitely not. There is much truth in the saying that: 'A poor seaman can sail successfully by great reliance on instruments but a good seaman should not need them.'

In a way excessive instrumentation gives an unfair advantage to the inferior sailor. If he had to make do without them, his awareness of his boat, the sea and his own sensitivity would increase rapidly and he would in time become a far better seaman.

This argument has gone on for many years and indeed there was strong opposition to the radio D.F. set when it was first introduced. The question is, where does one stop? Radar, Loran, Weather Facsimile and Decca are at present not generally allowed in the more significant racing. Certainly, a catamaran benefits more from extensive use of instruments than does a trimaran, because it does not heel so much and gives little

64. *(Opposite) This chart of the fourth leg of the Round Britain Race 1974 shows how the tactics of sailing free in a multihull may pay off on a long leg.* British Oxygen's *course allowed her to sail consistently faster because she maintained a reaching course throughout. The wind shift to the north came at exactly the right moment, and from 2015, 19th July she had a reach to Lowestoft.*
Three Cheers *had been averaging less throughout, being harder on the wind, while the wind shift gave her a slow spinnaker run in light airs over the last 60 miles.*
Obviously the danger of this tactic lies in the risk of the wind backing instead of veering; however, 5° freer had given British Oxygen *such a lead that she would probably have won the leg in any case. This speed difference is more apparent in multihulls than in monohulls.*

indication of when to change sail. A wind speed indicator is of great help here as it tells one exactly when a sail change is needed.

In very light weather, particularly at night, a wind speed direction indicator is most useful as it is difficult to sense the true wind direction in pitch black darkness.

A combination of the apparent wind indicator and speedometer will assist enormously in getting the best out of a multihull. For instance, when reaching under the genoa, the sails are trimmed to get the maximum speed on the desired course, which may be 60° off the apparent wind. All one has to do then is to steer the boat by the wind indicator to keep the angle constant and when, for example, the boat accelerates down a wave, it is necessary to bear away momentarily to keep the wind at the angle to which the sails have been trimmed. In this way the maximum possible speed will be maintained.

The log/speedo is an essential instrument, not only for racing but for navigational safety; but weed fouling must be watched for at high speeds. Many multihulls have difficulty in finding a satisfactory position on the hull for the impellor; the usual reason for this is that the water flow under the hulls often goes in strange directions. Generally speaking, the best place for the impellor on a multihull is in the aftermost third of the yacht where the turbulence is less.

Such sophisticated gadgets as performance computors are, to may mind, a total waste of time, energy and money. Moreover, they add unnecessary weight and tend to distract people from the main object of winning the race.

The echo sounder is one of the most underestimated of instruments for both racing and cruising. Many people use it solely when closing the coast to stop themselves going aground, but it is one of the most valuable navigational instruments available, particularly the 100 fathom model, as it can frequently give a better position line than any D.F. fix, so anybody who contemplates long distance racing or cruising is well advised to buy one. At high speed, turbulence under the hull may have an adverse effect on the instrument and the transducer should be situated in a part of the hull where there is no turbulence, in the same way as the impellor of the log/speedo.

Finally, on the subject of instruments, it is always worth remembering that the compass and sextant are the two most reliable instruments available for navigation. How many of us know how to use them properly?

(iii) *Use of ballast*. Ballast, both human and otherwise, can be used with excellent effect to assist the yacht's speed. I do not agree with using water ballast unless it is water that is contained within the ship as drinking water, usually in jerry cans, because any additional weight pumped into the boat will serve to slow her down.

In strong winds on a long windward or reaching leg it helps performance to get as much weight to windward as possible, because heel will be reduced so it may be possible to increase sail area.

Downwind speed can be increased in craft with flattish stern sections by moving weight back aft. This applies more to catamarans than trimarans especially when they are surfing.

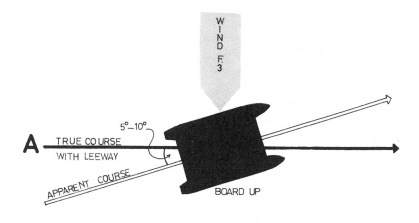

65. *Deliberate use of leeway by raising the boards can be valuable to some multihulls, especially those which make substantial leeway with the boards raised.*

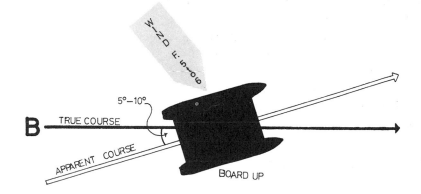

(A) In light winds a multihull will sail faster on a close reach than a beam reach, so leeway towards the objective can turn the apparent course into a faster true course.

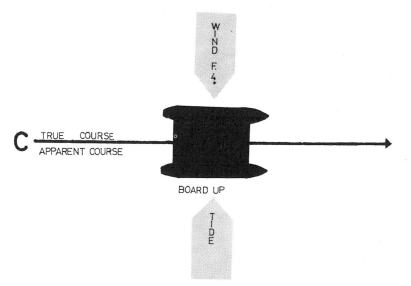

(B) In stronger winds the same theory may apply if the wind direction is further aft.

(C) In a wind against tide situation deliberate leeway may be made against the tide.

In very light weather ballast should be used to weight down the leeward outrigger or hull to give the boat some heel so as to put a bit of shape into the sails when close-hauled or reaching.

(iv) *Deliberate use of leeway*. On some multihulls it is possible on certain points of sailing to reach an objective faster by allowing the vessel to make intentional leeway. This applies especially to vessels which make a lot of leeway when their centreboards are up, and in particular the semi-circular hull shapes will make much leeway with the boards up.

Three occasions when this tactic can be used:

(a) In very light airs when the course presents a true reach to an objective a multihull will sail faster if the apparent wind can be brought further forward. Therefore, by a slight alteration of course, say 10°, the apparent wind can be brought much further forward and speed will increase. If the centreboard is then raised, leeway will be made towards the objective and the leg will be completed faster.

(b) In stronger winds the same principle applies except that the true wind will initially be abaft the beam when the yacht is on the desired course and she will alter course to windward to go faster and then pull up her board to make leeway.

(c) Leeway can be very useful when crossing a tidal stream at right angles on a reach. Instead of aiming down wind to stem the current, use can be made of the boat's natural drift to avoid losing ground down tide.

It is important to emphasise that these tactics will only work with multihulls that are very prone to leeway without their boards down.

(v) *Use of Tide*. As in any racing, every advantage possible should be taken of tidal currents. There is tendency for sailors of very high performance multihulls to pay only occasional lip service to the tides on account of the high speed of their craft. This is stupid. In very light winds and calm conditions, the tides play an extremely important part in a race, not so much because of the push that they give in a certain direction but because they generate wind. An excellent example of this occurred in the Crystal Trophy race of 1973 when *Three Legs of Man* was leading *Three Cheers* from abreast the Lizard towards the Wolf Rock. The wind was about force 1 directly from the Wolf and the tide was setting S.W. from the Lizard to a point some way south of the Rock. *Three Legs* elected to go on the port tack into Mount's Bay hoping for offshore winds, while *Three Cheers* deliberately sailed into the tide on the starboard tack. This pushed her into the wind thus generating an increased wind speed and more boat speed through the water. The result was a gain of about two miles, temporary as it turned out, but the small amount of tide helped *Three Cheers* little while the extra wind was a real bonus to a boat so easily driven and made a vast difference. This tidal advantage is not nearly so pronounced with monohulls.

Similarly it is vital when both tide and wind are contrary to cheat the former as

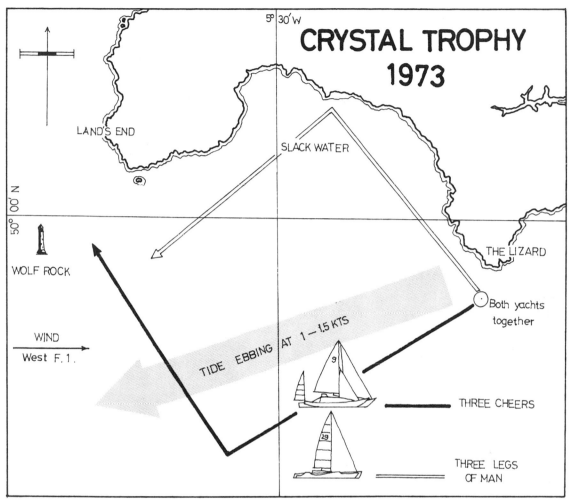

66. *A gain of two miles by* Three Cheers *in the light weather Crystal Trophy of 1973 was due to the extra wind speed over the deck generated by the tide, more than the tide itself.*

much as possible. If the tide and wind are travelling towards the yacht at the same speed then she will obviously be becalmed, though moving 'down hill' over the ground. If a very slight easing of the tidal stream can be found, wind will once more cross the decks and it may be possible to move forward again.

Extreme attention to this should be paid in light airs.

When beating on a long passage down a wide sea, such as the English Channel which is prone to strong tides, it makes little sense to bash backwards and forwards directly across it in any yacht, particularly a multihull. It is far better to hug the coast when the tide is against one and to stand out when the tide is running in the right direction. Thus, with cunning, a good seaman will pull every string in the book and use the tide to increase his windspeed over the deck as well as his ship's speed over the land.

(vi) *Sailing for more speed*. In strong conditions during a coastal race it will usually pay a multihull to sail reasonably close to the land in smooth water. This is because:

(a) All craft sail faster and more easily in calm water.
(b) Stability is greater and more sail can be carried.

It is often possible to average remarkable speeds under these conditions but a very sharp look out for squalls must be kept at all times. It should be remembered that many capsizes have happened in calm water under 'ideal' conditions, when the crews had not been prepared for the squalls which invariably accompany strong offshore winds.

Another tactic to increase speed is the use of a slight luff to cause a surf. If the yacht is going downhill in a seaway with a quartering wind she may be surfing every so often; she can be assisted to surf more frequently by giving her a slight luff which will make her pick up speed and get going more quickly on the front of a wave. The moment she does this she will start moving extremely fast, the apparent wind will move forward and she can be held on her original course, on the surf, for some time. The only disadvantage of this is that she will slowly claw to windward which may be undesirable.

To sum up, there is not a great deal of difference in racing tactics between monohulls and multihulls, so the points that I have mentioned should all be fairly obvious to any sailor with ocean racing experience. As a final thought, however, it is worth pointing out that over 50% of multihull capsizes have occurred during offshore races and this emphasises the point that alertness is even more necessary when a multihull is being driven hard.

5 Cruising

Anchoring—Manoeuvring Under Engine—
Drying Out—Going Aloft—Balance—Self
Steering

The cruising multihull will usually differ from its racing equivalent in that it will be heavier, have more accommodation and travel more slowly. Because of its weight, it may need more ground tackle than a stripped out racing machine.

Anchoring

(a) *Size of Ground tackle.* Because a multihull, even when fully loaded for cruising, does not displace anything like as much weight as a monohull, it does not need the same weight of anchor or chain. In general, it is acceptable to use pre-stretched terylene for anchor cable but it is advisable to have a length of chain between the anchor and rope cable.

A recommended size of main anchor chain and rope cable for multihulls is as follows:

LOA of Multihull (feet)	Minimum Chain Length (fathoms)	Main Anchor Weight (pounds)	Chain Size (inches)	Rope Cable Size (inches)
Up to 25	4	20	$\frac{1}{4}$	$1\frac{1}{4}$
25 to 30	4	20	$\frac{5}{16}$	$1\frac{1}{2}$
30 to 35	5	25	$\frac{3}{8}$	2
35 to 40	5	35	$\frac{7}{16}$	2
40 to 50	6	45	$\frac{7}{16}$	$2\frac{1}{2}$
50 to 60	7	60	$\frac{1}{2}$	$2\frac{1}{2}$
Over 60	8	75	$\frac{1}{2}$	3

A minimum of 30 fathoms of warp is advised up to 50 ft. LOA and 45 fathoms for larger vessels.

Many racing multihull sailors may feel that this table specifies too much chain and too heavy an anchor. This may well be true of the 46 ft. racing trimaran that displaces 7,000 lbs., but it is definitely not true of the same length craft which displaces double that weight.

(b) *Types of anchors.* The C.Q.R. anchor is my favourite overall general purpose anchor for any type of boat, multihulls included, because it is the best compromise for all types of bottom and is the least easy to drag or foul; it can also be stowed conveniently because of its shape. However beware of using it without any chain—it will drag easily, especially if the water is deep.

The Danforth anchor has extremely high holding power on a clean bottom providing that the pull on it is constant; if it is not, i.e. when the vessel swings 180° to the tide, it will pull out before digging in again and this gives it the opportunity to become fouled. It is a singularly useless anchor in weed as once it becomes clogged, it resembles a toboggan on the sea bed; in these conditions, particularly if the boat is being swung by the tide, a Danforth will often drag. In water where the bottom is known to be free of weed, the Danforth is excellent if two are laid in opposition to each other; this means that there will always be a constant pull on one or the other anchor and the ship will be extremely secure. Once a Danforth is in place, it has the greatest holding power of any anchor and is used for anchoring such things as oil rigs. Providing its limitations are known, it is excellent. A Danforth is the best anchor to use without chain.

In weed, the best anchor of any is unquestionably the fisherman's anchor. It has the capability to dig right through the weed on the sea bed and to get a fluke into the solid ground below.

(c) *How a multihull will lie to her anchor.* Because of a multihull's relative lightness, she is at anchor far more vulnerable to the wind than a monohull, which can cause great inconvenience to everyone in a mixed anchorage of monohulls and multihulls.

A particular example that comes to mind is when wind and tide are against each other. The heavy monohull will usually lie snugly to her anchor and the wind is unlikely to blow her over it against the tide. Quite the reverse can happen to a multihull; she may be blown at sufficient speed to make way against the tide and because of this may cause untold havoc and confusion in a crowded anchorage. Similarly, in a very strong cross wind which·is blowing at right angles across the tide, a monohull will usually lie head to tide. A multihull, however, may lie at 45° between the two, which again may cause danger and confusion in an anchorage. It is possible to avoid this by keeping the centreboard(s) down, but this can be a very risky practice. It is extremely easy for rope anchor cable to wrap around the centreboard when it is down, and if this occurs it is often hard to free the cable, particularly if it gets drawn up into the centreboard casing.

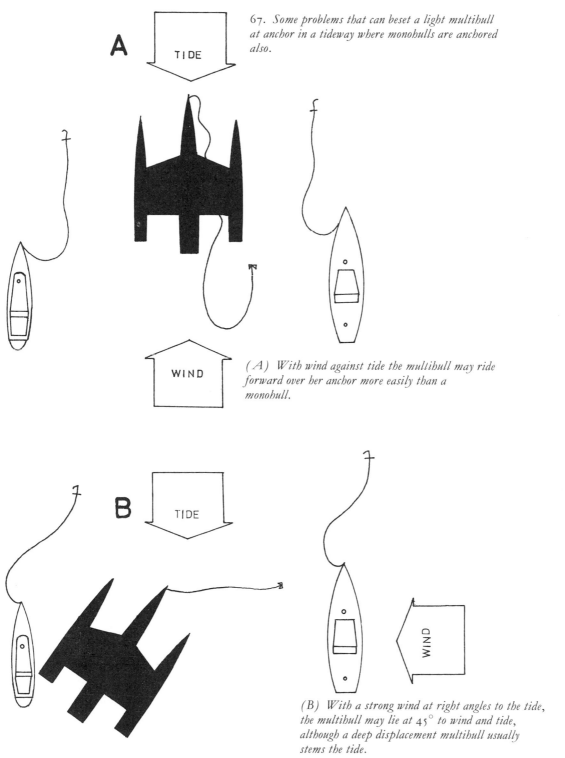

67. *Some problems that can beset a light multihull at anchor in a tideway where monohulls are anchored also.*

A

TIDE

WIND

(A) With wind against tide the multihull may ride forward over her anchor more easily than a monohull.

B

TIDE

WIND

(B) With a strong wind at right angles to the tide, the multihull may lie at 45° to wind and tide, although a deep displacement multihull usually stems the tide.

The solution which I prefer is always to lay two anchors, which used to be normal cruising practise in most yachts but gradually went out of fashion; however in a multihull it gives great additional security—both to the ship and other yachts anchored in the area. Where the anchors are placed is very much a matter of prevailing conditions; in a wind against tide situation, direct opposition is the best answer—but make sure the plates are up. In a wind across tide situation it is best to lay the main anchor up tide and the second anchor at 45° on the windward quarter. This will maintain the boat in a fairly constant position on both directions of the current.

When all chain cable is used, the weight of the cable gives a horizontal pull to keep the anchor on the bottom, but if only a small length of chain is used it is essential to pay out more rope than would be needed with an all chain cable. The normal figure for a totally chain cable is at least three times the depth of water at high tide and preferably more if a ship has swinging room. With a multihull, however, this amount should be increased to at least five times the depth of water. If only one anchor is used, the yacht has a large swinging circle when compared to a monohull using less length of chain. This is obviously undesirable and another very good reason for using a second anchor.

If the wind is constant and there is little tide, it is quite acceptable to lie to one anchor. If there is much wind, the boat will still surge backwards and forwards on her long length of rope cable. A good way of preventing this is to put a sinker down the cable; this is simply a weight—usually an old anchor stock of 30 or 40 lbs.—which can be slid down the cable on a shackle attached to a line which is paid out from the foredeck. This has the effect of damping the cable which reduces surging; it also places a more horizontal pull on the anchor which will reduce dragging.

Ideally, the second anchor should be the same weight as the main anchor if it is going to be used in conjunction with it. However, it is not really necessary to have a length of chain shackled to it, as with the main anchor, because this could prove a hindrance when used as an emergency kedge.

(d) *Securing points on a multihull's deck for anchor cable.* A trimaran presents no problem as the cable is secured to a cleat on the forecastle of the main hull in exactly the same way as it is on a monohull. This means that winches, fairleads and chain or cable stowage will usually be similar, if used at all. An anchor winch is best avoided if possible as it puts weight in the wrong place and cable stowage should be in the bilges.

A catamaran presents a more complicated problem; as there is no centre hull, the yacht may sheer around the anchorage far more than a trimaran if the cable is led to a securing point between the two hulls. This can be corrected rather unsatisfactorily, by securing the cable to one bow or the other. Inevitably, doing this will cause the boat to sheer but only in one direction which will be the opposite way to the 'securing' hull. Some catamarans anchor from the quarter which is a satisfactory solution to prevent

68. *(Opposite) The use of two anchors, particularly if they have rope 'cable', will give a multihull extra security and reduce her swinging. However, it may be a hazard as other boats lying to single anchors may swing towards her as the tide turns. Also a keen eye must be kept at slack water and anchor warps may have to be adjusted.*

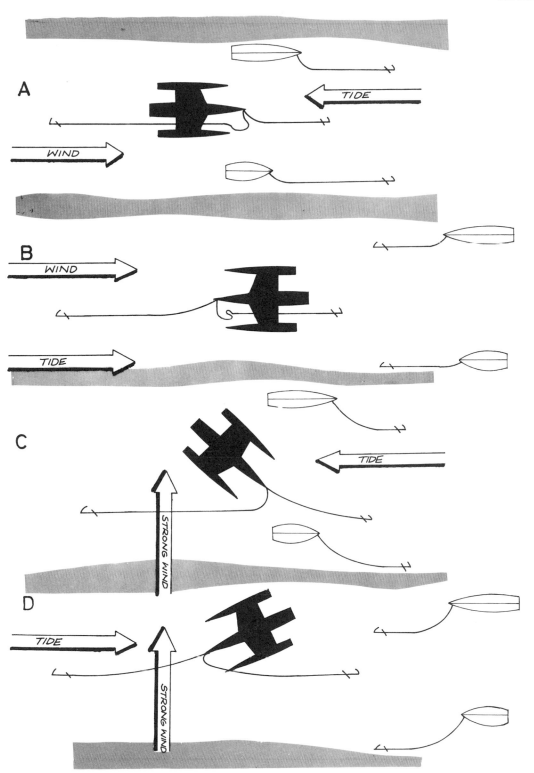

sheering but this can make it extremely difficult to get the cable in again. It also presents a lot more windage to the anchor which will put an extra strain on it. Another solution is the use of a bridle from both bows. The main cable is led through the fairlead of the main 'securing' hull until sufficient is out. A snatch block on the end of a short length of rope is then placed over the main cable and pulled in to the other bow so that the cable ends up being led out from the snatchblock which is amidships and slightly forward of the catamaran. There are other ways of making bridles but this is the simplest.

(e) *Mooring*. When picking up a mooring, it is usually best in a catamaran to aim to pick it up outboard of one or the other hulls. This is because it is easier to haul the buoy on deck if one is going too fast as all one has to do is walk back down the hull with the boathook still attached to the buoy. If the buoy goes between the two hulls when it has been caught with the boathook, there is a very good chance that it will not be seen again if the yacht is moving too fast.

In any manoeuvre such as picking up a mooring buoy, it should always be remembered that a multihull will lose all way very rapidly once she is pointed into wind. A long keel boat will carry her way for a considerable distance and it takes some getting used to for the sailor who has graduated from a monohull.

At a permanent, free swinging mooring, a catamaran should be secured by a bridle.

Manoeuvring Under Engine

Most multihulls are easy to drive under engine because of their lightness. However, at slow speeds in strong winds they will make considerable leeway which must be watched, and it often pays to have the centreboard(s) down if motoring up a river with a strong cross wind. This leeway can be particularly important if there is some urgent reason to stop while moving up a confined waterway. Such occasions frequently happen on congested rivers where yachts, ferries and moored craft all add to the problem, and if the plates are not down, immediate leeway could lead to dangerous results.

The majority of multihulls rely on long shafted outboard engines which are lowered into the water between the hulls of a catamaran or between main hull and outriggers of a trimaran. The outboard is a satisfactory solution as the price and weight of an inboard engine is usually greater; however, outboards are greedy on fuel and may suffer from severe cavitation problems in anything of a lop, because it is rarely possible to get the propeller deep enough to avoid aerated water or to prevent it coming out if the yacht is pitching and the crew move onto the bow. This gives an excellent reason for trying to do as much as possible under sail—always to be strived at by a good seaman.

In a trimaran where the engine is offset to one side of the main hull, it is important to remember that it will produce a turning moment of its own; thus if the engine is on the port side of the yacht, its use will cause a tendency to veer to starboard. This in its turn means that it will be very much easier to turn to starboard than to port while it

69. *When the engine is offset from the main hull the yacht will turn more easily in one direction than the other. The yacht shown above will have its smallest turning circle to starboard.*

may prove extremely hard to turn to port if there is a strong wind blowing from that direction. An engine which can be turned in its mounting will prove an enormous asset to manoeuvrability as both engine and rudder can be used to 'push' the water in the right direction to give turning moment.

In a fast multihull it is important that there should be no drag whatsoever from the propeller. In the 60 ft. trimaran *Gulf Streamer*, which is fitted with an internal diesel engine, Philip Weld found that a solid propeller slowed the boat by two knots on his Atlantic crossing in 1974. Moreover, if the engine was left in gear, the force of the water at 12 knots succeeded in turning the propeller and starting the engine! Thus a folding propeller is essential.

Drying Out

All multihulls should be able to dry out without any problems and open up a whole range of cruising areas which would not be available to a single-keeled monohull.

It should be remembered, though, when drying out:

(a) *Do not get neaped*. It is possible to dry out on top of a tide and then find that the following tides do not float the yacht, but a quick glance at the tide tables can avoid it. If the tides are falling off, do not take the bottom at the top of high water but wait an hour or so. If they are making it is of no consequence.

70. *Drying out does not always go to plan. Toria's main hull is suspended in mid-air, which says much for her strong construction.*

(b) *Do not sit on the ship's anchor.* This sounds obvious but it is surprisingly easy to do, particularly if the area on which the ship will dry has been subject to wind over current. It may not matter too much with a Danforth or C.Q.R. but a Fisherman's anchor will be distinctly prickly.

(c) *Always dry out on a soft bottom.* It is important that an even strain is put on all parts of the keels. If there is a rock or obstruction in the middle of a hull, a very localised pressure point could penetrate the skin, or leave long unsupported overhangs which could strain the overall structure.

(d) *Be careful of taking the beach on a potential lee shore.* It is not advisable to dry out on an open beach when a wind shift might make it a lee shore. If this does happen, the result could be severe pounding on the bottom as the tide floats her which might result in damage. This could be particularly severe if the bottom is of rock or very hard sand, and it may also make it hard to get off.

(e) *Always lay out a kedge to seaward.* This is important, as it may become the only way that the ship can be got off if the wind changes and blows on shore. It is vital to get the kedge out into deep water as far as possible from the yacht as soon as she has taken the ground. If the yacht is grounded on a straight open beach, the kedge should be laid at 90° to the shore line.

Going Aloft

This is usually done either by the use of steps on the mast or by means of a bosun's chair. In harbour, either method is satisfactory but at sea it may be safer to use a bosun's chair, as there is a more unpredictable motion at the top of a multihull's mast, even though the craft is more stable, and it is easy for a man to be flicked off like a fly. This has, in fact, happened and the sailor concerned was lucky to escape with his life because he landed in the trampoline. The unpredictable motion is due to the fact that any irregular sea movement under the hulls or outriggers (all waves are of different sizes) will be magnified greatly at the masthead; this does not matter nearly so much if one is securely seated in a bosun's chair, but it is very hard to hang onto steps, even if they are of the open hoop type, and any other steps should not even be contemplated. If mast steps are used, it is vital to wear a safety harness to secure oneself on the way and at the top. Unfortunately though, the snap link on the harness has to be unclipped at some stage to allow the wearer to move up or down before clipping on again. This was precisely the 'in between' situation when the accident happened in the case just described and the man fell wearing his harness which he had just unclipped while moving back down from the rungs below the masthead. The use of a jumar would have saved him.

Under any circumstances, the best time to climb a mast by any method is in a flat calm. If this is not possible, the yacht will be at her most stable when she is sailing directly down wind. This is a fundamental difference between a multihull and a monohull and in a moderate seaway, it is not advisable to go up the mast if the yacht is lying hove-to, or a-hull to wind and sea. Put her before the wind if it is vital to go up the mast.

If the sailor is singlehanded, the problem is, of course, more complicated and certainly more serious. The use of steps is the obvious but least attractive way of reaching the top and I prefer to use a method which I developed in *Binkie II* for the 1972 *Observer Singlehanded Trans-Atlantic Race*.

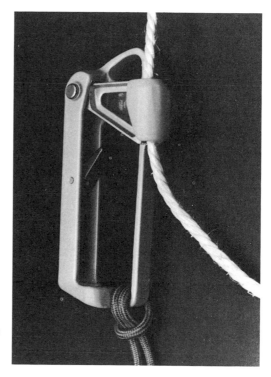

71. *A rope or halyard is placed between the hinged piece and the rope groove of the Jumar, which can be slid upwards, but will grip the rope when pulled downwards. Pulling down on the trigger allows the hinged part to open fully. The Jumar will take rope up to 2 inch circumference.*

This method uses a bosun's chair, a four- or three-part block and tackle which when extended is the full height of the mast, a sail bag and a jumar, which is a mountaineering device for climbing up ropes to escape out of crevasses or follow quickly up fixed ropes on a difficult route. The power ratio of the purchase depends on the strength of the individual and can be discovered in harbour. The stages of the operation are as follows:

Stage 1: Hoist one end of the fully extended purchase to the mast head on a halyard—

72. *A single handed method of climbing a mast, using a block and tackle. Left, the extended block and tackle is attached to a suitable halyard which is hoisted to the masthead and secured. Right, the bosun's chair is secured to the bottom end.*

preferably the main. Attach the bosun's chair to the bottom block of the tackle once it has been hoisted and the halyard secured. Get in the bosun's chair or equivalent.

Stage 2: Tie the bottom end of the jumar's six foot strop to the bosun's chair and attach the device itself to the down haul. It must be on a sufficiently long lead to allow it to be raised at full arm's stretch to allow maximum intake of rope at any 'pull down' of the downhaul. Attach the sailbag to a leg so that the downhaul can flake into it.

Stage 3: Hoist oneself to the top of the mast by pulling down on the downhaul. This will be done with the jumar in one hand which will slide up the rope without resistance.

73. *The climber gets into the bosun's chair, ties the bottom of the jumar strap to the chair and clips the jumar onto the downhaul.*

74. *(Below) He hauls himself up the mast by pulling down on the downhaul. The jumar is used as a handhold to pull down on and is then easily slid up the rope. Right, if the climber loses his hold the jumar will grip and prevent him falling. The tail of the rope should flake into a sail bag attached to climber's leg, but this is not shown in the photograph.*

If one loses hold of the rope with both hands, the jumar will automatically grip and it will be impossible to fall. At the top of the mast there will be a gap of nearly three feet between the climber and the masthead. This is because the jumar has been tied to the bosun's chair to give full arm's stretch so there will be a gap at the top of the same distance. The only way to surmount this is to pull oneself up the last few feet without using the jumar and then secure the downhaul to the bosun's chair with a convenient knot. The jumar can be left on the rope as insurance.

To descend, the jumar may be left on the downhaul and slid down the rope with the trigger held open as the climber lets himself down. The device will still be on the rope so if the climber loses his grip it will have the same 'life-saving' effect.

At the bottom, the block and tackle is lowered and the job is done.

The chief advantages of this method are:

(a) Safety. It is hard to come to grief using it.

(b) Ease of working at the masthead. It is extremely hard to do a job when standing in steps but relatively easy from a bosun's chair.

The disadvantages are:

(a) Length of time to reach the masthead. A lot of rope has to be hauled in before the masthead is reached—three or four times the height of the mast. In a mast over 60 feet high, it is an exceptionally long and laborious process. The higher one gets, the easier it becomes and the quicker one ascends. One has to be quite fit to do it.

(b) Practise is needed with the equipment. This is essential as it does take some getting used to.

(c) One must be careful that the downhaul rope does not get snagged on the deck so that one cannot overhaul it and descend again. This is why a hoop-mouthed sail bag is attached to one's leg to allow the downhaul rope to flake down into it as one ascends.

Mast climbing singlehanded will always be hazardous but the methods described will lessen the risks. If one elects to use steps, remember that a jumar attached to the safety harness can be a real safety device if it is used in conjunction with a secured halyard.

Balance

For ease of sailing, lightness of steering, comfort of crew and maximum speed, all sailing craft should balance well. This means that there should be neither lee nor weather helm on any point of sailing but it should be possible to induce either by sheet adjustments, centreboard adjustments or weight distribution.

In a conventional monohull, it is usually a simple matter of sheet adjustment to achieve reasonable balance. Most monohulls carry a little weather helm to windward which gives the helmsman an easy 'feel' of the ship when he is steering. Their balance can only be adjusted by playing with the sheets. If, for instance, the mainsail of a close-hauled sloop is eased, she should pay off slightly or carry less weather helm. If a ketch is well balanced on a reach and the mizzen is lowered, she should pay off. If the forward jib of a cutter is lowered, she should carry more weather helm and so will a sloop if her mainsheet is tightened. All these simple common sense rules of seamanship apply to

75. *Using a jumar to climb a mast with footsteps. Left, a strap of the jumar is attached to the body and the jumar itself is clipped to a halyard which is firmly secured; the jumar is slid up the halyard and the man climbs upwards. Right, if he falls the jumar will grip the halyard and prevent the climber from crashing to the deck.*

multihulls, but they apply with far more importance at greater speeds. A much smaller sheet adjustment is needed at speed to get the correct balance.

In larger multihulls of both types, the use of two boards is common to assist balance. This gives great flexibility as it means that the boards can be used instead of sheet alterations which might reduce speed. If, for example, the yacht is fore reaching with both boards down and carrying weather helm, she will immediately pay off when the forward one is raised. Similarly, if she is carrying lee helm on a reach with half the main board down, only a small bit of forward plate will be needed to instantly correct the problem.

In a very small or very light multihull, weight distribution will affect balance. If there is too much weight forward, the head of the yacht will be depressed and weather helm will result. Similarly, the yacht can be made to pay off if a lot of weight is put in the stern as the bows will be biting on very little water.

Down wind it is hard to get any boat to balance well, particularly when surfing occurs. One solution with a cutter rig is to sheet the staysail amidships so that if the ship starts to veer either way, the pressure of the wind on the staysail keeps her pointed in the right direction. It is obviously essential to keep the forward centreboard(s) up in a large multihull and to keep the weight aft. If this is not done, the yacht can easily 'gripe' to windward and broach.

Self Steering

There are many types of self steering gears on the market, and it is not intended to discuss the relative merits of individual makes in this book.

Generally speaking, there is not a great amount of difference between a fast mono-hull's self steering requirements and a cruising multihull's. The problem of self steering on an extremely fast racing multihull is, however, considerably greater. This is because the apparent wind direction can alter very quickly unless the wind strength is constant. This problem is not apparent when the vessel is close-hauled, but it becomes more so as the wind draws aft.

If the yacht is surfing at speed, it is extremely hard for any wind vane self steering to cope because the apparent wind will shoot forward as the yacht accelerates. On the whole, the horizontal pivot vanes, which are usually directional as well, prove better

76. *Windvane self steering gears are harder to use in fast multihulls.*

than the purely vertical vane in this situation. This is because they will still be depressed even though the apparent wind moves forward.

There is much to be said for compass orientated self steering gears in multihulls. These were not originally allowed in any of the big short handed races but recently they have become accepted, provided that the power supply comes from natural sources. It is now possible, but expensive, to obtain this power through the use of solar cells. These cells generate electricity by absorbing solar energy from ordinary daylight which is then transmitted to the battery power supply for the self steering. There are other ways of getting power, such as wind or water driven generators, but they are costly

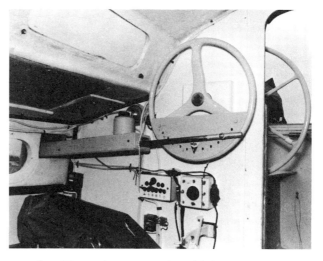

77. *Solar cell panel on* Triple Arrow, *used for charging the battery which powers the auto pilot.*

78. *Auto pilot fitted to the steering wheel of* Triple Arrow. *This Tiller Master gear has a compass fitted on top of it.*

on performance. A good compass orientated self steering gear should be able to cope with a multihull on any point of sailing but it will use considerably more power if it is having to work much harder due to the boat's yawing from side to side. The main disadvantage of the automatic pilot is that it cannot possibly steer such a good windward course as a human being or a wind vane gear. This is because the wind is constantly varying slightly in direction—may be only a few degrees—but the automatic pilot will only be true to the compass. This means that the yacht may be pinched or sailed too free because the self steering gear has not got the seaman's 'feel' for close-hauled sailing.

There is also a capsize danger in the use of an auto pilot, particularly if the yacht is being sailed singlehanded and the gear is coping in strong conditions. If, for instance, the yacht is on a broad reach with the apparent wind just aft of the beam and there is a rapid wind shift which puts her on a close reach, the vessel will be immediately over canvassed and could capsize if there was no one on deck. A wind vane gear would alter the course of the yacht onto a different heading but she would still be on a broad reach. A compass orientated auto pilot, however, will be faithful only to the compass and the wind shift may therefore be of very real danger to the yacht.

With all types of self steering gear, the most important thing to remember is that it is vital to get the multihull as balanced as possible before engaging it. If it is not balanced, the gear will have to work harder, wear and tear will increase and speed will be reduced. More power will be used if an automatic pilot is used.

To conclude, self steering is a tremendous asset if it can be used efficiently. Caution should be used in strong winds as the self steering gear cannot release the sheets or pay off in a squall.

The Amateur Yacht Research Society publishes an excellent book on the subject which should be read by anyone contemplating its use.

6 Accidents and Safety

*Capsize—Man Overboard—Dismasting and
Jury Rigs—Structural Damage—Damage by
Lightning*

Almost without exception, all accidents at sea happen for one reason: **human error**. The exception might be described as an Act of God.

This human error can be broken down further:

(1) Errors of basic seamanship by the crew of a vessel.
(2) Construction failures caused by bad workmanship.
(3) Design failures caused by a poor designer.

The Act of God accident, which is rare, is caused by phenomena such as tidal waves, whirlwinds, volcanic eruptions and war. There are very few accidents attributable to an Act of God although many people who have come to grief for one reason or another will try to wriggle out of the responsibility by blaming natural causes. This is extremely damaging to progress as it will inevitably bring suspicion on the type of vessel which has had an accident.

Because the multihull is a recent type of 'pleasure' sailing yacht (forgetting the Polynesians for a minute) it has gone through all the traumas and difficulties of any new innovation. If we look back at the history of the steam driven ship, the motor car and the aeroplane, we can read about the incredulity, distrust and dislike that these inventions caused to our ancestors. The aeroplane in particular was regarded as utterly unsafe and in defiance to the laws of nature. It was loudly condemned by politicians, clergymen and the general public and it had to prove itself before it became accepted. Every accident that happened to it was given enormous publicity and even today, many people will not step on board an aircraft even if they are paid to do so.

A similar situation prevails with the multihull today though on a far more limited scale as its primary use is for sport and pleasure. Generally speaking, all multihulls are completely accepted by a small percentage of people, some multihulls are accepted by a large percentage of people and all multihulls are detested by a small percentage of the sailing population. The first and last groups are of no particular concern because anyone who thinks that all multihulls in existence are acceptable is obviously both biased and wrong. Similarly, a person who is so narrow minded as to completely deny the possibility that some multihulls are seaworthy vessels must be discounted as not worth listening to. The truth is that there are no shades of pure black and white but a very large spectrum of grey in the middle. It is this section that must concern us.

As with aeroplanes, the happenings which have attracted the worst and most wide-spread publicity during the course of multihull development have, inevitably, been the accidents. Of these, the most spectacular has been the capsize.

The Capsize

There are many contributing factors to a capsize and some of these are the poor design features that have been discussed in Chapter 2. However, in most cases, capsizes have occurred through a lack of understanding, experience and seamanship by the crew of the vessel. It is extremely easy to blame the excessively tall rig of a vessel, its narrow beam or any other design factor but in the end it must always be the skipper and crew who should shoulder the blame for a capsize. If they do not know the safety limits of their craft, nor understand its capsize potential, they may be putting themselves and their ship in jeopardy.

Contrary to what most people think, 99% of all multihull capsizes have taken place because the yacht has been **sailed** over—NOT because she has been rolled over by enormous seas. Moreover, a high percentage of these sailing capsizes have occurred in relatively calm water when the crews were caught out by heavy squalls.

Capsize by wave action

The 1% which have happened because of wave action alone are extremely rare because a multihull will normally act as a raft once all sail has been taken off and slide with the breaking crests. The usual reason for a capsize purely by wave action is that the multihull is very heavily overloaded and as a result, digs her lee hull/outrigger into the sea and the rest follows over the top. A classic example of this happened to Tom Corkill in the South Atlantic during 1967 while sailing his 25 ft. Nicol designed Clipper class trimaran to South America. *Clipper* was 17 ft. wide and Corkill had already sailed her from Australia to Cape Town so had confidence in his own seamanship and the boat. On leaving South Africa, he was hit by a strong south-easterly gale on the second day out and started running before it. At once, he noticed that the ship was far too heavy with four month's supply of food and water on board; he was pooped, without damage, because the ship could not run fast enough to escape the breaking crests. Eventually, exhausted, he lay a-hull without sail and an hour later was capsized by an extremely large breaking crest. By a miracle he was rescued 18 hours later and survived to tell the tale.

As he realised at the time, the principal reason for the accident was that the boat was grossly overloaded thus reducing her buoyancy below an acceptable level. The result was that the leeward outrigger dug into the sea instead of sliding with the wave. Once

79. *Artist's impression of Tom Corkill's South Atlantic capsize when, incredibly as it was in a deserted part of the ocean, he was rescued.*

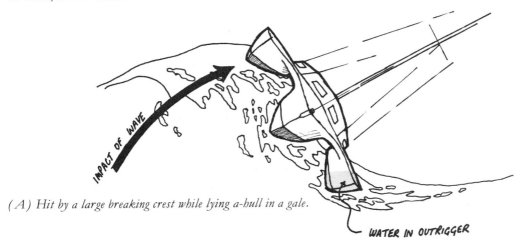

(A) Hit by a large breaking crest while lying a-hull in a gale.

WATER IN OUTRIGGER

(B) The partially flooded leeward outrigger immersed and then acted as a hinge.

NON-BUOYANT LEEWARD OUTRIGGER SUBMERGES AND ACTS AS A HINGE.

(C) The yacht followed over the pivot point of the lee outrigger and ended bottom up.

this had started, the process was accelerated because the outrigger, which had half filled, had so little buoyancy that it bit into the solid water deep down and formed a hinge for the vessel to flip over.

This unusual accident brings out a very relevant point. It is dangerous to overload a trimaran to such an extent that its buoyancy is reduced. This applies particularly to trimarans less than 35 ft. in overall length as they will need a far smaller weight increase to make them unsafe when lying a-hull. With the larger vessels, more weight can be added without risk.

The same danger of adding weight applies to a lesser extent to a catamaran because one of its hulls will have more buoyancy than the outrigger of a trimaran of equivalent size. A catamaran is therefore better equipped to surf sideways on the breaking crest of a wave than an overloaded trimaran. In some cases, it may pay to put weight into the windward hull of a catamaran when lying a-hull in a storm so that more relative leeward buoyancy is assured.

It is important to emphasise that in no case must the centreboards of either a trimaran or catamaran be down when lying a-hull in a severe gale. In the case of a trimaran which has its boards in the centre hull this is not so dangerous but it is inviting the sea to break off the board because the vessel may surf sideways on the crest while the board will be held by the 'solid' water underneath. If the board is down in the leeward out-rigger of a trimaran or the lee hull of a catamaran, this is extremely dangerous and inviting capsize. The reason for this is that the board will dig into the solid water and form a pivoting point for the boat to be rolled over. It is far better in all cases to have the centreboards up and the yacht will then side-slip to leeward with the breaking crests.

It must be clearly understood that from the point of view of capsize from wave action (not necessarily the construction viewpoint) a multihull will be safer the larger she is. This is because smaller multihulls will have a relatively small beam and a far smaller wave will stand a greater chance of capsizing her.

The Sailing Capsize

This is the most common of all capsizes and is accounted for by one of the following reasons.

(a) Sailing with too much sail up in rough irregular sea conditions.

(b) Overpressing a yacht on a close reach.

(c) A sudden squall which capsizes the boat before sheets are released.

(d) Centrifugal force while luffing, particularly with a reaching spinnaker set.

(e) Stalling at the top of a wave in a gale and being blown back down the front and capsized.

(f) Pitchpoling over the lee bow.

Obviously, many of these causes can combine together to accelerate capsize. We will examine them in more detail:

(a) *Sailing with too much sail up in rough, irregular sea conditions*

This is a mistake which is usually made when a boat is being pushed too hard or too fast in a race and a particularly steep sea combined with too much sail may account for a capsize. This is more likely to happen to a narrow multihull with a tall rig than a relatively wide vessel with a low aspect ratio rig.

Just such an accident happened to Nick Keig in *Tom Tom*, a Mark 1 Iroquois, off the Isle of Man in 1968 and as his description contains much information of value I have included it here.

'We had won the Isle of Man multihull trophy for four consecutive years and with the race only four days away we decided to spend the evening practising sail changing. The wind had been blowing about 7/8 from the S.W. all day but when we left the harbour it had moderated to force 5 to 6. Quite a big sea was running off Port St. Mary and where the tide was setting, about a mile off shore, the sea was very confused. We beat out through this and enjoyed one of the most exciting runs back that we had ever experienced. It was so much fun that we decided to do it again. We went about in the harbour and headed out to sea on the starboard tack with the number one jib and full mainsail set and both centreboards down. The wind was blowing from twenty to thirty knots but was still very gusty. Both the jib and main sheets were being hand held ready to let fly when suddenly a steeper wave than usual seemed to fall away and leave us suspended with a hull in the air. Immediately the rudders became inoperative and we had lost our balance so the sheets were let go. The area of bridge deck now exposed to the wind was enough to complete the capsize and within ten seconds or less, we were in the water and the boat was on her side. The automatic mast head buoyancy inflated but

80. *Nick Keig's* Tom Tom *after being washed ashore on the Isle of Man.*

within seconds it had burst and the complete 180° capsize took about twenty seconds.

'A rope was always mounted under the bridge deck for such an emergency and this now proved invaluable. It helped us to get out of the water and also gave us something to hold onto on the slippery surface of the inverted bridgedeck.

'I decided that before it got dark I should try and swim into the cabin and obtain the flares. This would have been a very difficult and dangerous operation and the thought of it filled me with horror. However, luck was with us and as I was preparing to go under, what should float into my hand but a red parachute flare! This was immediately dispatched into the gathering gloom and minutes later we were on the lifeboat cold and wet, but, I think, much wiser. These are the lessons we learnt:

(i) However experienced you are, a capsize occurs when you least expect it.

(ii) If the lee centreboard had been lifted it might have helped.

(iii) Catamarans with large bridge deck areas are at a distinct disadvantage over trimarans with wings that are not solid and have greater beam.

(iv) Emergency gear (liferaft, flares etc.) must be **easily** accessible if the ship is upside down. There is no question of re-entering the hulls.

(v) When beating and in danger of capsizing, I favour luffing. It slows the boat and takes the drive out of the sails quickly. Bearing away is slow and the boat accelerates dramatically.

(vii) Safety harnesses were not being worn and I feel in a capsize you are safer without them. However, I would still recommend their use at **all** times most strongly.

(viii) We were in the water three minutes and on the upturned boat for thirty minutes. We were already very cold and could possibly have survived for only two to three hours. Had we had a liferaft we could have inflated it as a tent and survived indefinitely. I would never sail without one again.'

Keig had logged 14,000 miles in *Tom Tom* but gave up catamaran sailing after this accident and built the successful trimaran racer *Three Legs of Man* with which he was later to win the under 35 ft. trophy in the 1974 Round Britain Race.

It is interesting to note that this accident may have been partially caused by wave action as *Tom Tom* was in an area of extremely confused water caused by a tide race. However, had she had less canvas up and the lee centreboard raised she might have been all right. Despite easing the sheets, the capsize could not be stopped because the wind had got under the large area of bridgedeck. This is an excellent reason for buying a multihull which is not completely decked in from stem to stern as so many modern production catamarans are. As Keig rightly points out, it is essential to have easy access to flares and liferaft when the boat is inverted. This can be easily arranged on a multihull with a little bit of thought.

It is extremely hard and hazardous to enter the hulls of a fully decked catamaran which has a central hatch when it is upside down. This is because there is quite a distance to swim under water before the air inside the hulls is reached. In a trimaran or catamaran which has direct access to the main hull or hulls, this does not present such a problem.

It is interesting to note the comment about luffing to decrease the danger of a capsize when beating. This is absolutely true as the acceleration caused by bearing away will add extra moment to the capsize motion and would cause a flip, particularly with the board down. When reaching, however, the situation is reversed as the centrifugal force and acceleration caused by luffing could do the same thing so it is essential to bear away. Obviously, therefore, there must be a point in the middle, somewhere on a close reach, where one will be uncertain which way to put the helm if the boat is on the verge of capsize. This is a most dangerous point of sailing for a multihull at speed and extreme caution should therefore be exercised when travelling close to the limits. I have found that by easing sheets **and** bearing away at the same time, the danger can be avoided, however, it does require a high degree of alertness by the crew and knowledge of the boat.

Finally, safety harnesses should, of course, be worn at all times but on a multihull, **they must be unfastenable at both ends**. The best type is that which incorporates a snap link that clips to the harness so that if the man is trapped below the boat he can release it instantly without having to find the snap link at the far end of the line.

There is no need for further elaboration on the subject of carrying a self-inflating life-raft; death from exposure can occur very rapidly and an inverted multihull must **never** be considered to be its own liferaft.

(b) *Overpressing a yacht on a close reach*

This sort of accident will usually only happen during a race when a yacht is being driven on the knife edge of capsize by a full crew. On most occasions the crew of the vessel will get away with it, providing their reactions are sharp enough, but all that is needed to cause a capsize is one simple thing to go wrong and the boat is soon upside down.

On 8th July 1967 the first Crystal Trophy Race for offshore multihulls started from Cowes, Isle of Wight. Up to the Nab Tower the trimaran *Trifle* and the catamarans *Mirrorcat* and *Snow Goose* were leading the field followed in fourth position by Bill Howell's catamaran *Golden Cockerel*. On rounding the Nab the course to Cherbourg put the fleet on a close reach with a westerly Force 5 blowing. Bill Howell takes up the story of how *Golden Cockerel*'s race finished.

'We had lost a bit of time between the start and the Nab with the result that *Trifle*, *Mirrorcat* and *Snow Goose* got out ahead of us and this made us more mad keen; we really felt we had to catch them. *Pelican* was having a lot more trouble behind us because she didn't have a very big spinnaker and she was only carrying it for a while. So when we got to the Nab Tower and turned on to a close reach, the wind was about Force 5, and we were sailing at about 45 to 50° to the apparent wind. We put up our number two genoa which actually is the biggest that we are allowed to carry under the rules. We weren't far off carrying a thousand square feet of sail. The *Cockerel* was doing about 14 knots (by the Harrier) and we were getting a certain amount of pounding, I wouldn't say it was serious, but we got the occasional wave slapping underneath the bridge-deck.

We have a flip device on our main sheet which we've used experimentally on occasions

and we were using it at the time. It's an adaptation of Roland Prout's design and hitherto it has always worked very well. Its only fault is the fact that it can be sparked off by a wave hitting the ship. We were catching up on *Snow Goose* but *Mirrorcat* and *Trifle* were way out in front at this stage of the game, going great guns, and *Pelican* and *Stiletto* were pounding up pretty hard behind us when the flip device on the mainsheet went out twice.

As we came out of the lee of the Isle of Wight the breeze plucked up a bit, and I decided that we had to take in the big genoa. I put on my wet suit and I went forward with young Quentin to change the headsail and left Duncan steering and Emile holding the mainsheet. *Golden Cockerel* has a double forestay and because we were racing fully crewed, I did a thing that I wouldn't ordinarily do if I was sailing on my own. Instead of dropping the genoa first and then putting the working jib up, we started trying to hank on the working jib first. Well, I remember looking at the instruments as I went out of the cockpit; the wind then was 25 knots. We were between 45 and 50° still of the apparent wind and we were doing 14 knots but occasionally surging up to 16. I was having a hell of a job forward with this young chap because with these short seas that were then building up, I should say about 8 or 10 feet, very short seas with not all that much space in between them, she kept on jumping and sometimes we were about three feet in the air, while we were trying to change the headsail. This meant that we were very slow hanking on the working jib. In any case, we had it all hanked on, and were just about to put the halyard on when I looked round and saw the weather hull begin to lift. As the hull lifted I screamed out at the top of my voice:

"Let go of the mainsheet, let go of the mainsheet."

'I was under the impression that the mainsheet hadn't been let go for I saw the hull lift to about 40° but then it started coming down again. I thought, "Thank Christ for that, Emile has let the mainsheet go", and when I saw it come down to 20° I thought that she was going to be okay. Then—much to my horror, the hull started lifting again and this time it went up very, very slowly like a slow motion picture. There was nothing fast about it at all. I understand that a member of the crew did get to the genoa sheet and start letting it out. He let it out about four feet—this was verified by Mike Priestly who was watching it—but the sheet snarled on the winch. What happened then was a slow continuance of the process and she skidded along on the flat outside part of the leeward hull in a vertical position. She went along there for quite some time, it seemed to me about 10 seconds or so, probably a little bit less than that, but it seemed a tremendously long length of time and even then I had the feeling that she might come back. I could see the genoa right next to me flapping in the sea and having hung there for quite some time all of a sudden she went over alarmingly quickly. I was trapped underneath the trampoline (the safety net forward) and I had my safety harness on as did young Quentin. I was wearing an old harness which I've been using for many years which has a snap hook only on the far end of its line. My line was too short and

81. *(Left) Bill Howell's* Golden Cockerel, *later to be called* Tahiti Bill.

I was caught underneath the safety net unable to escape from under the boat. The ship kept ducking me under and I thought "Christ, you know, I am going to drown here". I was getting the occasional gulp of air and actually I swallowed about five or six pints of salt water so I can't understand why I wasn't sick afterwards; may be it was just fear that stopped me being sick. I couldn't reach the end of the line to get the snaphook undone because every time I did the boat surged and I drifted away. Luckily, I had on a buckle harness which I managed, eventually, to get out of. I got on board and found myself standing there with five other members of the crew. One chap was trapped in the hull and we were all very concerned about that, so we started pounding on it and soon we were very relieved to hear young Raymond's voice. We said, "Raymond where are you?" and he said "I'm all right", rather upset because we were asking after him. We pleaded with him to come out, but he was very busy. He turned off all the sea cocks and things like that, which was irritating us because we thought, "that poor young bugger if he doesn't bloody well come out shortly . . ." but he turned them all off displaying great presence of mind and he also collected a few flares, because he realised that as the boat was lying upside down we wouldn't have any up top. He found some and pushed them out to us. Then, much to our relief we saw him surface like a big porpoise astern. The first thing he said to us was "Did you get those flares?" We said "No, bugger the flares, you come in!"'

The crew were then taken off by minesweeper and helicopter and *Golden Cockerel* was righted with some damage by a Dutch coaster.

This capsize by an extremely experienced seaman in a fully crewed catamaran was subject to a post mortem chaired by David Simonds, a director of Courage Breweries (Howell's sponsors at that time) who was steering when the accident occurred. All

82. Golden Cockerel *overturned off the Isle of Wight*.

83. *Howell and Hartman being picked up by a minesweeper.*

crew members made statements at this meeting and numerous outside persons representing many yachting interests were present. As a result, the capsize was exceptionally well recorded and the knowledge gleaned from it was of considerable importance for the future safety of multihulls.

So, what were the main causes of the accident? By and large, they were as follows:

(1) Over-canvassing the yacht on a reach due to the desire to win the race.

(2) Failure to release the genoa sheet due to a snarl of the sheet round the winch. The 4 or 5 ft. easing made no difference at all. The snarl was caused by a riding turn.

(3) The leeward centreboard was partially down. Although having it up might not have saved the day, the fact that it was half down could not have helped.

(4) The helmsman at the last moment luffed the yacht to windward which increased the wind speed over the sail and added centrifugal force. Although Howell's description does not include this, this did happen though possibly at a time where things had gone too far to make any great difference.

The capsize brought up many other important points of safety. Bill Howell again;

'I'll tell you this much about staying on a cat when it's upside down. All this talk about it being a comfortable life is all bull, you know. It's an uncomfortable bloody life because it's awful slippery there. We could hardly keep our feet. The dagger plate was sticking up so we attached our safety lines to it and everybody just stood there kept on deck by their harnesses. It was very, very difficult standing there.

'Somebody said straight away that there should be some hand holds under the bridge deck and I agree with them.

'We now struck another difficulty because our life raft was strapped underneath the safety net aft. We had a hell of a job getting this and eventually it had to be cut out from under the webbing as it was so buoyant that we could not get it out from underneath. This was difficult and took time.

'An interesting point is that she was lying broad side on to wind and sea so the hull in the air was protecting us from being swept by the waves. She wasn't lying head to wind, which made her comparatively comfortable. If I were ever stuck in the same position again I would inflate the life raft, leave the life raft attached to the boat and then get in it. You can lie there and you are not so exposed with a canopy and such like and then you wait until you have got a dead calm and dive under and get into the cabin and rescue what you can. I think that if you had to stay on the upturned bridge deck for twelve or twenty-four hours, you would probably end up slipping off, or the exposure would kill you. If you had a life raft, like we had, just leave that attached to it and then crawl into it and you could rest indefinitely, waiting for a break in the weather to re-enter the ship.'

Some form of under deck hand hold is vital and the necessity to be able to get at the life raft from both sides is obvious. Howell re-emphasises Keig's views on death from exposure.

What of the two people who were trapped down below after *Golden Cockerel* had inverted? Raymond Simonds, the chairman's 19-year-old son, had pushed Mike Priestly out of the hatch as the *Cockerel* went over and stayed below with ample air and complete coolness to turn off the sea cocks and rescue the flares. Having done this, he swam out without difficulty and surfaced due aft. Priestly, on the other hand was in the luckless position of having the boat fall on top of him and he had a harder time reaching the surface.

'I wasn't really convinced that it had happened until the mast actually hit the water and at that point we realised that it was time to get outside the cabin anyway. Raymond said "Get out Mike" and I was assuming he was coming too. I was closer to the door and I had my feet on the edge of the door as it was horizontal and I leaped out into the water right beside the vertical boat. It seemed to me that she then inverted almost instantly. It can't have been more than a few seconds and I can't have taken more than one or two strokes in the water before this great shadow appeared above me and I realised that it was the rest of the boat falling on top of me.

'I probably would not have got a broken head if it had come down on me but I would've been pushed under rather smartly. So I dived back into the cockpit which was self draining, unfortunately, in the wrong way and was filling up with water beautifully. The thing that occurred to me at that time was, that although I knew there was air in the hulls so presumably the *Cockerel* wouldn't sink, I wasn't sure she would float and I did not want to be a hundred feet down with the air bubbles. My chief thought at the time was to take the breath of air that was available and to get out as best I could, so I went back under the opposite hull and it seemed to be a hell of a struggle in clothing and seaboots to get out through the rigging. It's bad enough on deck when the yacht's the right way up, but I found I had to fight my way through a lot of gear. I suppose in the end it wasn't all that difficult but let's say it wasn't nearly as easy as I expected it to be.

'Under similar conditions at night it would have been a much more serious problem. I could at least see what was happening to the boat, which way it was coming down, I could even see some of the rigging under the water, but at night—quite a problem.'

Although it is not relevant to this accident, the thought of being trapped inside an inverted multihull is particularly horrific. All hatches must, therefore, be capable of being opened easily from both sides.

This dramatic and well documented capsize firmly brings home the following points:

(1) Excess sail may only be carried with extreme circumspection.

(2) **All** sheets must be freed if the yacht does not right after the main has been let out. Sheets must be free to run to avoid snarls with not too many turns on the winch.

(3) Any lowering of the leeward centreboard in a catamaran may assist this type of capsize.

(4) If the vessel is luffed at the last moment on a reach, this will add power to the capsize moment.

(5) Safety harnesses must have snap links at each end of their safety lines.

(6) Self inflating life raft, flares and life jackets should be easily and instantly accessible from both sides.

(7) Underdeck hand holds are essential. A fixed rope is satisfactory.

(8) Multihulls are difficult to stand on when inverted but will generally lie a-hull so may give some shelter behind the windward hull. This will only be of a temporary nature and death from exposure will come quickly if the self inflating life raft cannot be used.

(9) It is possible to stay inside, once inverted—provided the person keeps his head and does not panic. Such things as fumes from salt water and battery acid are dangerous and will be covered later.

(c) *A sudden squall which capsizes the boat before the sheets are released*
This is a cause of capsize which has occurred when a yacht is close under the land when squalls may whistle down from high hills. It may also happen in the tropics when sudden squalls may hit very quickly and, indeed, line squalls are by no means unknown in temperate climates. It is normally possible to anticipate such squalls and the crew of a multihull must be extremely alert if there is any likelihood of these conditions.

Such an incident happened to Brian Cooke in *Triple Arrow*, the trimaran which he sailed in the 1974 Round Britain Race. *Triple Arrow* is a light (7,300 lbs.) foam sandwich, Simpson Wild design with an overall length of 49 ft. and a beam of 30 ft. She has a moderately high aspect cutter rig with a 50 ft. mast. She is designed on the semi-submersible float principle in that the outrigger, which is long and thin, is frequently under water when she is hard pressed. There is no reserve of buoyancy as the outriggers are connected to the main hull by two box girder sections.

Cooke was lying fourth in the Round Britain Race when the capsize occurred. This story, published in the February 1975 edition of *Yachting Monthly*, tells the tale in Cooke's own words.

'We had run down from Muckle Flugga the northern tip of the Shetlands towards Lerwick in a N.N.E. Force 5 wind under spinnaker and full main.

84. Triple Arrow.

'After rounding the southern tip of Bressay Island we came on the wind with Lerwick about 4 miles away, but could not make the course to the finishing line which was north by west approximately. In view of the likelihood of short tacking, the No. 2 genoa was set instead of the No. 1 which would normally have been set in the prevailing conditions but which is cumbersome to sheet in quickly. The full main was set but no staysail. We were in the lee of the land, but covered about $1\frac{1}{2}$ miles towards Lerwick without incident and then ran into a calm about $\frac{1}{4}$ mile off the land. A breeze then made and we continued on our way, gradually opening out from the land.

'There was then another calm which lasted long enough for *Triple Arrow* to lose all way. At this stage, we were about $\frac{1}{3}$ mile off the Ord with Lerwick in sight two miles away with both Eric Jensen and I in the cockpit ready to let go the sheets if a sudden puff came.

'A sudden disturbance appeared on the surface immediately ahead in the form of little spikes of water (not the usual ripples which appear when wind makes horizontally on a calm sea). We both saw this as it appeared but before the turns of the genoa and main sheets could be taken off their respective winches, an almighty gust hit the yacht— I believe from the starboard beam and coming down off the hills at an estimated angle of 45° to the horizontal. With no way on at all, and the sails pinned right in, the whole force of the wind was in a capsizing moment and I estimate that the 180° flip took less than 10 seconds. It was fast enough for Eric to be catapulted out. I hung on, not believing the boat would go over until it was evident there was no hope of her coming back and got caught under the boat from which position I found it very difficult to swim under the trampoline and out beyond the float as my oilskins seemed to provide considerable buoyancy at first. The capsize was at approximately 1205 BST on 16th July.

85. Triple Arrow, *after the capsize.*

'I suppose we were fortunate to capsize in daylight. Getting caught under the boat at night could have been tricky and rescue could have been more protracted.

'I do not consider that there was anything basically wrong with the boat which contributed to the capsize. I believe that if any other multihull in the Race had experienced the same conditions, she would have similarly succumbed. *Triple Arrow* is after all 30 ft. beam. I further believe that such an impossible whirlwind or whatever it was, would not likely be experienced at sea—although conjecture on what would happen if caught involuntarily in a waterspout is interesting to say the least.

'There was no hope of righting the yacht ourselves.

'The yacht floated high on the water and it was only a short time before she had drifted into more exposed water.

'Rescue came after about 45 minutes when the lifeboat coxwain ordered us off the yacht as I had incurred an eye injury which looked much worse than it was.

'The lessons that we learnt from this capsize were as follows:

(i) The life raft **must** be stowed so that access can be gained to it with the yacht overturned. We had done this and recovered the raft quite easily in case it was necessary. It contained distress flares which would have been needed had rescue not been fairly swift. Despite its heavy weight, the raft floated.

(ii) Our main supply of distress flares were stowed in a water tight container near the cabin entrance so as to be easily accessible. They could not be recovered without diving down and into the boat from underneath—a risky undertaking.

(iii) Our survival beacon was stowed in the main cabin in an easily accessible position if the yacht was upright but it was virtually impossible to recover it from this position with the yacht capsized. There would appear to be a very strong case in a multihull for keeping it on deck adjacent to the life raft although I have never seen this done.

(iv) Access into the boat from the outside or vice versa when capsized by means of a water tight hatch which can be opened from both inside and outside would seem very important. *Manureva* has one fitted. One is to be fitted underneath the starboard sponson on *Triple Arrow* at the end of the season.

(v) Hepplewhite Automatic Sheet Release is to be fitted to *Triple Arrow*. I am surprised that this equipment is not more widely used as from the experienced multihullers I have spoken to who have this gear—notably Bill Howell and Alain Colas—they say that they would not feel happy sailing singlehanded without it. I doubt if it would have saved *Triple Arrow* in the conditions met with which caused its capsize, but it should save a yacht from capsizing due to a very sudden **horizontal** wind or when for any other reason the yacht reaches a steep angle of heel. The gear can be adjusted for degree of heel.

(vi) The modest area of the mainsail (300 sq. ft.) has decided me that I can handle it with a two fold purchase instead of the present three fold purchase. This should be an additional safety factor as the sheet will run out quicker with a two fold rather than a three fold purchase.

(vii) The question of masthead buoyancy arises and considerable thought has been

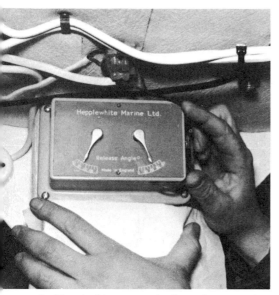

86. *Hepplewhite automatic sheet release gear is a safety aid for singlehanded sailing. Left, shows how the release angle is set—here at 25°. Right, is the clamp, in this case holding the main sheet, which will be released when the angle of heel exceeds 25°. Obviously the sheet must be free to run if the gear is to be effective.*

given to this. Discussing this with experienced multihull men, opinions seem to be sharply divided as to the merits of masthead buoyancy in a sizeable trimaran.

'I personally feel that as far as *Triple Arrow* is concerned, the disadvantage on a fairly tall and heavy mast of having the weight and windage aloft of an effective float, might be the final cause of a capsize, whereas without it a capsize might not occur. I doubt if *Triple Arrow* could be righted without outside assistance if she capsized with a masthead float fitted as I believe she would lie with the mast 10–20° below the horizontal. I cannot substantiate this statement and certainly do not wish to be able to from personal experience. Once is enough!'

It is interesting to note from this description that Cooke does not lay any blame for the accident on *Triple Arrow*. In my opinion the accident would not have happened so rapidly, and might have given more time for the crew to release the sheets if the outriggers had been slightly more buoyant or at least had had a reserve of buoyancy in the crossbeams. The Ord is a notorious place for bad squalls and the three leading yachts *Three Cheers*, *Gulf Streamer* and *British Oxygen* all experienced hard gusts. In *Three Cheers*, both main and genoa sheets had to be instantly freed and *Gulf Streamer* almost lifted her centre hull out of the water in a squall which made Phil Weld release all his sheets. When *British Oxygen* was hit they too did not have time to release the main sheet and one of the gusts succeeded in tearing the sheet track away from the boat. However, the squall which flipped *Triple Arrow* must have been a particularly vicious one, almost an Act of God, as it came off the hill at an angle of 45°. Had this happened with the sheets released and the sails out they might have got away with it but with the sails sheeted hard in—the worst position for them in squally weather—the capsize occurred with inevitable rapidity. Cooke re-emphasises the importance of having life raft, all flares, and in this case, survival beacon readily accessible **outside** the cabin. This is obviously sensible and not always done by multihull sailors. Life jackets should also be added to the list.

The question of masthead buoyancy and 'capsize' hatches is a debatable one. I cannot, under any circumstances, agree with the sense of providing a multihull with masthead buoyancy of any sort. To do so puts a considerable amount of windage and weight in the wrong place. So much so, that it can have the undesirable effect of helping to cause a capsize because the inertia at the masthead is enormous. It is also a strong psychological factor in putting the sailing public off multihulls and might suggest that a multihull is potentially unsafe and has to be sailed with extreme caution. Such a design technique cannot be right, and it is interesting to note that many vessels with masthead buoyancy are narrow beamed catamarans with a high aspect rig. As previously mentioned, **all** multihulls are capsizable but some are far easier to invert than others. The majority are very hard to capsize but there is a small percentage which are not. Most of this latter group have masthead flotation.

87. *A masthead float puts weight and windage in the wrong place, so should not be accepted.*

88. Triple Arrow's *capsize hatch is under a bunk mattress.*

A 'capsize hatch' is a more sensible safety idea than masthead buoyancy as it can be fitted to any multihull without detriment to strength provided it is well built and in a sensible position. The only disadvantage that it has is additional expense, and a possible psychological one in that the crew can see it and know why it is there! Personally, I prefer to sail without one as I feel it is vital to sail a boat within her limits and I am not planning to capsize. On the other hand, if I was sailing Round the World single handed as Alain Colas did in *Manureva*, I might consider it. It is all a matter of personal choice. One thing, though, is certain and that is that it is a difficult business re-entering an upturned multihull.

In similar vein, a pendulum automatic sheet release gear is another anti-capsize feature that is fitted to some craft. Generally, this is an efficient gear which works on the pendulum basis in that it automatically releases the sheets at any required angle of heel. However, there is a fundamental weakness in pendulum release gears. If the boat capsizes quickly, the rate of roll may cause the acceleration or centrifugal force on the pendulum to exactly balance the downward pull of gravity on the pendulum so that in relation to the hull (and in this case, the release operating mechanism) the pendulum stays in its central position and will not release the sheets. This could apply particularly in the case of a broach. A gyroscopic device would work, but not a pendulum.

It is, despite this, useful for single handed sailing when there may be no crew on deck to release the sheets in an emergency. This is particularly true of a catamaran which may give less warning of a capsize and flip more quickly than a trimaran. Many people regard it as the final multihull safety device. Here again, I prefer not to use it, but to sail in a low aspect ratio craft and rely more on human alertness.

The question of when to let go the sheets is important. In all cases, the answer should be 'too early'. However, in racing this loses time and the tendency is usually to hang on until the last possible moment. If this is done, there must be a very good guarantee that the sheets can be released instantly. Five things will assist this:

(a) Alertness.
(b) Quick release cleats.
(c) As few turns on the winch as possible.
(d) The smallest purchase possible on the main sheet.
(e) Ensuring that the sheets are clear to run, and in the last resort—**a sharp knife.**

We have already discussed alertness at some length but there is no harm done in re-emphasising it. Alertness is of far more importance on a multihull that a monohull, particularly in squally conditions. Rapid reactions may be vital to prevent a capsize in a sudden gust.

Quick release cleats are essential to ensure the fastest possible 'spill' of wind from the sails but remember that certain types are better than others. Some cleats only serve to jam the rope under exceptionally high loads. Also, always ensure that the sheets are free to run and are not being sat on or lying tangled in the cockpit. It is advisable to have the minimum number of parts to the main sheet purchase possible to ensure the main sheet can be rapidly released and the fewer turns that are round a winch the quicker the sheet will run. The American catamaran, *Imi-Loa* was capsized because the genoa sheet had four turns around the winch and could not be released quickly enough because the Samson braid had meshed together. Not all braided ropes will do this, but it is probable that they may not slip of their own volition if more than three turns are on the winch. They will have to be flicked off which adds time.

Remember also that it may be necessary to let go the headsail sheets as well as the main sheet in an emergency. The main sheet will always run out more slowly because of its purchase so there may be reasons for releasing the headsail first, especially if it is a big one.

The last resort, a sharp knife, should always be remembered by every sailor who puts to sea in any yacht, especially a multihull. Certain skippers will not hoist sail without a knife close to the sheet winches and the final resort is to cut the sheets (expensive!).

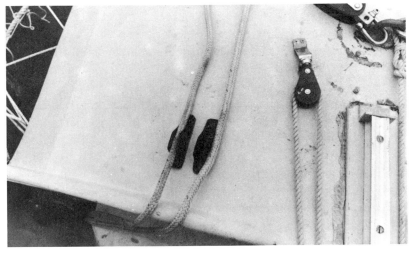

89. *Quick release cleats.*

(d) *Centrifugal force while luffing, particularly with a reaching spinnaker set*
As we have seen, it is a dangerous mistake when reaching to luff up in order to avoid a capsize. This is because it causes centrifugal force and increases the wind speed, and therefore pressure, over the sails. The combined effect has a capsizing moment which may well prove fatal. This danger is even more apparent if the boat is being luffed broadside to heavy breaking seas as wave action can be a further contributory factor. Usually a capsize of this nature is directly attributable to the inexperience of the crew or the man at the helm. It is therefore essential that the skipper makes absolutely sure that he has briefed everybody on board as to the correct course of action to take in these circumstances. It must always be borne in mind that the natural tendency on a monohull is to **luff up** in order to ease the ship in a squall and as most multihull novices graduate from monohulls their natural reaction may be to do likewise.

There is also a capsize danger when altering course from a run onto a reach, particularly when racing in a strong wind. If, for instance, the yacht has been running towards a buoy in a Force 6 or 7 wind, there will be very little wind speed over the deck because of her speed through the water. As a result, she may well be carrying full sail and the moment she rounds the buoy the apparent wind could well go from 5 to 30 knots in the space of seconds. If this is not appreciated by the crew, there will be a capsize risk as she rounds the mark and she will be carrying far too much sail. It is therefore advisable to make a rough calculation of what the apparent wind speed will be once the mark is rounded and to shorten sail accordingly before the buoy is reached.

90. Centrifugal force and lift from a spinnaker can combine in a dangerous capsize moment if the yacht broaches while running.

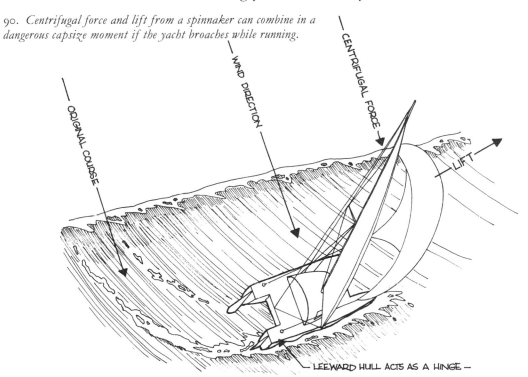

In moderate to strong winds, there is considerable potential danger from a spinnaker if a broach occurs. This is because a spinnaker has lift and should a luff or broach occur, the wind pressure on the sail will increase in an upward direction. This will produce a very rapid capsize moment as the direction of lift will serve to raise the weather hull or outrigger out of the water extremely fast. Several capsizes have happened because of this and it has been found that even if the spinnaker sheets are cut or released it is often too late because of the rapidity with which this sort of capsize can happen. A capsize with a spinnaker will be extremely fast.

A spinnaker must always be watched very closely if it is being used on a reach as the lift factor is potentially hazardous. A good rule is that if the end of the spinnaker boom is pointing forward of the weather hull or outrigger—**watch out!**

(e) *Stalling at the top of a wave and being blown back down the front and capsized*
This is an unusual type of accident and there is only one case of it happening to my knowledge. This occurred in the 1970 Round Britain Race when Mike Butterfield capsized in the MacAlpine-Downie designed *Apache Sundancer* (see page 149), a 40 foot long catamaran with a 19 foot 6 inch beam and a draught of 7 feet with the centreboards down. She had a 'flying saucer' type of masthead flotation and was lying in third place on the last leg down the English Channel. The wind was from the west gusting up to gale force 9 and *Apache* had been trying ineffectually to beat against wind and tide under reduced canvas for some hours off the Nab Tower. Butterfield decided, wrongly as he later admitted, to try and make over the ground by using the whole of the mainsail and at midnight, the fully battened mainsail was set, unreefed, with the working jib. His reason in doing this was largely on account of the fact that the reefing system did not work properly. The boat was pinched in the squalls and allowed to sail in the lulls. *Apache* managed for a time. Because the mainsail was fully battened there was no tendency for it to flog. The centreboards were down. However, both the crew were extremely tired and the concentration needed to maintain steering on the knife edge of paying off, which could cause a possible capsize over the beam, and luffing too high, so that the vessel would stall in irons and be pushed backwards down the front of a steep wave, was too great. Two particularly steep waves followed in quick succession; *Apache* stalled on the first and, with no weigh on, slid backwards and sideways down the steep front of the second to gently capsize over her centreboards at the bottom. The masthead float did its job initially but soon broke off and *Apache* totally inverted. Luckily, Butterfield and his crew were saved by a Dutch coaster but *Apache* was not so lucky and was later destroyed, somewhat unnecessarily, by Trinity House who deemed her to be a hazard to shipping.

This sad tale of an extremely rare capsize brings out a number of points.

(1) Too much sail was carried which in itself was dangerous but also forced the helmsman into steering a dangerous course. Had the ship been carrying considerably less sail it would have been possible for *Apache* to bear away more and sail faster over the waves in greater safety.

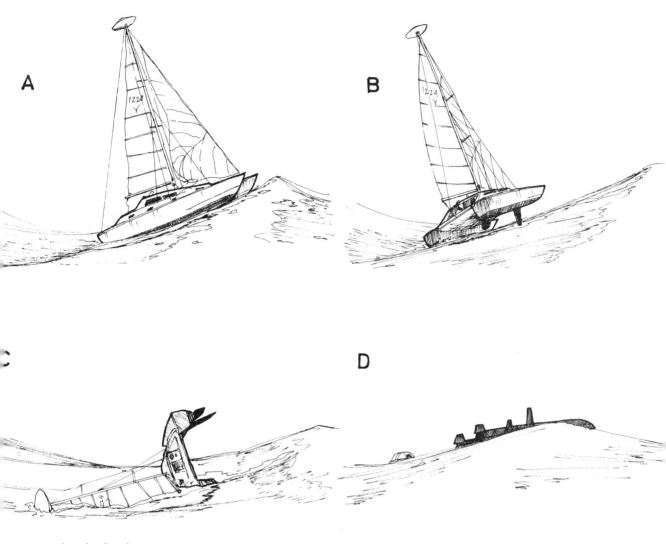

91. Apache Sundancer *capsized in a gale force wind when (A) the yacht stalled in irons at the top of a wave. (B) She started to make sternway and began to broach beam on to the sea and wind. (C) She capsized gently to port over her lee centreboard. (D) With the yacht totally inverted and the masthead float broken off, the crew took to the liferaft.*

(2) Because they were beating to windward, the centreboards were down. Had the leeward one been raised and the windward one down she might not have capsized.

(3) There is always a danger in getting pushed backwards by a wave if the ship has stalled in these circumstances. The action of the rudders may tend to swing the vessel broadside on to the sea, and the after end of the leeward hull or outrigger may dig in. Any sail or masthead buoyancy carried will then accelerate the capsize process.

(4) A similar danger arises if one is caught in stays and goes backwards in storm conditions. Because of this it may be safer to gybe round.

(5) Butterfield and Ellison became separated from *Apache Sundancer* because the painter of their self inflating life raft, which was attached to the inverted yacht, pulled out from the raft. Had this not happened, they might have been able to save the ship. The reason that it pulled away is that it is designed to do so to stop the life raft from being dragged down with a sinking ship. To prevent this it is best to lash the raft to the upturned catamaran (preferably to the trampoline to prevent chafe) or attach it by a fresh painter to the life raft's hand ropes.

(f) *Pitchpoling over the bow*
The final type of capsize invariably happens because of design failures, and when it does provides the most violent and dramatic way of reaching the inverted position.

Both catamarans and trimarans have suffered from being pitchpoled and in all cases the reason for the accidents was poor design. This was because the designer had not given enough lift or buoyancy to the forward ends of the hulls/outriggers with the result that the ship surfed at a steep angle down an enormous steep wave, had insufficient lift to prevent the bow digging in and somersaulted. Similar accidents have happened to monohulls and the famous example of *Tzu Hang* is a classic. Amazingly, the Smeeton's ketch did not sink, as many monohulls would have done, and they lived to tell the tale. Although a multihull will not sink, it will not necessarily be much better off in its inverted position. It is also likely that crew members may be injured in such an accident because the impact of 'digging in' at fifteen+ knots is like hitting a brick wall in a motor car.

Alain Colas, who fitted extra sponsons to give *Manureva* greater lift told me that he found that **lift** forward was more important than buoyancy when surfing down the gigantic seas of the Southern Ocean in a storm. I am sure that this is true after my own experiences in *Three Cheers* and anyone who is contemplating deep water sailing should make sure that his multihull has sufficient lift in the forward hulls or outriggers. In a catamaran, this lift can often be achieved by a knuckle in the hull or good, flared bows.

It is easy to tell whether or not a multihull has sufficient lift by surfing in a rough sea. If there is the **slightest** tendency to dig, this could be magnified to pitch-poling proportions in an ocean storm and the skipper would be best advised to sell his craft and buy a better design. A catamaran which is fully decked between the bows is more vulnerable to 'digging in' than one which has a bridgedeck that starts further aft—it also has more windage which could assist a capsize.

ACTION WHEN CAPSIZED
Righting and Recovery. If we accept from the beginning that all multihulls **can** capsize, it is only seamanlike and realistic for every skipper to have some form of plan in his mind should the worst happen. In a monohull, every skipper should give instructions

92. Apache Sundancer, *40 ft length with a 19 ft 6 in beam and a draft of 7 ft with the boards down.*

to his crew on what action must be taken if the ship is to be abandoned and the same applies, in a slightly different context, to the multihull.

The first and most important point has already been made, and that is that the life raft **must** be accessible from both sides together with the flares, life jackets and survival beacon. As soon as possible, it should be inflated and, providing it is not too rough, secured to the bridgedeck where it can be used for shelter. Remember that one of the principle dangers in a capsize may be death from exposure.

It is quite likely that there may be crew members inside a hull when the boat overturns. There is no immediate cause for panic as, providing they are in a hull, and not in the bridgedeck of a catamaran, they should have a plentiful supply of air for some time. There is always the possibility that someone may have been injured in the capsize by being thrown against something and it is essential that somebody, preferably the skipper, does an immediate check by shouting for each member by name to determine whether or not everybody is all right.

One very important danger that must be borne in mind is that of asphyxiation by the action of salt water mixing with battery acid. This is a cause of death which has happened on past occasions (not in multihulls to my knowledge) and is particularly hazardous because it is not always possible to tell whether or not one is being asphyxiated. Obviously, any batteries will be inverted after a capsize and it is therefore important for the skipper to make sure that everyone knows the need to evacuate as quickly as possible any hulls in which batteries are stowed.

From experience of past capsizes we know that all multihulls float surprisingly high in the inverted position and it may be possible to live in an upturned hull if the capsize has occurred in mid-ocean. Obviously, to do this, adequate ventilation would have to be arranged by cutting a hole in the bottom of the hull. This could have the effect of almost sinking the hull of a catamaran which does not have internal buoyancy, but it should have no adverse effect on a trimaran which has its central hull supported by its outriggers. If the hulls can be lived in, a jury floor will have to be arranged.

As far as righting an upturned multihull is concerned, more has been written than has been achieved in practice. There are no cases in existence where an offshore multihull has been righted by its crew after a capsize 'in anger', although cases exist where a boat has been deliberately capsized and righted in 'laboratory' conditions of absolute calm with a fresh and enthusiastic crew. From all practical points of view, the best advice that can be given is—forget it!

The Amateur Yacht Research Society has done an extensive study on this subject and all the theories that have been put forward may be found in the pages of their journals. Anybody who wishes further information on the subject should contact them.

This is not to say that it is impossible for a crew of an upturned multihull to right the vessel but just that it has not yet been done for real. Some ideas involve flooding a hull or outrigger and using the mast as a lever to get her on her side, when the natural forces of wind and water in conjunction with human assistance might get the boat

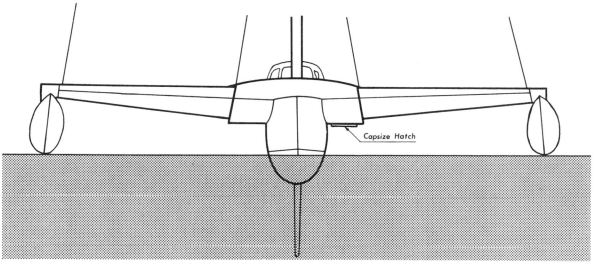

Capsize Hatch

93. Triple Arrow, *above, in normal trim and below, in capsized trim when she floated extremely high. Note the position of the capsize hatch fitted after the capsize.*

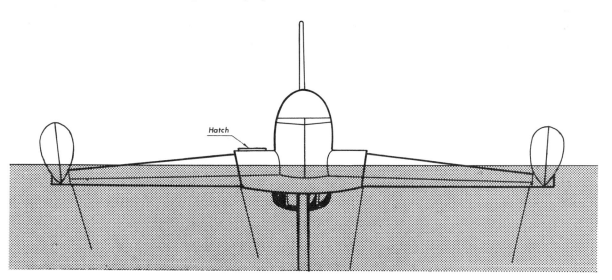

Hatch

upright. I do not intend describing this theory in detail as it is still—a theory—and well documented by the Amateur Yacht Research Society. To my mind, it is far more important for the crew to concentrate on survival from the moment the accident happens.

There is a fair amount of knowledge available about the recovery of a multihull by another ship. The first important point to realise is that it is very difficult to tow an inverted multihull with her mast still in position. If this is done, it must be done extremely slowly and in a forwards direction. *Triple Arrow* was towed stern first by her centreboard with the result that the boom, centreboard, sails and mast were all damaged to some degree. This is obvious. Once the mast has been removed, an inverted multihull will tow reasonably well in a forwards direction. A catamaran will require a bridle and a trimaran must be towed from the bow of its main hull. It is still important for the tow to be as slow as possible because the natural sheer of an inverted multihull will give it a tendency to dive towards the bottom.

The best way of righting the craft is to crane it up by one hull so that it is in a vertical position with the lower float or outrigger still in the water. This is then pulled towards the base of the crane which then lowers the boat the right way up. Needless to say, this puts a considerable strain on the vessel and should give the owner some idea as to how well built it is!

Capsize Conclusions

I have said a good deal about capsizes and this may give the reader the impression that the multihull capsize is a common event. This is by no means the case as the percentage of multihull capsizes is amazingly small. Sadly, most of them occur on occasions when the boats are being driven to their limits such as in racing, and they attract the maximum amount of publicity thereby giving the multihull a poor reputation. However, providing the multihull skipper knows what the potential dangers are, he should have little problem in avoiding a capsize. Always remember that PREVENTION IS EASIER THAN CURE.

To conclude, this short list of capsize safety precautions is worth remembering.

(a) Always shorten sail early in gusty conditions.
(b) Always be aware of the 'tripping' danger from the lee centreboard.
(c) Stow the liferaft, flares, lifejackets and survival beacon **outside** the cabin in a position where they can be reached if the yacht turns over.
(d) Make sure the sheets are free to run and can be released as quickly as possible.
(e) Ensure that the crew are briefed and **ALERT**.

Man Overboard

Too many people have lost their lives unnecessarily through being washed overboard from a yacht. In the 1973 Whitbread Round the World Race for monohulls, three people were drowned, and this sort of accident is probably the most tragic and avoidable of all mishaps. Forgetting for a moment, **why** people fall overboard, let us look at the reasons **why** they are often not picked up.

The main difficulty, particularly at night or in a gale, is locating the man. It is quite amazing how hard it is in broad daylight to find a person who has been washed into the sea. Even if he is wearing bright oilskins, and a lifebuoy and beacon have been thrown to him, it is often immensely hard to find him again if there is a rough sea running.

This difficulty is accentuated if the ship has been running, under spinnaker or running sails which are boomed out, because it will take that much longer to lower downwind canvas before a search can be made. The yacht may then have to tack back along her track and in a high sea stands a very good chance of missing the unfortunate man who has gone over.

The problem is even more accentuated with a multihull. This is because the speed of the vessel will be very much greater on a reach or a run than a monohull in strong conditions and the boat may therefore be that much further away making the problems of the search more difficult.

It is therefore, extremely important that crew members carry some form of locating means on them such as mini-flares, wrist strobe lighting, and a whistle at all times. Obviously, this is particularly relevant in foul weather.

The lifebuoy and safety beacons should always be thrown to a man directly he has fallen overboard and the latter device should have a flashing light on it.

A new and important safety system is currently being developed. *Sea Trail*, the invention of a British sailor, Ewen Southby-Tailyour, is a device that leaves a trail of phosphorescent dye in the water as soon as it is activated. This leaves a trail in the sea which can be followed back to the scene of the accident. It has the advantage of 'direction' in that even if the ship has to tack across it, the trail can be picked up by day or night, and will, eventually, lead the ship to the right place. Evaluation trials are still in process and this device should be an enormous asset to sailing safety.

On a light multihull which carries no headway, it may be possible, if the ship is beating to windward when the man goes over, to recover him by going about without releasing any sheets so that the 'hove to' yacht drifts down to leeward to the man in the sea. Just such an accident occurred to the author on *Three Cheers* in the middle of the North Sea during the 1974 Round Britain Race.

'Our normal procedure when changing the forward headsail on *Three Cheers* going to windward is to pinch the boat to such an extent that her speed is minimal and there is little movement on the foredeck. This needs considerable concentration on the part of the helmsman, for the moment she pays off she accelerates and the foredeck becomes a dangerous and jerky platform. If the weather is too rough to use this method—usually force 6 and above—we either steer downwind which is costly on time, or heave to.

'The accident happened at 0800 on July 18. We were close hauled on the starboard tack in a force 5, gusting 6, S.W. wind. *Gulf Streamer* was in sight two miles on the port quarter and *British Oxygen* was well to seaward of us and an estimated hour ahead. I was on watch at the time and called Martin to steer as I considered that the time had come to change down from the No. 1 to the No. 2 jib. The sail change went without a hitch, and, as I hoisted the No. 2, Martin paid the boat off and started to winch in the sheet. However, the sheets had fouled themselves into a "steel ball" at the clew of the sail due to the flapping of the jib before it was sheeted home. The only way to sort out the mess was to lower it and, without thinking (and ever conscious of the enemy closing on the port quarter!), I dropped the sail and rushed forward to sort the problem out. This action was ill considered for *Three Cheers* was now pounding to windward at about nine knots and the forecastle was like a trampoline. Within seconds I was bounced overboard to leeward. Fortunately, I still had hold of a lifeline and only half of me was in the water. Martin, seeing my plight, immediately put her into the wind to stop her and rushed forward to help me back aboard. By the time he reached me the pull of the water had got me and I was gone—a flash of yellow in a rough, grey sea. The next thing I remember was a very painful bang on my left thigh as I went under the boat (she was still turning) and hit the skeg at about five knots. I came up the other side to find her hove to on the port tack with staysail aback, some 30 yards upwind. Fortunately, she carries no weigh when she comes about and it was, therefore, a matter of no action to be taken by anyone other than *Three Cheers* who, like a real lady, drifted straight back to me and held out her starboard outrigger to a very thankful hand. The problem of course, did not end there because I now found that I could not climb back on board. I was wearing seaboots, longjohns, trousers, shirt, two sweaters, oilskin trousers with braces and a fisherman's smock that came down to my knees. After a vain attempt we concluded that a halyard was the only answer and after lowering all the sails except the mizzen (the leeway was pushing me under), Martin got a rope around me and winched me up on deck.

'It took a long time to get going again for everything was by now in a foul tangle including the errant sheets of the No. 2 jib. By the time we were on our way, exactly an hour had passed from the moment I went in. This hour had cost us a further hour in missed tide at the Lowestoft end.

'The moral of the story is that had I been wearing a safety harness I would not have become separated from *Three Cheers* and although I would have gone overboard, Martin could have winched me in on a halyard from the forecastle. Had Martin been forced to carry out the complicated evolution of sailing round in a circle to pick me up, I think that I could possibly have drowned. I was swallowing water so fast in the rough sea that, weighted down by clothing I could not have got out of, I feel that drowning could not have been too many minutes away. In point of fact, I was not separated from the boat for more than a couple of minutes. Neither Martin nor I consider ourselves to be careless in the matter of wearing harnesses and we both use them when we feel the need to. However, the real moral is, that even if a person feels that a harness is unnecessary for the prevailing conditions, he has forgotten the possibility of human error and the one moment of carelessness which could, in my case, have cost a lot more than the race.'

94. *(Right) The sequence of events when the author fell overboard from* Three Cheers *about 100 miles offshore from Newcastle in the 1974 Round Britain Race, with the wind blowing SW force 6. (A)* Three Cheers *was on the starboard tack and X marks the spot from which the author fell; he was injured as the skeg hit him when he went under the yacht. Martin Read tacked the yacht, which carried no way through the wind, so (B) she became automatically hove-to on the port tack with the staysail aback and made leeway towards the author. (C) Recovery was effected by using the spinnaker halyard.*

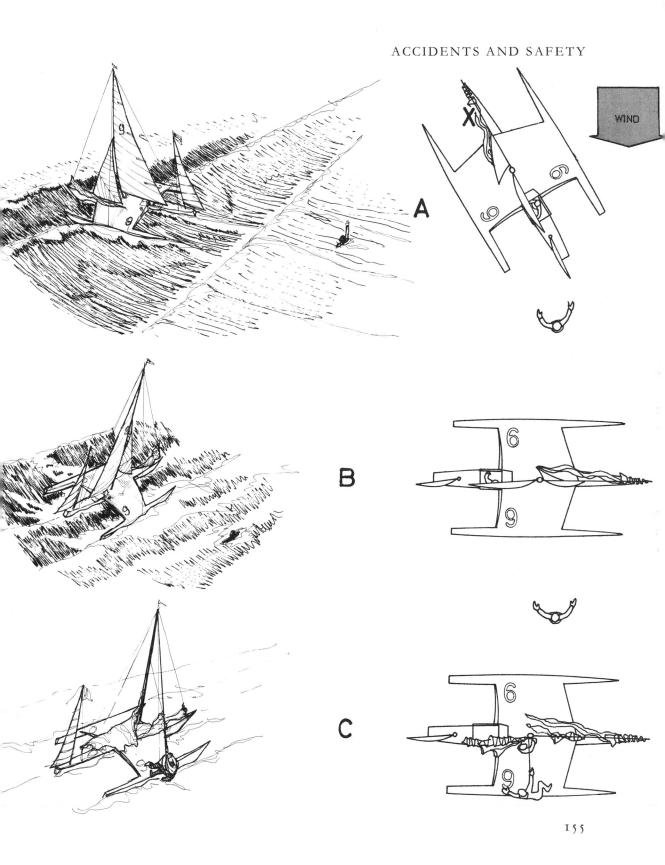

The point about wearing safety harnesses can not be over emphasised. I, like many people before me, learnt the hard way, but was sufficiently lucky to survive.

What is interesting, however, is that *Three Cheers* from the moment she was hove to (simply by putting the helm over and going about without touching the sheets) was directly upwind of me and therefore able to drift down without any further control by the helmsman. Luckily, Martin Read instantly appreciated the situation and did not alter the sheets or sail round in a circle to pick me up—which might have proved fatal in the rough conditions. This could not possibly have happened in a monohull because of the headway that would have been made during the tack. This would have resulted in the monohull heaving to and:

(a) Making very little leeway because of her deep displacement.

(b) Missing me by a considerable distance, if she had drifted sideways and to leeward, because her headway during the tack would have taken her too far.

It also brings out the point that it is possible to sail backwards in a multihull and Martin could have used this capability, had it been necessary, to position *Three Cheers* so she would have drifted onto me.

Because she was making considerable leeway (at least a knot) when I eventually regained hold of her, she was heeled over so that the outrigger was well down in the water. Even so, I could not get out of the sea because of the considerable weight of water that my clothes had soaked up and the fact that I was injured. Because of this, a halyard had to be used. On a high sided catamaran, this would be the only safe way to get a man out of the sea if the yacht was being sailed shorthanded. If a halyard is used to get the man out it is important to remember that the 'business' end of it may well not reach him in the water if there is insufficient rope or wire. It is therefore prudent to throw him a line as soon as possible with a bowline tied in the end of it which he can put his arms and shoulders through so he cannot drift away from the ship. The rope can then be attached to the halyard and the man pulled out at leisure.

Obviously, this evolution of immediate rounding up and heaving to so that the ship makes leeways towards the man in the sea can only be used if he has gone overboard with the wind forward of the beam. If the ship is on a reach, then it will have to come back to him on a reach and if running will have to tack back. However, in all cases, it may prove easier and safer to heave to to windward of the man rather than luffing to him as one would to a mooring buoy, and allow the yacht to drift onto him. This also provides a lee in which to pick him up.

This manoeuvre should be practised by all multihull sailors until they are familiar with it.

Finally, it should be emphasised that the bow of any multihull that is pounding fast to windward is a very hazardous spot!

Dismasting and Jury Rigs

The most usual cause of dismasting on a multihull is a compression strain which causes the mast to buckle in the middle and collapse. This strain is caused because the initial shock of a gust of wind cannot be taken out by the immediate heel of the yacht in the same way as happens with a monohull. This results in a compression load on the mast which may cause a failure.

On a multihull which is stayed to its extremities, i.e. the cap shrouds are chainplated as far outboard as possible, there will always be more strain on the lower shrouds than on the cap shrouds themselves. This is because the compression load on the mast increases this strain at half height, as there is less length of wire to give flexibility, and the main lateral centre of effort from the sails is somewhere in the middle. As a result, it is important that the lower shrouds are correctly set up and the rigging is strong enough for the job. Usually, the lower shrouds should be slacker than the cap shrouds to allow for the stretch and upward pull on the outrigger from the cap shroud when the yacht is sailing. A good tip is to always look up the mast track when the boat is sailing and to adjust the rigging for that, rather than do it when the yacht is stationary in harbour.

Generally speaking, most multihulls should have a thicker mast section than a monohull to allow for this compression strain.

In the event of the mast breaking, a jury mast is easier to rig on a multihull than a monohull because it provides a more stable platform and a wider staying base. Brian Cooke rigged a jury rig on *Triple Arrow* after the yacht had been righted in Lerwick harbour in order to cross the finishing line to complete the third leg of the 1974 Round Britain Race.

'It would seem from our experience that if a trimaran should be dismasted (which was effectively how we found ourselves after the mast was removed and the yacht righted), that it is not difficult to fix up an effective jury rig.

'Ours was our 18 foot spinnaker pole set in the mast pot with guys to keep the foot firmly in place. The pole was easily stayed by spinnaker guys and down hauls and the halyards were barber haulers led through snatch blocks shackled to boom eyes at the "head".

'Two sails were set—the storm jib as foresail and the staysail (with the foot as the luff) acting as mainsail. This was thought out and rigged in about 30 minutes and could easily have been done singlehanded over a longer period.

'This rig in a force 3 breeze just forward of the beam gave us 3+ knots in smoothish water. It would therefore appear that such a rig would be adequate in a dismasted, light displacement, easily driven multihull to sail to a far distant port without requesting rescue, providing the course is a reach or a run.'

Cooke had the misfortune to be dismasted 'in anger' later on that year because of a faulty terminal joint in one of the lower shrouds. In a force 4 wind the mast collapsed to leeward as the result of the compression load set up by the lower shrouds breaking.

They had considerable difficulty freeing the mast because it had trapped itself underneath one of the outriggers and this could have proved dangerous in a rough sea as the outriggers might have been holed. As soon as the mast was cleared, the same eighteen foot spinnaker pole was re-erected as a jury mast.

'Erecting a spinnaker pole in a seaway is entirely a different matter. After a dismasting in the Channel in Force 4 in a short sea, lying a-hull with wind abeam, it took two very tired men four attempts before an 18 foot pole was satisfactorily set up.

It would seem that to do the job single handed, fairly kind conditions must prevail with this length of pole. With a third hand, I believe a 24 foot pole could be rigged in fairly rugged conditions.

So that the staying of the jury mast is satisfactory when the wind freshens, it is best to lead the halyards to weather as additional stays instead of down the mast as usual where they would be doing nothing to support the mast.'

It is interesting to note from the first description how easily driven *Triple Arrow* was under her improvised rig. This will be true of all reasonably light multihulls and a dismasting should, on the whole, provide less problems than it would for a monohull.

95. Triple Arrow *under jury rig after her dismasting in the English Channel during December 1974; with it she easily achieved three knots of headway with the wind abaft the beam.*

Structural Damage

The commonest failures that occur to the structure of a multihull are:

1. *Rudder damage*

This is a fairly common complaint of ill constructed multihulls. It usually happens because the rudder pintles are either too weak or insufficient in number. As a result, the rudder usually breaks off completely.

The greatest strain on the rudder usually comes when surfing because considerable pressure may be exerted in keeping the yacht on a true course and preventing a broach. If a broach does occur, enormous strains will be put on the rudders. Other large stresses occur if the yacht is caught in irons and sails backwards. This can be prevented by stops on the transom if the rudder is mounted right aft.

On a catamaran it is possible to sail with one rudder provided that the speed of the yacht is not too great. If the catamaran is close hauled, or on a reach, it will be hard to steer the yacht if the remaining rudder is on the windward side. In all cases, sail must be reduced immediately to take the strain off the remaining rudder.

Similarly, a trimaran will only steer easily with a jury rudder if the vessel is not sailing too fast. To try and maintain high speeds using a makeshift steering oar will usually result in a broken oar.

In both cases it is vital to try and balance the yacht by sail adjustments and with a bit of practice, it may even be possible to steer by altering the sheets. This will usually be easier in a multihull which has a two masted rig as many more permutations are possible.

2. *Breaking up*

The reasons for a break up are usually bad design, bad construction or a combination of both. There is little point in elaborating on this as both design and construction have been discussed in a previous chapter. What is relevant is the action to be taken if the ship shows any signs of break up.

In the case of a trimaran, the usual place for a break up to start is in the crossbeams. Cracks may appear and loud noises will certainly be heard. If this does happen, the first thing to do is to stop the yacht, and, if possible, lie a-hull with the damaged side to windward. There will be far more strain on the beams if they are to leeward because the immersed outrigger will be straining upwards. Assuming that some form of repair is feasible or that the yacht can still be sailed, shelter must be sought as soon as possible. When deciding on which place to shelter, it is advisable to try and keep the damaged side to windward during the sail there in order to keep the stresses to a minimum.

Obviously this will not always be the case, particularly if the rigging is stayed to the extremities as the cap shroud may tend to pull the outrigger off in an upward direction. However, if the minimum of sail is carried so that the strains come more on the lower shrouds the ship may survive.

Ideally, the least strain on the ship will come when it is sailing directly before the wind. However, this may not always fit in with the proximity of shelter.

A catamaran is not so likely to break up at the 'armpits' but may be more prone to damage from wave action underneath the bridge deck structure. This could eventually lead to a break up and has done so on past occasions to certain poor designs which had the bridge deck too low. Once again, the smallest amount of sail and a downwind course may be the only road to safety.

3. *Wave damage to deck structure*
This is almost always caused by overloading a multihull with too much weight. This results in the yacht being unable to move fast enough or being insufficiently buoyant to escape the damaging effects of large breaking crests. Obviously, square sided cabin tops, large windows and badly fitting hatches invite this sort of damage. Generally speaking, wave damage is less commonplace to a multihull than a monohull because a multihull will be more buoyant and ride a wave better.

4. *Holed while sailing at speed by a floating object or collision*
This represents a fairly serious risk to a fast multihull as a floating log can inflict severe damage if it is hit at high speed. Apart from keeping an excellent look out, there is little that can be done to avoid such accidents. If a collision of this sort, or indeed with another boat occurs, the first essential action is to weight the craft so that the damage part is, if possible, out of the water. Repair may then be feasible in calm weather by

96. Repair may be possible in calm weather by lifting the outrigger with an inflatable dinghy.

97. *Damage from lightning can be avoided by lowering a small chain from a masthead shroud to the water, to act as a conductor.*

lifting a hull or outrigger by means of an inflatable dinghy underneath it. It is important to have bilge pumps that are permanently fixed in all hulls/outriggers and can be operated from the main accommodation or cockpit.

Damage by Lightning

This rare cause of damage applies to all sailing boats and is more common in the tropics and sub-tropics rather than temperate climates. Philip Weld who owns *Gulf Streamer* had one of his earlier trimarans damaged in this way. There was no lightning conductor between the mast and the water and the result was a series of holes in the hull around the chain plate of one of the shrouds not unlike bullet holes. No one was aboard when the lightning struck. This danger can be avoided by trailing a chain from a masthead shroud in the water. The lightning will run down the shroud and chain into the water where it will be earthed. The back stay is usually the best shroud to use on a multihull.

7 Heavy Weather

*General Pros and Cons of Multihulls in Heavy
Weather—Action taken by Multihulls—
Heavy Weather Indications*

General Pros and Cons of Multihulls in Heavy Weather

Heavy weather, together with the capsize problem, gives more worry to prospective multihull sailors than anything else. Surely, they say, in gale conditions a multihull is far more likely to be damaged by wave action, rolled over, pitch-poled or pooped than a monohull. What happens, they argue, if a multihull broaches? Will a multihull be capable of clawing to windward off a lee shore in a full gale? What about leeway?

The easiest way to analyse the handling of multihulls in storms is to look at specific examples and deduce indications from them.

Before we do this let us discuss the dangers which face a yacht in extremes of bad weather. By heavy weather I refer to winds of force 6, 22–27 knots, and above.

The principal dangers to a multihull from heavy weather which apply to a greater or lesser extent to monohulls are:
(a) Leeway.
(b) Broaching and capsize.
(c) Pitch-poling.
(d) Pooping.
(e) Structural damage from breaking waves.

The safety factors in heavy weather which could also apply in some cases to monohulls but are particularly associated with multihulls are:
(a) Speed.
(b) Great beam and lack of ballast.
(c) Shallow draft.
(d) Unsinkability.

Here is a brief summary of the main dangers to a multihull in a storm.

(1) *Leeway*

All yachts when hove to or lying a-hull will make leeway downwind; some may make headway as well. In a near gale or storm the leeway will be increased because:

(a) The top two or three feet of sea will be aerated and will allow a vessel to slip sideways more readily than if the water was denser.

(b) There will almost certainly be a wind-induced current which will mean that the

162

top four to six feet of sea may be moving down wind at speeds of up to 2 knots after a prolonged blow.

The multihull is much more liable to make leeway than her monohull equivalent because:
(a) She will not draw as much (assuming centreboards are up).
(b) She will be far lighter, size for size, and therefore, more easily driven to leeward.

This means that the dangers of a lee shore are very much greater for a multihull than a monohull. Therefore, it is vital that all multihulls have the capability to claw off a lee shore to windward in gale conditions. Sadly, this is by no means the case and there are many production yachts which would not be able to do this. Most of these are vessels which do not have centreboards and rely for their windward ability on V-shaped hulls or low aspect keels. However, a well designed yacht which has a good windward performance, should be able to make to windward in a seaway against winds of gale force. Small multihulls have more to fear from the lee shore, as they are harder to drive to windward in a storm.

(2) *Broaching and Capsizing*

Lack of ballast and large beam cause a multihull to resemble a steerable raft in a gale. As a result, she will not be so vulnerable to the capsize moment as a monohull for she will slip sideways with the breaking crest—even if the yacht has broached. Provided that the centreboards are raised there is no part of the hull deep enough to dig into the solid water beneath the top two or three feet of aerated water. A monohull, however, has a deep, permanent keel which will stick like glue in the solid water below three feet. This can, and frequently does, produce a situation where the monohull may be knocked down onto her beam ends by a breaking crest and, in extreme cases, rolled over.

The capsize danger to a multihull will increase if:
(a) The yacht is too heavy thereby encouraging the hulls/outriggers to dig in from lack of buoyancy.
(b) The centreboards have been left down encouraging a 'trip'.
(c) The outriggers of a trimaran are too thin and easily pushed under water where they act as a hinge.

(3) *Pitch-poling*

This danger will be present when the multihull is running in extremely heavy weather before a full gale. As we have seen, it is essential to have lift and buoyancy forward to avoid the bows digging in leading to a somersault. Running at speed will be examined in detail later in this chapter.

(4) *Pooping*

This is an extremely rare danger as the catamaran or trimaran will normally be travelling fast enough to escape the full fury of the breaking crest of a wave. If it does happen, it is because the yacht is too heavy and too slow.

(5) Structural damage from breaking waves

Here again, the multihull will be less vulnerable to this type of damage than a monohull because it will give before a wave and slide away from it. A monohull, however, will try to resist the impact of a breaking crest with the result that it may be damaged. Once again, a multihull which is overloaded will be more liable to wave damage.

We will now briefly look at the safety factors inherent in a good multihull.

(a) *Speed*. Speed is an advantage in two ways. Firstly, it provides a yacht with the capability to escape an approaching storm. This is a very real advantage to the fast multihull but one that should never be relied on as a final solution to heavy weather. Obviously, it has more relevance to the coastal cruising yacht than the ocean voyager.

The advantage of speed was brought home to me during a summer cruise in *Three Cheers* during September 1974. We had spent four weeks cruising the French and Spanish coasts with four on board and were bound for Plymouth from Corcubion on the north-west coast of Spain. A particularly vicious gale had recently gone through during the course of which former British Prime Minister Mr. Heath's *Morning Cloud* sank in the English Channel with loss of life. We sailed on the evening of the tragedy with a strong S.W. wind which the forecast promised would decrease. This however, was not to be and in ominous tones the announcer told us that Hurricane Becky was developing 400 miles west of Finisterre. With a force 6 following wind we rushed northwards through the night of September 3rd/4th averaging $10\frac{1}{2}$ knots. On the 4th, the wind increased further and the 1800 forecast warned of severe gales in the English Channel. Accordingly, we hove-to on the night of the 4th/5th to avoid getting north into the really rough stuff where the forecasts were predicting force 8–9. I was also keen to stop in deep water before we reached the Ushant continental shelf where the shelving effect of the sea bed could cause worse seas. A comfortable night was spent lying hove-to with only the reefed mizzen set to keep the yacht's head up and *Three Cheers* sat like a duck with both centreboards raised, making about a knot and a half of leeway in the right direction.

Although it was blowing force 8, the forecast was unchanged the next day and we decided to continue our rapid run for Plymouth. Accordingly, the staysail and a bit of main were hoisted and we continued a comfortable average of $10\frac{1}{2}$ knots in the right direction.

As we passed Ushant, the forecast became far worse and predicted a very intense wave depression coming in from the Atlantic. Winds of force 9 and above were forecast, so in an increasing gale and rising sea we ran for Plymouth at *Three Cheers'* best possible speed.

When land was sighted the seas had built up and the wind was freshening all the time from the south-west, so we were thankful to pick up our mooring in Plymouth. Although it was blowing a good force 8 when we arrived, this was as nothing to what followed as six hours later shore stations were recording gusts of hurricane force all down the south coast. Had we been in a slower craft, we would undoubtedly have been caught in the worst summer storm of the year (and several years for that matter) so it was purely due to our speed that we escaped it. The point was really brought home to me when I discovered subsequently that some friends of ours who had left Spain at the same time in a 40 ft. monohull sloop had been caught by the storm and really pasted.

The other advantage of speed in a multihull is that when running before a gale, even under bare poles, she has the capability to escape the enormous breaking waves that so often damage a monohull. This is because the multihull's speed will allow her to run fast enough to avoid the full impact of the breaking crest.

(b) *Great beam and lack of ballast.* The multihull is so wide and so light that she resembles a raft in storm conditions. This has the immediate advantage in some cases of allowing her to surf sideways on the breaking crests without resistance to the sea when lying a-hull.

This sounds quite terrifying and was not at first appreciated as an advantage by multihull sailors. Many people thought that the yacht would trip over its leeward hull or outrigger and that lying a-hull was therefore dangerous. Practical experience, however, has shown that this is not so as the whole boat will slide to leeward **provided** she is not overloaded and has her centreboards up. In the case of a trimaran it is also essential that the outriggers are not too narrow and have ample buoyancy.

(c) *Shallow draft.* This leads straight on from beam and ballast, as the less draft a multihull has, the more easily she will be able to slide with the breaking crests rather than resisting them when lying a-hull. If she has her centreboards down, they may well be broken off or serve to capsize the yacht. If it is undesirable to make leeway in a catamaran when hulling the windward board can be left down or partly so but the skipper may well run the risk of breaking it in half or damaging the casing.

Another somewhat curious advantage of shallow draft is that in the final resort, when a multihull is being driven onto a lee shore by storm, it may be possible to beach the ship through the surf. This would almost certainly mean death by drowning for the crew of a heavy displacement monohull as she would ground some way out and break up. However, there is no keel to prevent a multihull from beaching right inshore, and providing the coast is not rock bound, the crew may survive. This has happened at least twice.

(d) *Unsinkability.* Finally, a great safety advantage of the multihull lies in the fact that it is positively buoyant. Many single hulled vessels have been dragged to the ocean bed by the lead or iron that constitutes their ballast once they have been swamped in a gale. This cannot happen to a trimaran or catamaran if it is built correctly.

Action Taken by Multihulls in Heavy Weather

The action that a multihull takes in heavy weather will depend on four things. These are:

(a) Proximity of shelter.
(b) Dangers of a lee shore.
(c) Direction in which the yacht wishes to sail.
(d) Knowledge of the multihull's behaviour pattern in storm conditions.

If shelter can be reached before the full fury of the storm breaks most skippers will try to use the speed of their craft to reach harbour. However, it must be emphasised that this can be dangerous if the harbour is on a lee shore and the skipper is not too sure of his navigation. It is doubly so in a multihull that has a poor windward performance in extreme conditions.

The lee shore may be one of the greatest dangers to a multihull in storm conditions and if there is no possibility of making harbour it is vital that as much sea room as possible is gained to offset the possibility of being driven onto the land. Remember also that sea conditions worsen where the ocean shallows. The deeper the water and the less the currents, the better the sea state will be. It is important that skippers have some previous knowledge of the amount of drift that their multihull makes when lying a-hull so they can calculate a dead reckoning position.

The direction in which the vessel is making may well decide the best course of action to take in a storm. If the wind is free it will pay to run before the gale but if the wind is contrary, lying a-hull will keep the ship up to windward better.

There may not be a choice in a really severe 'ultimate' storm and only knowledge of the best course of action to be followed for a particular yacht will ensure survival.

The three principal methods of weathering a storm in a multihull are:

(a) Lying to a sea anchor.
(b) Hove-to and a-hull.
(c) Running before.

It is very easy to be too dogmatic about the course of action to be followed by a multihull in heavy weather. This is undesirable as there is still insufficient knowledge available to draw too firm conclusions. This particularly applies in survival storms of hurricane force winds, as relatively few multihulled yachts have experienced this frightening aspect of the sea. However, the information available does allow us to record indications of the correct course of action.

(1) *Lying to a sea anchor*

The theory of riding to a sea anchor is that it prevents the yacht from surfing down a wave and digging in at the bottom where she might broach or pitch-pole. It is also meant to keep the ship's head or stern to the seas so that the waves will rush past her without causing damage.

There are very few examples of lying to a sea anchor in a multihull for the good reason that it is not usually the best way to weather a severe storm.

David Lewis, in his catamaran *Rehu Moana* used one on various occasions. *Rehu Moana* was at this stage fitted with permanent low aspect ratio keels which were 1 ft. 3 in. deep aft, rising to almost nothing forward.

'I first used the sea anchor from one quarter in three sharp force 8–9 gales we encountered off Cape Agulhas in December 1966. I feared that the steep seas on the shallow Agulhas bank with a strong south-west flowing current against a south-west gale would possibly produce capsizing conditions. The experiment was so satisfactory that I used the method again in the only other gale we encountered, force 9 off the Bay of Biscay in the spring of 1967.

'The sea anchor consisted of three full sized motor car tyres (fenders) and a couple of fathoms of 2 in. anchor chain or a small anchor streamed on 40–50 fathoms of 2 in. nylon warp (stretchy).

98. *A sea anchor from the quarter, as used by David Lewis in* Rehu Moana *will present a greater length of yacht to the run of the seas.*

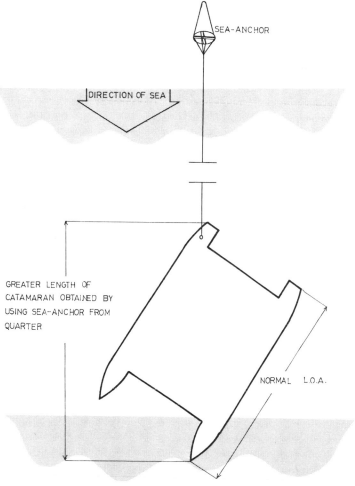

SEA-ANCHOR

DIRECTION OF SEA

GREATER LENGTH OF CATAMARAN OBTAINED BY USING SEA-ANCHOR FROM QUARTER

NORMAL L.O.A.

'The distance from one stern to the opposite bow perpendicular to the run of the seas must have been about 70 feet—a big steep wave would have been needed to upend the cat. (I still wonder how she would have faired in the sub-Antarctic seas where I recently took such a beating.) However, I was always happier in *Rehu Moana* in gales than in the Scottish double-ender with "Colin Archer-like lines", *Isbjorn*.'

This method of using a sea anchor has the advantage of presenting a longer length of ship to the run of the seas as the yacht is at an angle of 45° to the seas due to the anchor being secured from the quarter; this will help to prevent a pitch-pole capsize. It is important to note that Lewis used nylon warp as cable because of its elastic qualities; this is essential for any sea anchor because rope that has no stretching qualities will cause the ship to snub violently, which will increase friction and possibly pull out fittings or break the cable.

This course of action might be inadvisable for a trimaran due to the possibility of pulling off an outrigger. The strains involved are enormous and it should be remembered that the yacht will need very strong securing points for the cable.

On the whole, the greatest advantage of a sea anchor would be in a situation where the multihull might be carried onto a lee shore in a gale. If she was unable to claw off to windward, a sea anchor would be the only thing that could prevent her making leeway onto a hostile coast.

Alain Colas also used a sea anchor but in this case from the bow of *Pen Duick IV* (now *Manureva*) on his return to France from the Pacific Ocean for the 1972 Singlehanded Trans-Atlantic Race.

'Returning home singlehanded from La Reunion non stop via the Cape of Good Hope, I met with a force 9 to 10 gale and unprecedented steep—frighteningly steep—head seas in the Bay of Biscay, thus being forced to heave-to. At the time I felt I had to keep the boat's head straight against the onslaught and I kept my reefed mizzen up with a sea anchor paid out from the bows for the last ten hours. This helped until it broke into pieces but by that time it was possible to get organised and make a little headway under reduced canvas.'

It was important not to make leeway at the time and the sea anchor certainly proved useful.

Lewis also found that lying a-hull and running before a storm presented little problem to *Rehu Moana* (an extremely heavy catamaran), so the sea anchor theory does not necessarily prove anything. It would seem, however, that there must be more chance of structural damage to a vessel using a sea anchor as the yacht is held almost stationary while the waves can break upon her. Personally, I feel that there may be less risk to the ship in letting her run or lie a-hull; the multihull's lightness, shallow draft and beam are her advantages and enable her to float like a cork, but they cannot be fully utilised when riding to a sea anchor.

In a race, the sea anchor may have a tactical use in keeping the yacht to windward in a storm while rivals are blown downwind.

(2) *Hove-to and Lying A-Hull*

For multihulls these techniques, which are distinctly separate for monohull vessels, can best be discussed together. In fact heaving-to with foresail backed to windward and a small bit of mainsail set in the conventional way is not considered a method of weathering a storm in multihulls where the wind is blowing so hard that no sail can be carried with the possible exception of the storm jib when running before or the mizzen when lying a-hull. Also this method of heaving-to is not suitable for a multihull in very heavy weather as it will present windage high up which can help cause a capsize and encourage leeway. Strictly, lying a-hull means hove-to under bare poles with the craft free to be carried sideways by the waves and wind. However a tactic which sometimes proved effective for multihulls in very severe weather may, with certain reservations, have the benefits of lying a-hull and heaving-to, as with a mizzen only set she will head up to perhaps 50° of the wind, yet will surf sideways with the breaking crests, provided

99. *'Transatlantic Incident' from a painting by Laurence Bagley, shows* Gancia Girl *hove-to under mizzen in a force 10 storm while Minter-Kemp tries to bail the starboard outrigger.*

that there are no flat surfaces such as keels or boards which will prevent her doing so.

In the 1968 Singlehanded Trans-Atlantic Race, two multihulls were hit by a survival storm with winds in excess of hurricane force and seas which were recorded by three independent observers as reaching heights of 50 ft. on occasions.

In the trimaran *Gancia Girl*, Martin Minter-Kemp recorded winds of 60 knots and lay hove-to throughout the storm. Minter-Kemp estimated that the trimaran was making three knots of leeway downwind despite the fact that his boards—which were in the outriggers—were half down. He kept the mizzen up throughout the storm as he felt that it helped to keep the yacht's head up to the seas. At one stage in the gale he realised that the yacht was heeled too far to leeward and noticed with horror that one of the hatches had come adrift from the starboard outrigger which had half filled with water. At this stage, *Gancia Girl* must have been in imminent danger of capsize in the same way as Corkill went and Minter-Kemp moved all the available weight to windward to compensate for the filled outrigger which he could not bail effectively. Amazingly, *Gancia Girl* survived the storm largely because of her foam sandwich construction which kept the outrigger extremely buoyant despite the water it had taken in.

'We lay like that all day at about 55° to the wind. The motion was extremely lively but *Gancia Girl* resembled a raft throughout and at no stage was I really frightened by the thought of capsize. I did not experience the phenomenon of surfing sideways as did Bill Howell in *Golden Cockerel* but then I did not experience enormous breaking crests of six foot or more.'

Although Minter-Kemp had experienced hurricane force winds the seas were not as bad as those experienced by *Golden Cockerel* 150 miles nearer the storm centre. If they had been, there is little doubt that having even half the boards down would have been extremely risky. This is because of the tripping tendency discussed earlier. *Gancia Girl* was also grossly overweight and this might have further aggravated a capsize.

'I had not yet realised that the secret of multihull performance is extreme lightness. I had loaded the yacht with all sorts of goodies and when Tom Follett, the great exponent of living on the minimum possible, came aboard in Plymouth, he shook his head with amazement when he saw what I was taking. As I had accepted food from everyone, I had enough for at least two crossings and fifty gallons of water in addition to a mass of gadgetry.'

Bill Howell's *Golden Cockerel*, a Choy catamaran with asymmetrical hulls of 43 ft. LOA and 16 ft. beam had, as we have seen, already capsized off the Isle of Wight in 1967. The big storm of June 11th hit *Golden Cockerel* in the early hours of the morning.

'At 2 a.m. in the morning I was woken by a bad thrashing on deck as the Hepplewhite sheet release gear had flipped open. At the time we were going to windward under the working jib with both centreboards down when the boat heeled right over to a gust and the sheets were released. I rushed on deck to find that the sheets of the jib had wrapped themselves into a huge "steel ball" which was flailing across the foredeck. I dropped the jib and noticed that the Brookes and Gatehouse windspeed indicator was stuck against the 60 knot stop. The air was full of spray and blinding rain while the noise was fantastic. The seas were 20–30 ft. high, or more, and their crests were being torn off by the force of the wind. We were well above gale force 8—wind speed was more than 50 knots—it was whole gale 9 or storm force 10. I think it was the worst gale I have ever been in at sea. It was the most terrifying, as I was in fear of capsizing the cat if I should make a wrong move.'

Howell's first tactic was to run under storm jib and then bare poles, with both centreboards up. However, as he was going in the wrong direction at about eight knots, this was highly unsatisfactory. His mind was made up for him when *Golden Cockerel* broached after the self-steering had tripped.

'To my surprise, I looked at the wind vanes and instead of bending behind me, they were bending at right angles to the boat. The vanes had not been able to take the strain of running so the steering oar had snapped out and the boat broached in such a way that I did not know she had. When dawn came, I raised the reefed mizzen and lashed the helm to leeward. The wind which had dropped to 40 or 50 knots then came back again at 60+ knots and this combination of sail and rudder kept the ship's head pointed up into the wind and sea. Every wave had a breaking crest of at least six feet and the *Cockerel* would take each one at about 45°. One in fifty hit her sides (everybody said "Thank God I am not in a multihull") and the whole boat would surf sideways for fifty yards or more in the breaking seas. This was terrifying initially but after an hour or two, I just ignored it. I felt happy as long as the mizzen kept her head up and now I would not be worried about lying a-hull.'

Golden Cockerel had a minimal draft of 22 inches, and Howell is insistent that the shallower the draft the safer the yacht will be. Even low aspect keels or skegs could, he feels, dig in the solid water below the surf and trip the yacht. To some extent, I am sure that he is right and this is borne out by David Lewis who lay a-hull in *Rehu Moana* before she had low aspect ratio keels fitted. In a force 9+ gale off Iceland he experienced similar sideways surfing conditions:

'*Rehu Moana* lay a-hull without sail with the seas on the quarter. Cooking presented no difficulties. When a large sea broke against her she would slide crabways before it, easily and without strain. Even when one caught her fair on the beam she would skid sideways without so much as a creak out of the hulls or centreboard cases. Lying a-hull and moving downwind at about 1½ knots the yacht presented an oblique section of about 30 ft. of herself to the gale.'

It is interesting to note that *Rehu Moana* used the same tactic of lying a-hull in a force 10–11 gale in the 1964 Singlehanded Trans-Atlantic Race and in both cases her boards were raised. Lewis did not use the tactic of lying to a sea anchor until **after** *Rehu Moana* had been fitted with low aspect keels.

I have taken these two somewhat dated examples of catamarans lying a-hull because they are well documented and in no way exaggerated. Although *Rehu Moana* was a far heavier yacht than *Golden Cockerel* she only drew three feet with her boards raised and still experienced the sideways surfing phenomenon.

When the phenomenon occurs, it is initially frightening because the windward hull is lifted before the leeward one. This means that the yacht may be pushed well over momentarily before she starts slipping sideways. Once the sea gets under the leeward hull the capsize moment is instantly reversed and the yacht slides horizontally sideways. This instant reversal can be so quick that in *Rehu Moana*'s case it once snapped the mast in two. Bill Howell put as much weight in the windward hull as possible to keep it down and this must obviously be seen as a sensible course of action.

It would therefore appear that the indications show that buoyant catamarans can lie safely a-hull provided that they do not have large flat surfaces underneath which could trip them up. However, I feel that a very small catamaran may stand more chance of being overwhelmed because stability increases more quickly than heeling moment as size increases.

Lying a-hull in a trimaran presents a somewhat more complex problem than a catamaran because the 'leeward hull' is in this case an outrigger which will have less buoyancy than the leeward hull of a catamaran. If one thinks of a trimaran heeled over to lee when lying a-hull, it does resemble a catamaran if, for a moment, one forgets the windward outrigger which will be up in the air. However, here the comparison ceases as the mast(s) are on the main hull (if we forget the weather outrigger, the main hull becomes, in effect, the windward hull) and their capsize moment should be less in a wide trimaran than in a narrow catamaran. She more closely resembles an 'Atlantic' proa which keeps its outrigger to leeward.

It would therefore seem that there is a compromise with the trimaran between the buoyancy of the leeward outrigger and the capsize moment of the mast and the rest of the boat when it is lifted by the surfing crest.

From my own experience of lying a-hull in *Three Cheers* I know that it is not, in any way, a pleasant experience. This description was written on return to England from the U.S.A. in 1972.

'We had sailed from Newport R.I. on August 12th 1972 bound for Plymouth, England after competing in the Singlehanded Trans-Atlantic Race. Murray Sayle was crewing for me after having lost his mast on the way over in *Lady of Fleet*.

'We were about 450 miles N.N.E. of Bermuda when the storm started on the 15th. Its first indication was a rapidly falling barometer and the backing of the wind from S.W. to S.E. By 0100 on the 15th the wind was blowing hard from the N.E. at about force 7 and at dawn a yellow-grey sky boded ill for the future. Throughout the day the wind increased and by 1500 it was blowing force 9 (we had no wind speed indicator so wind speeds are approximate guesses). The seas were frighteningly steep with breaking crests. Unfortunately, we were right in the middle of the Gulf Stream so a wind against current situation prevailed and the seas were exceptionally steep. We started lying a-hull

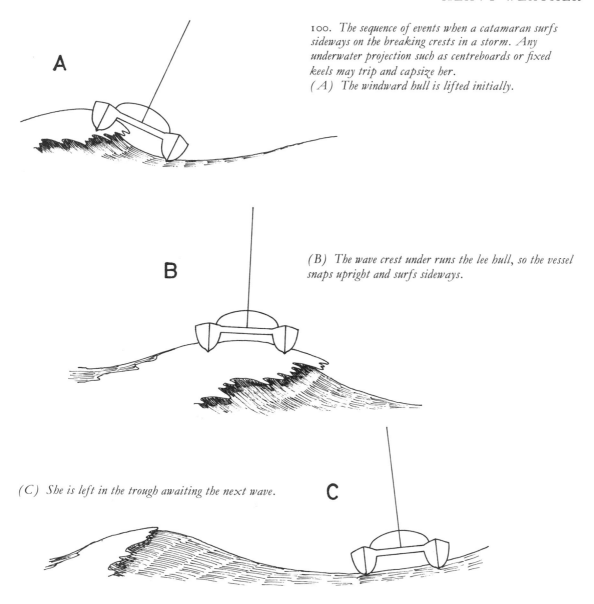

100. *The sequence of events when a catamaran surfs sideways on the breaking crests in a storm. Any underwater projection such as centreboards or fixed keels may trip and capsize her.*
(A) The windward hull is lifted initially.

(B) The wave crest under runs the lee hull, so the vessel snaps upright and surfs sideways.

(C) She is left in the trough awaiting the next wave.

with both boards up and were both frightened by the rapid way in which the yacht would suddenly heel up to 30°+ (we had no inclinometer) before levelling off. Neither of us had ever been in a trimaran in such weather and we were very worried by the danger of being rolled over.

'As the day wore on, the wind and sea increased and at 1800 I decided to try and run before it under bare poles. Accordingly, I steered the boat downwind and as soon as she was pointing in the right direction she took off at about 18 knots (instrumented) down the steep front of a wave. The wave was so steep that *Three Cheers* seemed to be running down it at an angle of 45° to the horizontal and I felt sure she must dig in at the bottom and pitch-pole. The whole stern of the boat was momentarily completely out of the water and for one awful moment, I had a feeling of total helplessness as she thundered down and forward in a welter of spray. I uselessly waggled a tiller controlling a rudder that bit only on air. At the bottom, or may be half way down, the rudder bit deep into the water again and control was regained. The buoyant and well flared bows lifted her up, and apart from some spray over the deck, there was no tendency to broach or pitch-pole. Nevertheless, both of us had been so frightened by the incident that we put her a-hull once more and lashed the helm to leeward.

'As night fell, we estimated the seas to be at least 30 ft. in height (they looked as high as the mast) and they were still extremely steep and breaking. Gradually, we became used to the quick lifting moment of the weather hull and slowly we realised that may be, after all the yacht was quite safe in this position. By dawn the worst was over.'

I discovered on return to England that we had been on the north edge of Hurricane Betty and although we had no wind speed indicator, I am certain that we had winds in excess of force 10 so it had been a good trial for the boat. Certainly, I have never been in a worse storm, before or since.

I was not conscious of surfing sideways for anything like the distance that Bill Howell describes in his 1968 storm. However, we were both conscious that the boat was, on occasions, bodily shifted sideways but for how far I would not like to say as we were down below and not looking out! I am sure that we had steeper waves than *Golden Cockerel* but possibly the breaking crests were not as large. The frightening aspect was the initial heel when the main hull was lifted by a crest as the yacht reached a steep (30°) angle of heel before the crest under-ran the leeward outrigger and lifted her back again.

One interesting fact to point out is that at no time did I feel that the wind could get underneath the windward outrigger and help cause a capsize. I was far more concerned about the sea state. Many others who have survived similar storms in trimarans have found the same and I believe that this is because the whole structure of the yacht is blanketed most of the time in a storm by the sea itself, with the mast and rigging presenting the windage. The only time the weather outrigger is really exposed is momentarily when the main hull is on the crest. The speed of the passing wave then lifts the leeward outrigger and cancels any capsize effect.

I am also fairly sure now that a reefed mizzen helps on a multihull that is lying hove-to in a storm. This is because it serves to point the bows into the sea more and this presents a greater overall length to the run of the seas.

Three Cheers is a very light (7,000 lbs.) buoyant multihull with buoyant outriggers and a reserve of buoyancy in the wings. What of a heavily laden trimaran with long thin outriggers?

Alain Colas told me after his singlehanded voyage around the world in *Manureva* in 1973 that lying a-hull would have meant death to him in some of the 'ultimate' storms in the Southern Ocean. This is extremely interesting as it does show how important outrigger design may be. *Manureva*'s outriggers are extremely narrow and there is no reserve of buoyancy in her crossbeams. As a result, it is far easier for her outriggers to dig in sideways and to act as a hinge for the yacht to flip over. Because of this, Colas is convinced that running before an 'Ultimate Storm' is the only salvation for a trimaran in these conditions.

I am sure that for *Manureva*, he is 100% right, particularly as the yacht was very heavily laden with extra radios, batteries, generators, spares, provisions and water. Allegre designed her as an ultra-light singlehanded Atlantic racer, and not for long voyages round the world. This extra weight would serve to decrease buoyancy and make lying a-hull more hazardous.

Without any doubt, Colas experienced some exceptionally bad weather in his voyage around the world, but so also did Nigel Tetley. Tetley found that *Victress*'s ultimate salvation lay in lying a-hull with no sail up, even in conditions when he judged wave height to be up to 80 ft. and winds to be of hurricane strength.

The reason for this difference in opinion between two men who thought about little else for months is reflected in the design differences of the two yachts. *Manureva*'s long

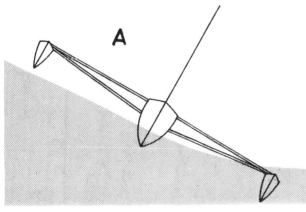

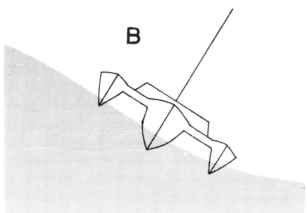

101. *Colas considered lying a-hull in* Manureva *(A) to be suicide, yet Tetley did it in* Victress *(B) —why?*
This scale diagram shows how Manureva's outriggers, which are designed to be almost totally submersible when sailing, will provide less buoyancy and will tend to dig in sideways when she is lying a-hull in a storm and is slammed to leeward by a huge breaking crest. Victress, *on the other hand, despite her narrower beam, would surf sideways more easily because the lee outrigger never submerged; had it done so, she might have capsized. Moreover the outboard side of her V-shaped hull and outriggers was angled out further from the vertical than* Manureva's, *giving less lateral resistance.*

thin outriggers must have a greater potential for digging in sideways than *Victress*'s buoyant V-shaped outriggers, which will tend to slide to leeward when the yacht is heeled. The former's large beam can in no way compensate for the narrow outriggers.

This, therefore, means that there must be many shades of grey in between the two types of design. Into this area fall most of today's modern trimarans.

So—can we specify the best course of action for a trimaran to take in survival storms? The answer on the whole is NO, for the unsatisfactory reason that it all depends on the configuration of the yacht. Generalisation may not only be nonsense, but may lead people into a dangerously fixed attitude of mind. So many variables are possible that the good seaman will only discover the right solution for his particular trimaran through experience, trial and error, and much thought.

However, we do have indications that the best trimaran configuration for lying a-hull may incorporate some of the following features:

(a) Buoyant outriggers that are not too narrow and prone to dig in sideways.
(b) A reserve of buoyancy in the connecting structure between outrigger and main hull.
(c) Shallow draft uncluttered by fixed keels.
(d) A mizzen.

(3) *Running Before*

Provided that the wind and sea are going in the right direction, running before a storm may well provide the best solution for a multihull. For some yachts caught in an ultimate storm it may be the only solution. The principal dangers from this are:

(a) Broaching.
(b) Running too fast, digging in at the bottom and pitch-poling.
(c) Running too slowly and being pooped.

Much can be done to avoid broaching by using the storm jib because as soon as the yacht starts to broach the pressure of wind on the sail will push the bow back again. If the jib is used in this manner it must be sheeted flat amidships using both port and starboard sheets. It will then not have too much forward drive which is desirable and will act as a vane to push the ship's head downwind if she tries to broach. If the jib is used for forward drive (in other words it is set full) it will have a tendency to push the bow down. This is highly undesirable. Bill Howell found this in *Golden Cockerel* during the 1968 storm previously described. He wrote:

'The only time when we were running very fast under the jib gave me the distinct impression that the sail was pushing the bow in. I have found this in lighter winds with the genoa and I am sure it applies to all fore and aft sails. On this occasion, we were running extremely fast and I found that the lee bow was tending to get within a foot of the water surface at the bottom of a surf. As soon as the jib was lowered this distance increased from one to two feet.'

One of the most important things to do if the decision has been made to run before is to shift some weight aft so as to assist the bows from digging in. This will also have the effect of preventing a broach as it will reduce draft up forward so there will be less water for the bows to bite on. Also, if the yacht has a wind vane gear, it is advisable to remove it completely, because the vane may act as a mizzen in that it will push the stern round and help a broach. It is also liable to get damaged and as it will be unable to cope with any self steering it is better removed.

In a very light racing multihull such as *Three Cheers* which has the rudder mounted right aft, as with most multihulls, there may be times in a really bad storm when it is lifted right out of the water and the yacht surfs at nearly 20 knots. This is, naturally, somewhat alarming but the loss of control is only momentary. A multihull with large full sterns will be at a greater disadvantage than one with slim 'canoe' type sterns. This is because the sterns will be lifted that much higher increasing the pitch-pole danger and the rudders may then come out of the water thereby increasing the danger from a broach.

Tom Follett, a seaman of colossal experience in both monohulls and multihulls felt it to be a worrying experience as well.

'I **prefer** a multihull (tri or proa, that is, as I have no catamaran experience to speak of) under any heavy weather conditions I can think of except the old "lee shore" thing. But—even then— I don't know. A trimaran might do just as well.

'I've never been caught in a "lee shore" position with any sort of yacht where it blew so hard I couldn't work to windward. Fortunately. But I did heave to twice with *Three Cheers* and found her quite comfortable. About force 8 to 9 both times. I reckon I could have worked to windward both times if I'd needed to but didn't try since it really wasn't necessary. Reefed mizzen and storm jib would have given me some headway I'm sure.

'Off the wind—let her go if there's sea room. Had some really exciting rides on the way over for the OSTAR 1972 blowing hard from the right direction a couple of times with really big seas running. No problems. Most of the time frightened to death and, consequently, not getting the best out of the boat but did about 180 miles per 24 hours at the worst which would have a single hull on her beam ends practically all the time assuming she could float that long.

'Force 10 or more? Off the wind under bare poles I think one would be quite happy. What's that you say? "Let's have a go"???—well, many thanks—just remembered an important appointment with my broker. Can't make it right now!'

It is arguable that some fast racing multihulls may need slowing down by trailing ropes, or ropes with small sea anchors attached such as a car tyre. This is because the aim of running before must be to keep **company** with the breaking crests, not to over-take them and crash into the back of the wave before it. If the boat goes too fast, the danger of pitch-poling must increase and if she goes too slowly, the danger of pooping may be present. Many fast multihulls have found that trailing warps is a successful way

102. *Alain Colas.*

of keeping control over the speed of their craft and furthermore, the ropes act as an extension of the hull and the broaching effect is therefore reduced. In a slow multihull, warps should not be necessary but they may be in a very fast one. Similarly, a fast multihull will need considerably more lift up forward than a slow one. Alain Colas found this is *Manureva* on his singlehanded voyage around the world in 1973.

'Down South, I came across a severe blow every so often, but they were generally blowing from the west and since I was going east I kept pressing along square-rigger style. That way I hardly ever shipped green water over the stern, as I was surging along in **company** with the big fellows. This technique could only be used since I had fitted anti-pitch-poling devices forward, on either side of the main bows and on the outer side of the bows of the floats. They worked like the tips of one's skis, lifting the boat out of that dreaded back of the wave you were catching up, once you had surfed down a powerful hillside. My feeling is that these special forward "bulges" (call them what you like best) **brought me back home**: There came a time when heaving to with or without drogue, would have been **suicidal**; hence one had to keep her going, and with the necessary speed not to be pooped and smashed, or to be taken broadside to by one of those quartering seas (from another direction than the general pattern) which would have certainly found a way of capsizing any size of yacht. The problem with our kind of yachts, is that once capsized they stay that way, which would not have been very pleasant half way between Cape Horn and South Georgia.

'To summarise the analysis, to my mind you should never go to such places where you can meet an "Ultimate" storm, unless you have given yourself a fair chance, that is to say a seaworthy boat able to face for quite a while with mizzen up and drogue out from the bows, remembering that **if things do become "Ultimate" running is the only answer provided your boat is fitted for it and there is sea room!**

'By the way, praying does not hurt either.'

178

Colas mentions an important point not previously brought out and that is the cross wave or quartering wave. All storms involve wind shifts and the wind shifts in their turn involve changes in sea direction. As a result, cross waves can be a very real hazard in a storm and the helmsman will have to be extremely vigilant in his steering to ensure that the yacht takes the seas on her stern and does not get laid over by them. Similarly, the 'freak' wave of unusual height, size or steepness must be continuously watched for. It may be that taking the seas slightly on the quarter will reduce the risk of pitch-poling as the ship will not be going down the sea at such a steep angle. However, doing this, may be more likely to cause a broach and if the boat feels 'right' it is usually better to run at right angles to the run of the seas.

103. *Storm seas. To lie a-hull?*

104. *Storm seas. To run before?*

Bill Howell, like Colas, believes that the ultimate safety of a multihull in storms of hurricane strength must lie in running before, despite his experience of surviving such a storm a-hull in *Golden Cockerel*. However, he emphasises the point that steering is critical and that a broach, caused by a fatigued helmsman could prove fatal.

Heavy Weather Indications

As we have seen, there are various options open to the multihull sailor in extremes of heavy weather and the action that he takes depends largely on his knowledge of his craft and its design.

The following list of miscellaneous **indications** is included for general guidance:

(a) Searoom is vital to multihulls that are caught in storms.

(b) All boards should be raised in survival conditions.

(c) Lying a-hull is safer for the buoyant yacht that has no flat underwater projections. Most catamarans can lie a-hull safely but not all trimarans—particularly those with extremely narrow outriggers. A mizzen helps to keep the bows of the yacht up into the wind which presents a longer section of boat to the run of the seas.

(d) Overloading will never assist a multihull in heavy weather. In some cases it may be dangerous, particularly in a light trimaran with narrow outriggers.

(e) Forward lift and buoyancy is vital when running before.

(f) The speed of the yacht when running should be such that she keeps company with the breaking crests. This speed can be adjusted by trailing warps if speed is too great, or raising the storm jib if the boat is too slow.

(g) A sea anchor can be used from the quarter or bow of a catamaran or the bow of a trimaran to reduce leeway in a storm but is probably not useable in an ultimate storm. Its chief use is in keeping a yacht off a lee shore. Remember it may be hard to recover!

(h) Careful use of weight can assist a multihull in heavy weather. If running, keep the weight in the stern, if lying a-hull, keep it to windward.

In the end, the ultimate survival of a multihull in heavy weather will depend entirely on the good seamanship of her crew. Preparations for heavy weather should be made in exactly the same way as they are on a monohull but particular attention should be paid to securing everything well below and above decks. The motion of a multihull in a gale can be very violent and such things as batteries, tool boxes etc. should be well lashed down. It is important to make sure that the life raft, flares and life jackets are easily accessible from both sides and that everyone always uses a safety harness (unfastenable at both ends) if they go on deck.

Weathering a gale in a yacht of any configuration is never a pleasant experience. In a good multihull, however, the crew should not have any reason to fear the storm any more than the crew of a good monohull **provided** that they understand their yacht and the different techniques involved.

Appendix I

A layman's guide to the International Offshore Multihull Rule (I.O.M.R.)

by Major-General Ralph Farrant, C.B. with extra details from Vic Stern

The rating given by using this rule is the result of an attempt to calculate the average speed any multihull should achieve round a course, in a 10 knot breeze. It is referred to as 'induced speed' in the rule. This wind strength has been chosen as a reasonable average strength for the duration of a race; a different wind strength could be used, without difficulty if experience in any country should suggest that a change were desirable.

At this wind strength the rating is one-eighth of the calculated boat speed and the time correction factor (TCF) is the same as the measured rating multiplied by the propeller correction factor which for a boat without an installed propeller or a retractable propeller is 1.000.

In order to calculate this potential induced speed, the rule uses measurements of the driving force determined from sail areas and measurements of the resistance (drag) of the craft, determined from waterline length, weight and hull length-to-beam ratio. Because of the complex resistance laws for craft having the wide range of speeds typical of multihulls, different coeficients, based on tank test date, are used for hulls of different speed potential. This up-to-date application of resistance laws makes the mathematics look somewhat complicated, but the measuring is straightforward and a small computer can easily deal with the calculations.

Measurements are required for the following:

Length over all (LOA) and waterline (WL) including outboard rudders which may extend both LOA and WL.

Length-to-beam ratio of hull(s) (L/B).

Weight (i.e. displacement) in sailing trim. See below.

Sail Area: For a sloop, the rated S.A. is the area of mainsail including roach reduced by an efficiency factor according to type, plus area of largest genoa modified by a factor which diminishes as the genoa area exceeds the foretriangle area, plus one quarter of any extra area in a drifter, plus one tenth of any further extra area in the spinnaker.

The L/B ratio is used to determine the wetted surface to sail area ratio which is needed for the final formulae. Different values are used for 'fat' hulls, i.e. ratios less than 8 : 1 to compensate for their extra resistance compared with 'thin', or fine hulls.

Other factors also examined are:

Displacement/length ratio for bow-wave drag.

Speed/length ratio for hull wave making (Froude number).

Speed/Length Product for skin-friction drag (Reynolds number).

Using coeficients from tank test data and the above measurements and ratios, a trial 'induced speed' is calculated. Using this speed the resultant Froude and Reynolds numbers are examined; if they fall above certain limits—1.34 and 200 respectively—the induced speed is recalculated using the coefficients appropriate to craft of that speed potential, thus giving as accurate an induced speed (VB) as possible.

Then measured rating (MR)=0.125 VB
and TCF=MR × propeller correction factor (1.0 for no propeller)
and corrected time=elapsed time × TCF.

As weight is such an important factor in a multihull's performance, the rule is quite specific about the items which may be on board when the craft is weighed. A specific amount of optional equipment, varying with measured weight, is allowed for in the rule; additional equipment on board, over this optional weight allowance, constitutes an owner's self imposed speed penalty. The attention to detail is further shown by the rules about the number of crew. In the rated weight, allowance is made for the weight of the crew at 200 pounds per man (this figure is intended to include the man's pro rata share of the weight of stores and liquids including stove fuel consumed during an average race) and the owner has to declare the standard number of his crew. The rating form gives the rating for this standard crew complement but it also gives rating for one more and one less, either of which conditions may be declared before starting.

It is interesting to note, as a guide to the practical outcome of racing under the I.O.M.R., that if the VB of a fast craft happened to come out as 8.00, then her TCF could be 1.000 and her corrected time would be the same as her elapsed time. The American ORcat *Patty Cat II* is an example of this situation. With a fully battened mainsail and retractable props her parameters are:

Measured weight	8,576 lbs.	
Length overall	44.01 ft.	
Waterline length	36.75 ft.	
Height of foretriangle	53.54 ft.	Her TCF is 1.0001.
Base of foretriangle	15.46 ft.	The addition or subtraction of
Mainsail area	472 sq. ft.	one crew member alter her rating
Mainsail efficiency factor	80%	by 0.6%. A change in sail area of
Genoa area	728 sq. ft.	1% results in a change in rating
Drifter area	(less than genoa)	of 0.4%.
Spinnaker area	1,802 sq. ft.	
Optional equipment	134 lbs.	
Standard crew	8	

Author's Note
General Farrant has deliberately not included the four induced speed equations, or the three others which have to be used after doing the trial calculations, in order to keep this appendix as simple as possible. Copies of the full rule are obtainable from most national yachting authorities. Although this rule is still in its infancy it offers the most sensible approach to multihull handicapping that has yet been devised. In the course of time it may well alter slightly.

Appendix II

The Boundary of Short Handed Sailing Performances

by G. Boxall, M.A. (Cantab)

Author's Description

This appendix has been compiled by Gerry Boxall and is included primarily as a comparison of multihull and monohull performance over the 1970 and 1974 Round Britain Races as well as the 1968 and 1972 Single-Handed Trans-Atlantic Races. However, it is far more than that; from it can be drawn numerous conclusions and indications, none of which will be pointed out because one of the aims of the appendix is to allow the reader the pleasure of working these out for himself.

The points shown on the graphs, both of multihulls and monohulls, have been joined up as a smooth curve and are intended to show the maximum performance over a range of boat lengths and courses so far achieved. All boats were plotted initially but for clarity the points shown on the graph give the locus of the upper limit of the boundary of the particular parameter chosen. As will be seen, high levels of efficiency and successful results do not always go together.

It is hoped that the reader will find interest from these graphs in comparing his own performance or that of other yachts, either multihulls or monohulls, against the plotted limits. In years to come, we shall undoubtedly see these limits pushed higher and higher but it is debatable whether size will necessarily always win short handed races.

Abbreviations and plotting symbols used.

RBR	Observer Round Britain Race
OSTAR	Observer Singlehanded Trans-Atlantic Race
LOA	Length Overall in feet
LWL	Waterline length in feet
V	Speed in knots
R	Rhumb line distance in nautical miles
VR	Average speed over rhumb line distance in knots
t	Time over rhumb line distance in hours and decimal hours
C	Catamaran
T	Trimaran
P	Proa
M	Monohull
⊙——⊙	Multihull
△- - -△	Monohull
⊙² or △¹⁴	Suffix number indicates 2nd or 14th in race or leg

Note: The trimaran *Manureva* was originally called *Pen Duick IV*; for simplicity she is referred to as *Manureva* throughout.

BOUNDARY OF SHORTHANDED SAILING PERFORMANCES.

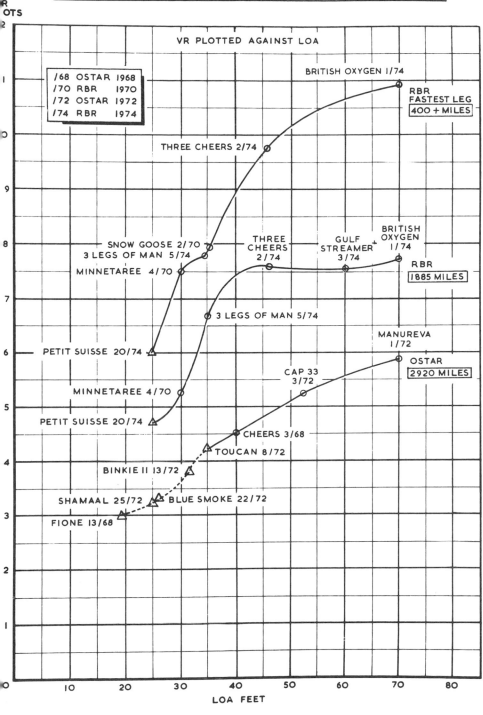

VR PLOTTED AGAINST LOA

/68	OSTAR 1968
/70	RBR 1970
/72	OSTAR 1972
/74	RBR 1974

BRITISH OXYGEN I/74

RBR
FASTEST LEG
400 + MILES

THREE CHEERS 2/74

SNOW GOOSE 2/70
3 LEGS OF MAN 5/74

THREE CHEERS 2/74

GULF STREAMER 3/74

BRITISH OXYGEN I/74

MINNETAREE 4/70

RBR
1885 MILES

3 LEGS OF MAN 5/74

MANUREVA I/72

PETIT SUISSE 20/74

CAP 33 3/72

MINNETAREE 4/70

OSTAR
2920 MILES

PETIT SUISSE 20/74

CHEERS 3/68

TOUCAN 8/72

BINKIE II 13/72

SHAMAAL 25/72   BLUE SMOKE 22/72

FIONE 13/68

LOA FEET

TABLE 1 **ROUND BRITAIN RACE 1974**

Place	Yacht	Type	LOA	LWL	√LWL	Total 1885 miles t	Total VR	Total VR/√LWL	Leg 1 (230 miles) t	Leg 1 VR	Leg 1 VR/√LWL	Leg 2 (460 miles) t	Leg 2 VR	Leg 2 VR/√LWL	Leg 3 (420 miles) t	Leg 3 VR	Leg 3 VR/√LWL	Leg 4 (470 miles) t	Leg 4 VR	Leg 4 VR/√LWL	Leg 5 (305 miles) t	Leg 5 VR	Leg 5 VR/√LWL
1	British Oxygen	C	70.00	60.00	7.75	244.43	7.71	0.995	35.53	6.47	0.835	47.18	9.75	1.258	61.33	6.85	0.884	43.13	10.90	1.407	57.25	5.33	0.688
2	Three Cheers	T	46.00	43.00	6.56	245.62	7.67	1.169	36.72	6.26	0.954	47.18	9.75	1.486	59.03	7.12	1.085	53.97	8.71	1.328	48.72	6.26	0.954
3	Gulf Streamer	T	60.00	56.00	7.48	247.80	7.61	1.017	38.18	6.02	0.805	51.28	8.97	1.199	54.20	7.75	1.036	54.82	8.57	1.145	49.32	6.18	0.826
4	Manureva	T	70.00	67.00	8.19	267.25	7.05	0.861	45.17	5.09	0.621	52.73	8.72	1.065	58.50	7.18	0.877	53.05	8.86	1.082	57.80	5.28	0.645
5	Three Legs of Man	T	35.00	33.75	5.82	276.22	6.82	1.172	41.57	5.53	0.950	58.37	7.88	1.354	61.65	6.81	1.170	66.55	7.06	1.213	48.07	6.35	1.091
6	Burton Cutter	M	80.00	69.00	8.31	282.48	6.67	0.803	45.25	5.08	0.611	61.78	7.45	0.897	58.66	7.16	0.862	62.48	7.52	0.905	54.30	5.62	0.676
7	Quailo III	T	55.00	39.25	6.26	289.62	6.51	1.040	44.98	5.11	0.816	64.47	7.14	1.141	64.88	6.47	1.034	61.33	7.66	1.224	53.95	5.65	0.903
8	Triple Arrow	T	49.00	45.00	6.71	313.50	6.01	0.896	37.15	6.19	0.923	48.27	9.53	1.421	109.67	3.83	0.571	65.17	7.21	1.075	53.25	5.73	0.854
9	F.T.	T	35.00	28.00	5.29	342.23	5.51	1.042	43.75	5.26	0.994	65.70	7.00	1.323	83.05	5.06	0.957	82.05	5.73	1.083	67.68	4.51	0.853
10	Superstar	T	35.00	32.00	5.66	368.67	5.11	0.903	52.65	4.37	0.772	75.60	6.09	1.076	82.03	5.12	0.905	75.92	6.19	1.094	83.47	3.65	0.645
11	Tyfoon V	M	34.50	24.00	4.90	376.85	5.00	1.020	52.10	4.42	0.902	86.25	5.33	1.088	82.33	5.10	1.041	79.02	5.95	1.214	77.15	3.95	0.806
12	Josephine M	M	35.00	26.50	5.15	381.50	4.94	0.959	52.87	4.35	0.845	88.45	5.20	1.010	80.72	5.20	1.010	77.33	6.08	1.181	84.13	3.63	0.705
13	Chough of Parkstone	M	30.00	21.00	4.58	382.45	4.93	1.076	53.60	4.29	0.937	88.08	5.22	1.140	79.60	5.28	1.153	81.80	5.75	1.256	79.37	3.84	0.838
14	Frigate	M	38.75	30.25	5.50	383.87	4.91	0.893	45.63	5.04	0.916	72.53	6.34	1.153	115.88	3.62	0.658	72.42	6.49	1.180	77.40	3.94	0.716
15	Snow Goose of Wight	C	36.80	33.50	5.79	385.23	4.89	0.845	51.70	4.45	0.769	94.85	4.85	0.838	75.48	5.56	0.960	75.03	6.26	1.081	88.17	3.46	0.598
16	Morning Song	M	33.50	24.14	4.91	388.18	4.86	0.990	51.97	4.43	0.902	85.97	5.35	1.090	83.07	5.06	1.031	89.22	5.27	1.073	77.97	3.91	0.796
17	Outlaw	M	48.50	38.75	6.22	390.25	4.83	0.777	54.03	4.26	0.685	99.03	4.65	0.748	79.43	5.29	0.851	82.42	5.70	0.916	75.33	4.05	0.651
18	Albin Ballad	M	30.00	22.60	4.75	391.03	4.82	1.015	55.50	4.14	0.872	99.12	4.64	0.977	78.66	5.34	1.124	78.02	6.02	1.267	79.73	3.83	0.806
19	Loiwing	M	34.50	25.60	5.06	402.20	4.69	0.927	52.35	4.39	0.868	102.13	4.50	0.889	79.97	5.25	1.038	89.40	5.26	1.040	78.35	3.89	0.769
20	Petite Suisse	M	24.75	20.00	4.47	403.47	4.67	1.045	59.78	3.85	0.861	99.22	4.64	1.038	81.68	5.14	1.150	79.12	5.94	1.329	83.66	3.65	0.817
21	Eroica II	M	31.14	24.14	4.91	407.68	4.62	0.941	59.10	3.89	0.792	102.15	4.50	0.916	79.23	5.30	1.080	76.02	6.18	1.260	91.18	3.35	0.682
22	Cherry Blossom	M	32.00	24.00	4.90	408.22	4.62	0.943	59.67	3.85	0.786	108.28	4.25	0.867	74.13	5.67	1.157	77.47	6.07	1.239	88.67	3.44	0.702
23	Zeevalk	M	39.50	35.50	5.96	419.63	4.49	0.753	55.83	4.12	0.691	101.75	4.52	0.758	84.83	4.95	0.830	93.92	5.00	0.839	132.13	2.31	0.388
24	Shamaal II	M	25.50	20.00	4.47	428.50	4.40	0.984	58.03	3.96	0.886	108.55	4.24	0.949	79.72	5.27	1.179	90.00	5.22	1.168	91.20	3.34	0.747
25	Minnetaree	C	30.00	27.00	5.20	431.65	4.37	0.840	46.97	4.90	0.942	78.53	5.86	1.127	125.65	3.34	0.642	75.23	6.25	1.202	105.32	2.90	0.558
26	Shesh	M	29.25	23.34	4.83	436.65	4.32	0.894	57.07	4.03	0.834	104.70	4.39	0.909	82.27	5.11	1.058	93.82	5.01	1.037	94.80	3.22	0.667
27	Ron Glas	M	47.00	36.00	6.00	470.50	4.01	0.668	63.38	3.63	0.605	119.78	3.84	0.640	82.93	5.07	0.845	93.43	5.03	0.838	110.97	2.75	0.458
28	Mex	M	35.00	27.25	5.22	471.10	4.00	0.766	56.08	4.10	0.785	112.37	4.52	0.784	84.63	4.96	0.950	103.55	4.54	0.870	114.47	2.67	0.511
29	Helen II	M	26.00	20.00	4.47	472.08	3.99	0.893	61.23	3.76	0.841	132.77	3.47	0.776	85.33	4.92	1.101	94.97	4.95	1.107	97.78	3.12	0.698
30	Croda Way	T	34.75	32.50	5.70	503.58	3.74	0.656	43.73	5.26	0.923	76.55	6.01	1.054	269.80	1.56	0.274	67.90	6.92	1.214	45.77	6.66	1.168
31	Galway Blazer	M	42.00	32.00	5.66	505.72	3.73	0.659	67.22	3.42	0.604	146.53	3.14	0.555	99.75	4.21	0.743	123.47	3.81	0.673	68.75	4.44	0.784
32	Gancia Girl	T	42.00	41.00	6.40	507.63	3.71	0.580	60.25	3.82	0.597	164.00	2.81	0.439	101.57	4.14	0.647	100.02	4.70	0.734	81.97	3.72	0.581
33	Catch 34	M	34.00	30.00	5.48	511.47	3.69	0.673	54.23	4.24	0.773	124.75	3.69	0.673	118.95	3.53	0.644	109.72	4.28	0.781	103.82	2.94	0.536
34	Boule d'Ecume	M	26.00	19.50	4.42	517.55	3.64	0.824	65.92	3.49	0.790	149.28	3.08	0.697	94.77	4.43	1.002	123.92	3.79	0.858	83.67	3.65	0.826
35	Airedale	M	29.50	24.00	4.96	545.33	3.46	0.698	64.25	3.58	0.722	171.72	2.68	0.540	94.53	4.44	0.895	119.58	3.93	0.792	119.25	2.56	0.516

No.	Name																			
36	Pulau Tiga	T	44.00	33.00	5.74	547.42	3.44	0.599	51.97	4.43	169.12	2.72	0.772	120.07	3.50	0.610	93.40	5.03	0.876	112.87	2.70	0.470
37	Heavenly Twins	C	26.14	21.50	4.65	554.77	3.40	0.731	75.95	3.02	160.02	2.88	0.652	97.07	4.33	0.619	130.05	3.61	0.776	91.68	3.33	0.716
38	Sherpa	M	26.00	25.00	5.00	566.33	3.33	0.666	68.80	3.34	156.78	2.93	0.668	119.62	3.51	0.586	132.10	3.56	0.712	89.03	3.43	0.686
39	Eclipse of Mylor	M	28.00	24.00	4.90	718.50	2.62	0.555	104.85	1.52	170.07	2.71	0.310	152.83	2.75	0.561	132.62	3.54	0.722	158.13	1.93	0.394
40	Windsor Life	M	24.00	17.50	4.18	733.50	2.57	0.615	99.32	2.32	178.18	2.58	0.555	166.33	2.53	0.605	126.42	3.72	0.890	163.25	1.87	0.447

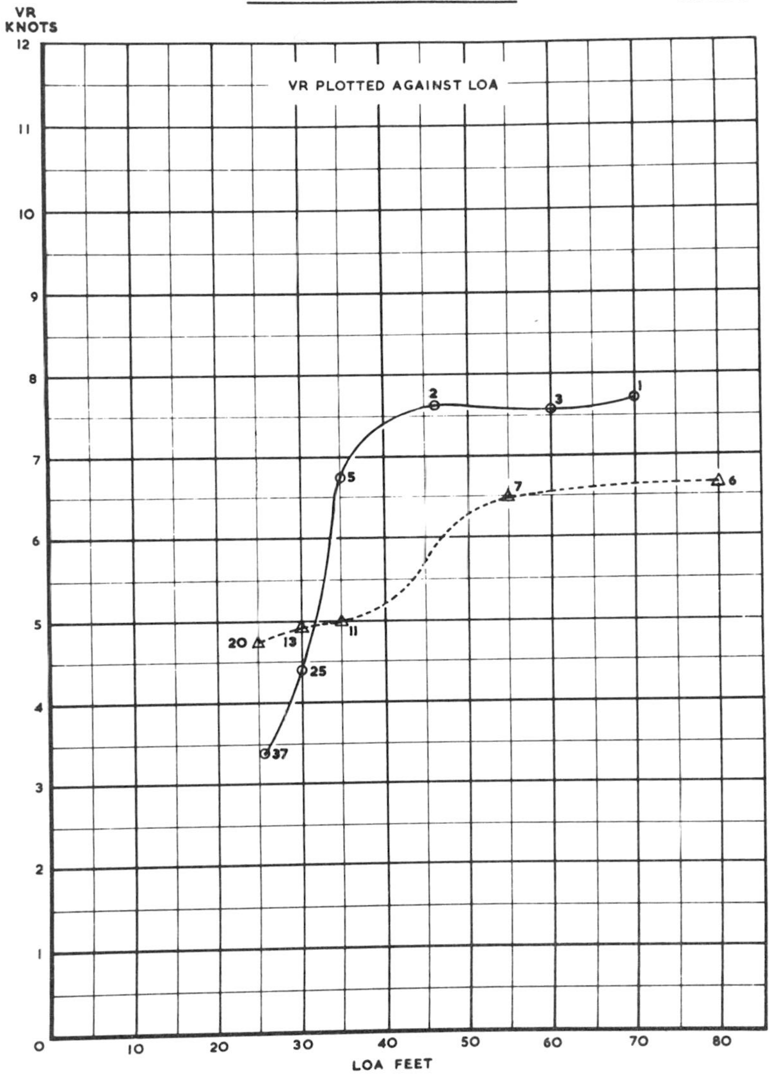

RBR 74 FASTEST LEG (200 + MILES)   GRAPH 2

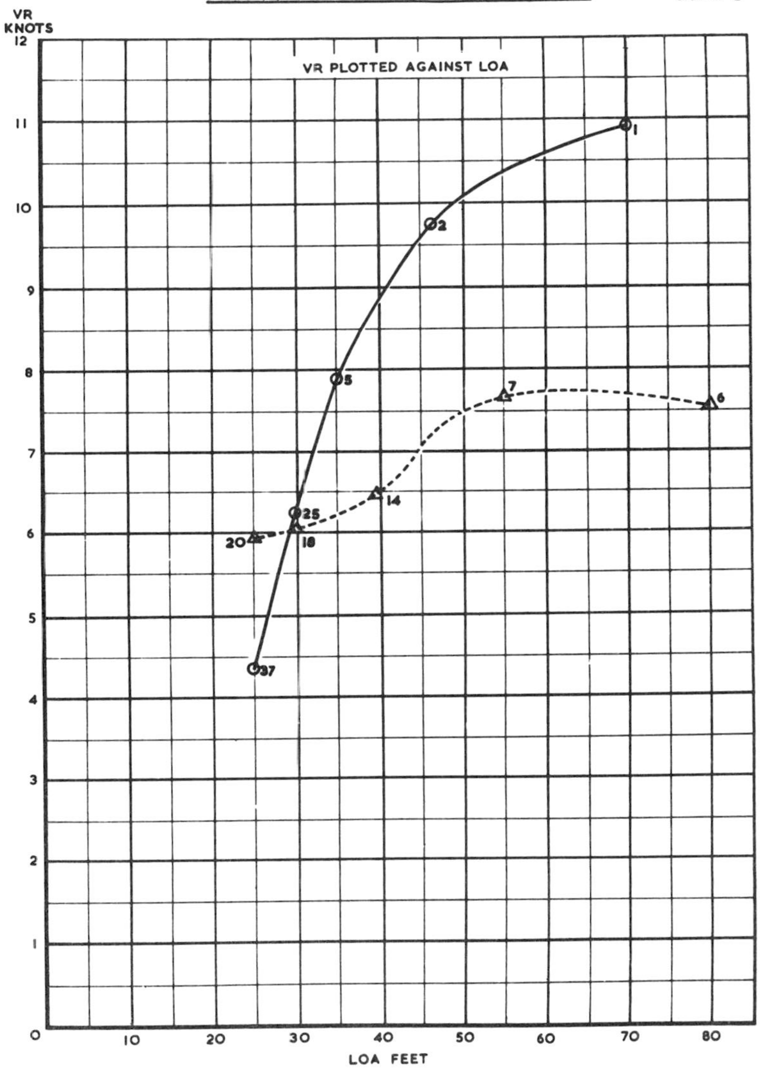

VR PLOTTED AGAINST LOA

VR KNOTS (vertical axis) — LOA FEET (horizontal axis)

RBR 74 OVERALL RACE   GRAPH 1

VR PLOTTED AGAINST LOA

VR KNOTS (vertical axis) — LOA FEET (horizontal axis)

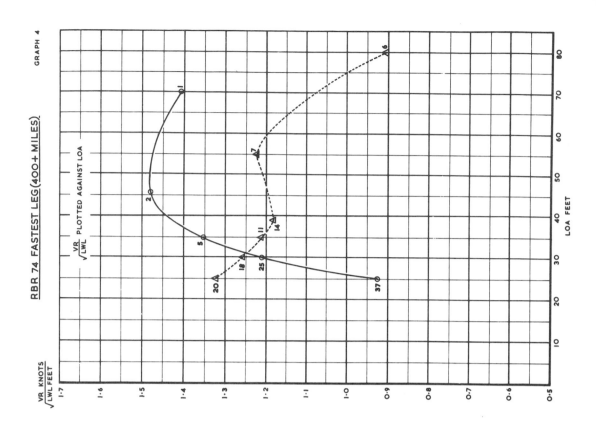

RBR 74 FASTEST LEG(400+MILES).

GRAPH 4

$\dfrac{V_R \text{ KNOTS}}{\sqrt{\text{LWL FEET}}}$

$\dfrac{V_R}{\sqrt{\text{LWL}}}$ PLOTTED AGAINST LOA

LOA FEET

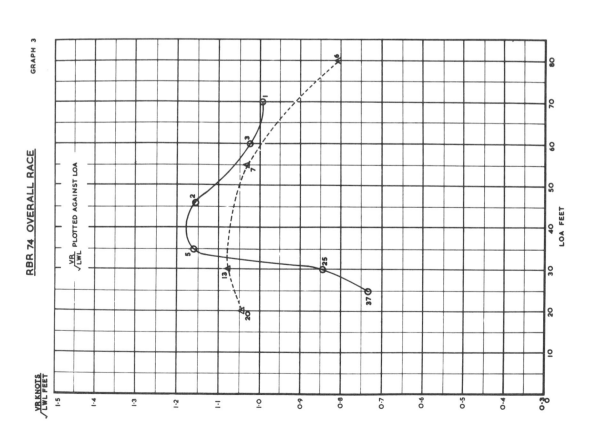

RBR 74 OVERALL RACE

GRAPH 3

$\dfrac{V_R \text{ KNOTS}}{\sqrt{\text{LWL FEET}}}$

$\dfrac{V_R}{\sqrt{\text{LWL}}}$ PLOTTED AGAINST LOA

LOA FEET

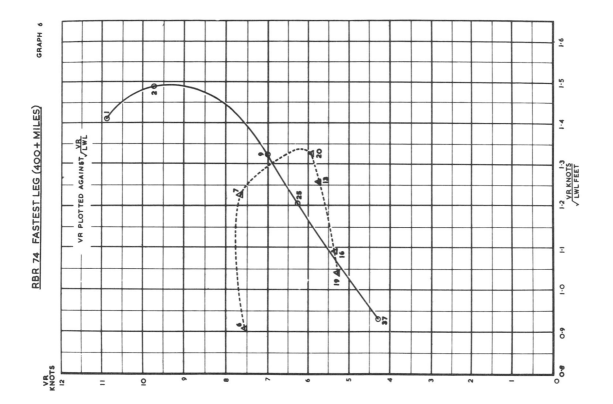

GRAPH 6

RBR 74 FASTEST LEG (400+ MILES)

$\dfrac{VR}{\sqrt{LWL}}$

VR PLOTTED AGAINST $\dfrac{VR}{\sqrt{LWL}}$

$\dfrac{VR\ KNOTS}{\sqrt{LWL\ FEET}}$

VR
KNOTS

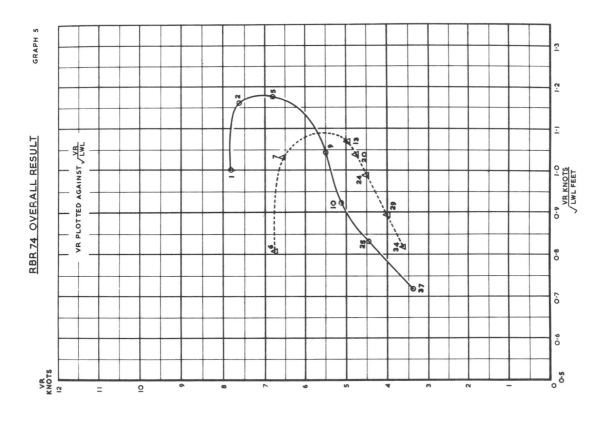

GRAPH 5

RBR 74 OVERALL RESULT

$\dfrac{VR}{\sqrt{LWL}}$

VR PLOTTED AGAINST $\dfrac{VR}{\sqrt{LWL}}$

$\dfrac{VR\ KNOTS}{\sqrt{LWL\ FEET}}$

VR
KNOTS

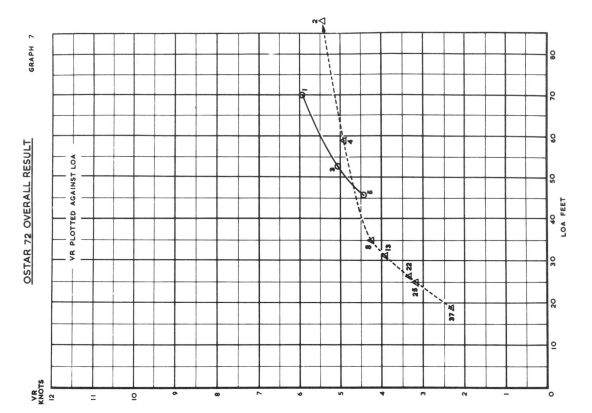

OSTAR 72 OVERALL RESULT

--- VR PLOTTED AGAINST LOA

GRAPH 7

VR KNOTS (vertical axis): 12, 11, 10, 9, 8, 7, 6, 5, 4, 3, 2, 1, 0

LOA FEET (horizontal axis): 10, 20, 30, 40, 50, 60, 70, 80

TABLE 2　OSTAR 1972

Total (2920 miles)

Place	Yacht	Type	LOA	LWL	√LWL	t	VR	VR/√LWL
1	Pen Duick IV	T	70.00	66.00	8.12	493.25	5.92	0.729
2	Vendredi Treize	M	128.00	116.40	10.79	519.23	5.62	0.521
3	Cap 33	T	52.90	46.00	6.78	581.66	5.02	0.740
4	British Steel	M	59.00	45.00	6.71	595.47	4.90	0.730
5	Three Cheers	T	46.00	43.00	6.56	659.07	4.43	0.675
6	Architeuthis	T	55.00	49.00	7.00	683.92	4.49	0.641
7	Strongbow	M	65.00	57.00	7.55	684.77	4.26	0.564
8	Toucan	M	34.50	31.20	5.59	684.90	4.26	0.762
9	Sagittario	M	50.70	45.80	6.77	695.08	4.20	0.620
10	Whisper	M	53.50	39.00	6.25	707.25	4.13	0.661
11	Isles de Frioul	M	47.90	35.40	5.95	722.75	4.04	0.679
12	Polonez	M	45.20	37.00	6.08	736.92	3.96	0.651
13	Binkie II	M	32.00	24.00	4.90	762.17	3.83	0.782
14	Alea VII	M	34.80	24.30	4.93	790.85	3.69	0.748
15	Flying Angel	M	46.00	32.00	5.66	801.35	3.64	0.643
16	Wild Rocket	M	63.00	50.80	7.13	829.63	3.52	0.494
17	Aloa I	M	34.80	24.30	4.93	833.50	3.50	0.710
18	Cambronne	M	45.50	37.00	6.08	850.40	3.43	0.564
19	Concorde	M	44.30	31.20	5.59	865.32	3.37	0.603
20	Gazelle	M	47.50	34.00	5.83	866.12	3.37	0.578
21	La Bamba of Mersea	M	37.70	24.00	4.90	868.50	3.36	0.686
22	Blue Smoke	M	26.00	21.00	4.58	885.43	3.30	0.721
23	White Dolphin	M	32.30	24.10	4.91	919.28	3.18	0.648
24	Ron Glas	M	47.00	36.00	6.00	921.83	3.17	0.528
25	Shamaal	M	25.80	20.00	4.47	922.50	3.17	0.709
26	Blue Gipsy	M	28.00	21.30	4.62	944.50	3.09	0.691
27	Trumpeter	T	44.00	40.00	6.33	949.42	3.08	0.487
28	Mex	M	35.00	27.20	5.22	968.38	3.02	0.579
29	Surprise	M	38.20	26.00	5.10	988.75	2.95	0.578
30	Mary Kate of Arun	M	38.00	27.00	5.20	1001.28	2.92	0.562
31	Francette	M	25.40	19.60	4.43	1041.63	2.80	0.632
32	Miranda	M	38.80	32.00	5.66	1090.08	2.68	0.473
33	Tinie	M	29.20	21.00	4.58	1119.50	2.61	0.570
34	Scuffler III	M	32.40	26.80	5.18	1178.00	2.48	0.479
35	Laurie	M	34.00	24.00	4.90	1238.55	2.36	0.482

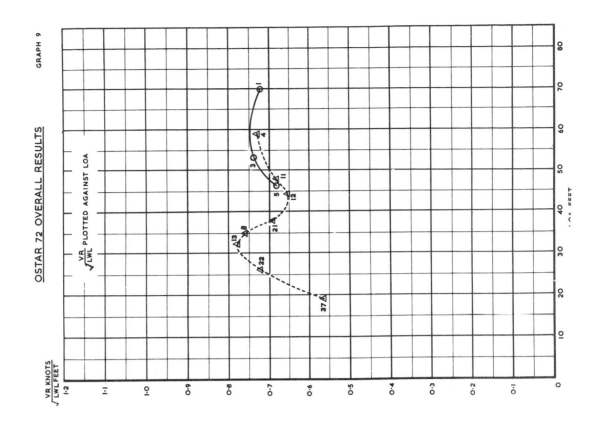

OSTAR 72 OVERALL RESULTS   GRAPH 9

VR PLOTTED AGAINST LOA

$\frac{VR}{\sqrt{LWL}}$

LOA FEET

VR KNOTS / √LWL FEET

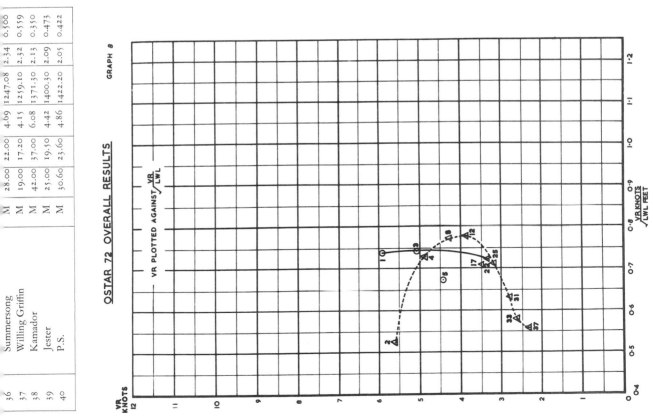

OSTAR 72 OVERALL RESULTS   GRAPH 8

VR PLOTTED AGAINST $\frac{VR}{\sqrt{LWL}}$

VR KNOTS / √LWL FEET

VR KNOTS

36	Summersong	M	28.00	22.00	4.69	1247.08	2.34	0.500
37	Willing Griffin	M	19.00	17.20	4.15	1259.10	2.32	0.559
38	Kamador	M	42.00	37.00	6.08	1371.30	2.13	0.350
39	Jester	M	25.00	19.50	4.42	1400.30	2.09	0.473
40	P.S.	M	30.60	23.60	4.86	1422.20	2.05	0.422

TABLE 3   ROUND BRITAIN RACE 1970

						Total 1885 miles			Leg 1 (230 miles)			Leg 2 (460 miles)			Leg 3 (420 miles)			Leg 4 (470 miles)			Leg 5 (305 miles)		
Place	Yacht	Type	LOA	LWL	√LWL	t	VR	VR/√LWL	t	VR	VR/√LWL	t	VR	VR/√LWL	t	VR	VR/√LWL	t	VR	VR/√LWL	t	VR	VR/√LWL
1	Ocean Spirit	M	71.00	55.70	7.46	308.17	6.12	0.820	43.32	5.31	0.712	68.33	6.73	0.902	57.58	7.29	0.977	70.07	6.71	0.900	57.83	5.27	0.706
2	Snow Goose	C	36.00	33.50	5.79	344.72	5.47	0.945	44.47	5.17	0.893	73.97	6.22	1.074	76.10	5.52	0.953	58.85	7.99	1.380	88.37	3.45	0.596
3	Trumpeter	T	44.00	40.00	6.33	358.48	5.26	0.831	43.07	5.34	0.843	75.28	6.11	0.965	71.88	5.84	0.923	70.95	6.63	1.047	92.02	3.31	0.523
4	Minnetaree	C	30.00	27.00	5.20	361.97	5.21	1.002	48.45	4.75	0.913	70.02	6.57	1.264	82.83	5.07	0.975	62.73	7.49	1.440	97.93	3.11	0.598
5	Golden Cockerel	C	43.00	33.00	5.75	396.87	4.75	0.826	74.98	3.07	0.534	78.27	5.88	1.023	68.33	6.15	1.070	74.33	6.32	1.099	70.95	4.30	0.748
6	Leen Valley Venturer	T	42.00	39.00	6.24	398.90	4.73	0.758	44.30	5.19	0.832	95.83	4.80	0.769	93.67	4.48	0.938	73.75	6.37	1.021	91.32	3.34	0.535
7	Electron	M	36.30	26.50	5.15	416.57	4.53	0.880	75.17	3.06	0.594	84.50	5.44	1.056	87.03	4.83	0.938	87.60	5.37	1.043	82.27	3.71	0.720
8	Gancia Girl	T	42.00	39.00	6.24	421.10	4.48	0.718	75.70	3.04	0.487	79.90	5.78	0.926	95.58	4.39	0.704	78.07	6.02	0.965	92.02	3.31	0.530
9	Myth of Malham	M	39.70	33.50	5.79	422.83	4.46	0.770	52.72	4.36	0.753	91.28	5.04	0.870	99.20	4.23	0.731	90.85	5.17	0.893	85.62	3.56	0.615
10	Three Fingered Jack	T	26.50	24.20	4.92	425.45	4.43	0.900	75.65	3.04	0.618	85.90	5.36	1.089	88.07	4.77	0.970	86.92	5.41	1.100	88.92	3.43	0.697
11	Rinaldo	M	35.00	26.50	5.15	430.27	4.38	0.850	75.38	3.05	0.592	84.33	5.45	1.058	88.45	4.75	0.922	92.78	5.07	0.984	90.32	3.38	0.656
12	Ishkoodah	M	28.50	22.00	4.69	436.08	4.32	0.921	72.08	3.19	0.680	80.98	5.68	1.211	93.90	4.47	0.953	94.65	4.97	1.060	94.43	3.23	0.689
13	Cymro	M	43.30	32.00	5.66	448.95	4.20	0.742	77.00	2.99	0.528	93.97	4.90	0.866	85.07	4.94	0.873	95.48	4.92	0.869	97.45	3.13	0.553
14	Speedwell	M	49.00	35.00	5.92	458.80	4.11	0.694	77.63	2.96	0.500	94.13	4.89	0.826	79.27	5.30	0.895	84.88	5.54	0.936	122.88	2.48	0.419
15	Binkie	M	25.60	21.00	4.58	471.13	4.00	0.873	77.60	2.96	0.646	98.42	4.67	1.020	81.08	5.18	1.131	103.77	4.53	0.989	110.27	2.77	0.605
16	Blue Smoke	M	26.00	21.00	4.58	485.45	3.88	0.847	77.83	2.96	0.646	95.40	4.82	1.052	86.17	4.87	1.063	104.20	4.51	0.985	121.85	2.50	0.546
17	Hurrying Angel	M	27.20	23.50	4.85	509.28	3.70	0.763	81.35	2.83	0.584	93.92	4.90	1.010	86.35	4.86	1.002	113.63	4.14	0.854	134.03	2.28	0.470
18	Kerry Blue	M	27.00	21.00	4.58	511.10	3.69	0.806	76.65	3.00	0.655	106.90	4.30	0.939	94.95	4.42	0.965	109.17	4.31	0.941	124.43	2.45	0.535
19	Slithy Tove	M	48.00	40.00	6.33	522.58	3.61	0.590	44.85	5.13	0.810	71.22	6.46	1.021	150.45	2.79	0.441	85.73	5.48	0.866	170.33	1.79	0.283
20	Renew	T	30.00	27.70	5.26	546.67	3.45	0.656	81.42	2.83	0.538	101.33	4.54	0.863	98.05	4.28	0.814	145.03	3.24	0.616	120.83	2.52	0.479
21	Apache Sundancer	C	40.00	35.00	5.92	capsized in Leg 5			46.40	4.96	0.838	70.35	6.54	1.105	67.20	6.25	1.056	75.42	6.23	1.052	capsized		

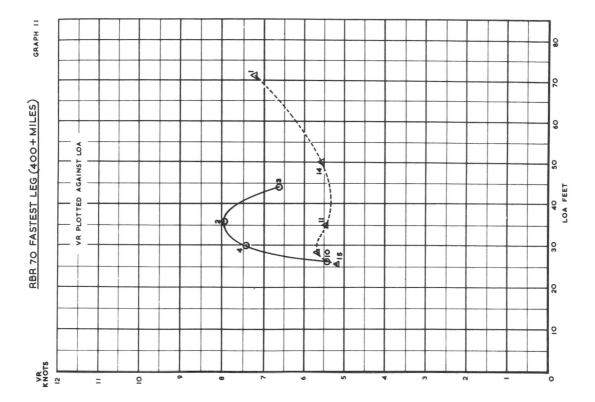

GRAPH 11

RBR 70 FASTEST LEG (400+ MILES)

VR PLOTTED AGAINST LOA

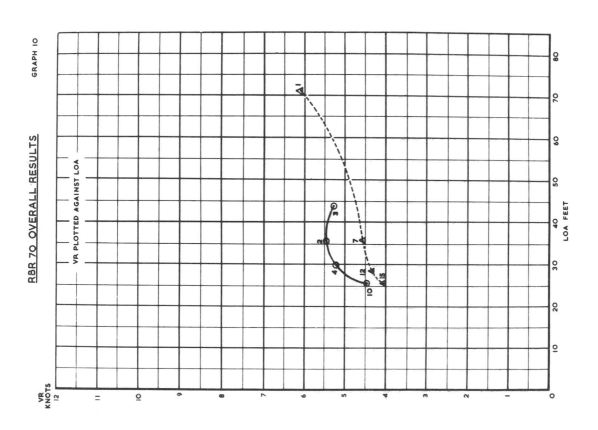

GRAPH 10

RBR 70 OVERALL RESULTS

VR PLOTTED AGAINST LOA

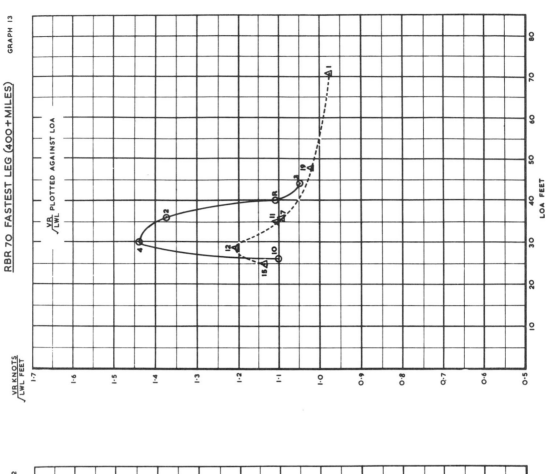

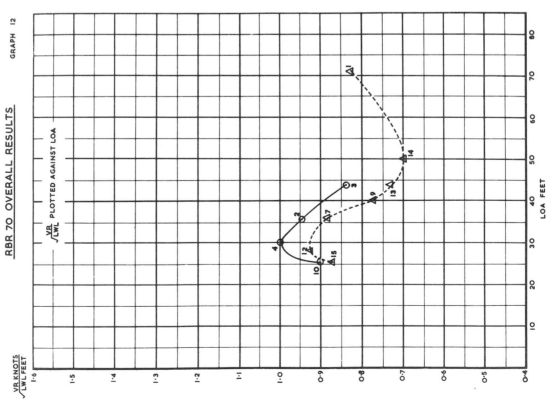

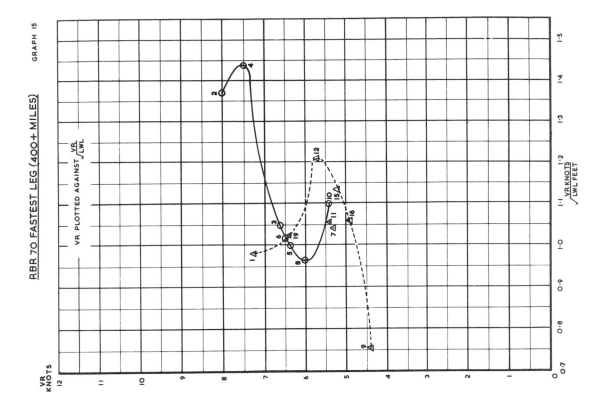

RBR 70 FASTEST LEG (400+ MILES)

GRAPH 15

VR PLOTTED AGAINST $\frac{VR}{\sqrt{LWL}}$

$\frac{VR\,KNOTS}{\sqrt{LWL\,FEET}}$

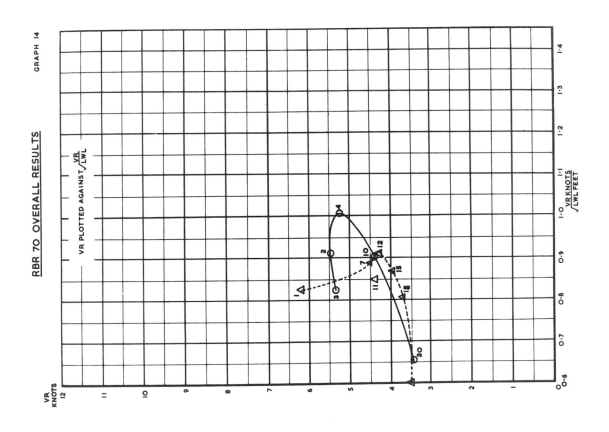

RBR 70 OVERALL RESULTS

GRAPH 14

VR PLOTTED AGAINST $\frac{VR}{\sqrt{LWL}}$

$\frac{VR\,KNOTS}{\sqrt{LWL\,FEET}}$

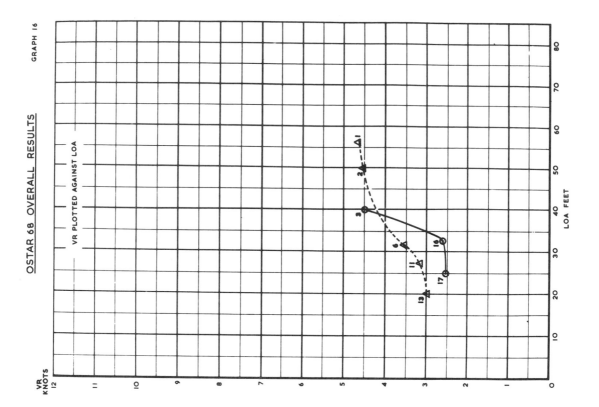

OSTAR 68 OVERALL RESULTS

GRAPH 16

VR PLOTTED AGAINST LOA

TABLE 4   OSTAR 1968

Total (2920 miles)

Place	Yacht	Type	LOA	L.W.L.	√L.W.L.	t	VR	VR / √L.W.L.
1	Sir Thomas Lipton	M	56.20	42.00	6.48	620.55	4.71	0.727
2	Voortrekker	M	50.00	39.60	6.29	637.70	4.58	0.728
3	Cheers	P	40.00	36.00	6.00	648.22	4.51	0.752
4	Spirit of Cutty Sark	M	53.20	38.80	6.23	706.28	4.13	0.663
5	Golden Cockerel	C	43.00	36.00	6.00	760.40	3.84	0.640
6	Opus	M	32.00	24.00	4.90	824.38	3.54	0.723
7	Gancia Girl	T	42.00	39.00	6.25	829.25	3.52	0.563
8	Myth of Malham	M	39.70	33.50	5.79	865.68	3.37	0.582
9	Maxine	M	34.80	26.00	5.10	901.78	3.24	0.635
10	Maguelonne	M	35.00	25.00	5.00	921.17	3.17	0.634
11	Dogwatch	M	27.80	24.00	4.90	924.22	3.16	0.645
12	Silvia II	M	36.00	25.50	5.05	960.27	3.04	0.602
13	Fiona	M	19.70	16.40	4.05	974.22	3.00	0.741
14	Mex	M	37.00	27.30	5.23	994.77	2.94	0.562
15	Rob Roy	M	32.40	27.00	5.20	1011.82	2.89	0.556
16	Startled Fawn	T	33.00	31.00	5.57	1090.13	2.68	0.481
17	Amistad	T	25.00	23.50	4.85	1146.08	2.55	0.526
18	Jester	M	25.90	19.90	4.46	1378.67	2.18	0.489

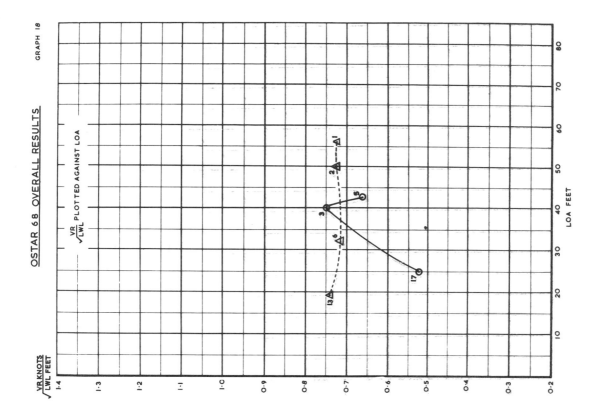

OSTAR 68 OVERALL RESULTS

GRAPH 18

$\frac{VR}{\sqrt{LWL}}$ PLOTTED AGAINST LOA

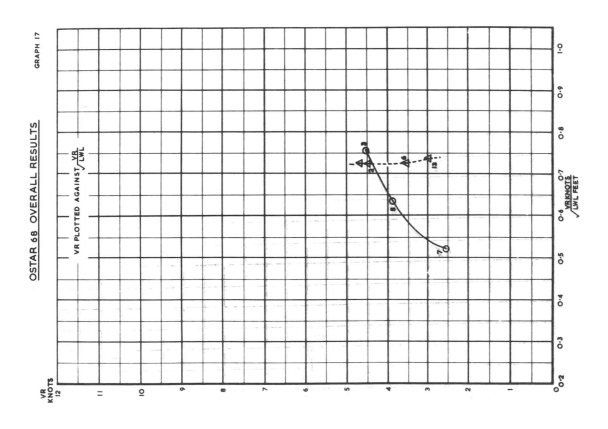

OSTAR 68 OVERALL RESULTS

GRAPH 17

VR PLOTTED AGAINST $\frac{VR}{\sqrt{LWL}}$

Index

acceleration, 78
accommodation, 50, 54, 55
a-hull, lying, 159, 162, 166, 169-76, 181
alertness, 79, 84, 85, 144, 152
Allegre, André, 42
Amaryllis, 27, 29
Amateur Yacht Research Society, (AYRS), 40, 124, 150, 151
American Multihull Sailing Association, 40
America's Cup, 86
Ananda, 36, 46
anchoring, 109-14
anchors, weighing, 80
anticipation, 84, 85
Apache Sundancer, 146-48
apparent wind, 78
Archer, Colin, 168
Architeuthis, 54, 55
armpits, 76
asphyxiation, dangers of, 150
asymmetrical hulls, 57-9
Atlantic Adventurers, 36
auto pilot, use and dangers of, 126

balance, 83, 120-2
ballast, 104, 105, 162, 165
Barton, Humphrey, 36
battens, 93-5
Baumann, Edith, 44
beachability, 50, 51, 115, 116
beam, 51, 54, 56, 57, 162, 165
Binkie II, 117
booms, 70
Boxall, Gerald, 53, 184
breaking up, 159, 160
Brisbane to Gladstone Race, 45
British Oxygen, 53, 62, 67-9, 81, 86, 100-3, 141, 153

British Petroleum, 41
broach, 84, 162, 163, 171, 176, 179
Brown, Woodridge, 33-36, 47, 57
buoyancy, 59-62, 74, 176, 181
Burton Cutter, 81
Butterfield, Mike, 146-8

Calais Douvres, 27
capsize, 51, 54, 83-6, 97, 98, 108, 123, 126-52, 162, 163
capsize conclusions, 152
capsize hatches, 140, 142, 143
capsize, righting and recovery, 148-52
catamarans, A, B and C classes, 38, 41, 45
centreboards, 65, 66, 75, 82, 83, 130, 137, 147, 152, 163, 181
centreboard casings, 75
centrifugal force, 145-6
Charles II, 24
Cheers, 40, 52
Chichester, Sir Francis, 41
Choy, Rudy, 38, 47, 57, 170
Clipper, 126-8
close hauled ability, 81, 82, 97
Colas, Alain, 43, 50, 60, 79, 140, 143, 148, 168, 174, 175, 178, 180
cold moulded wood construction, 71-4
collision, damage by, 48, 49, 160
Comminges, Comte de, 26
construction, 51, 70-6
construction weak spots, 75, 76
Cooke, Brian, 137-42, 157, 158
Copula, 37
Corinthian Yacht Club, 40
Corkill, Tom, 126-8
Courage Breweries, 134
crossbeams, 62-5, 73

Crossbow, 52, 53
Crystal Trophy Race, 41, 45, 53, 106, 131
Cunningham brothers, 37, 38
cutter rig, advantages, 92, 93

De Bisschop, Eric, 31
deck space, 50
De Germes, Captain, 27
De Kat, Joan, 44
design, 56-70
Dicey, Captain, 27
dismasting, 157, 158
Dodd, Edward, 17
Dominion, 30
Double Bottom, 26
double canoe, 18-20, 24
double outrigger, 23, 24
draft, 50, 51, 162, 165, 171, 176
drying out, 50, 115, 116

Ellison, Peter, 148
engine, manoeuvring under, 114, 115
Experiment, The, 24-7
exposure, dangers of, 130, 136, 137, 150

Farrant, General Ralph, C.B., 53, 66, 68, 94, 182, 183
Fearon, 30
Filloux, Jean, 37
flares, stowing of, 130, 137, 140, 150, 152
flush decks, 75
foam sandwich construction, 70-3, 170
Folatre, 39, 41
Follet, Tom, 43, 170, 177
Forbes, Colin, 41

Freedom, 38
Froude number (IOMR), 182
Fun, 38

Gancia Girl, 170
Golden Cockerel, 43, 44, 131–7, 170, 171, 174, 176, 180
Great Britain III, 53
Gulf Streamer, 53, 81, 82, 115, 141, 153, 161
gybing, 79, 80

Harris, R. B., 31, 38
Hartman, Emile, 133
Haslar, Colonel 'Blondie', 41
hatches, 76
headsails, 69, 79, 92, 93
Heath, The Rt. Hon. Edward, 164
heaving to, 92, 162, 166, 169–76
heavy weather indications, 180, 181
Hepplewhite automatic sheet release gear, 140, 143, 170
Herreshoff, L. Francis, 40
Herreshoff, Nathaniel, 27, 29, 30, 31, 40
Hirondelle class, 77
Hooks, 38
Howell, Bill, 43, 131–7, 140, 170, 171, 174, 176, 180
hull forms, 57–62

Imi Loa, 144
instruments, 82, 103, 104
insulation, 72–74
International Multihull Boatracing Association, 40
International Offshore Multihull Rule (IOMR), 45, 182, 183
Invention I and II, 24–6
Iroquois class, 129
Isbjorn, 168

Jensen, Eric, 139
jibs, 92, 93
Jumar, use of, 117–20
jury rigs, 157–8

Kaimiloa, 31, 32
Keig, Nick, 129, 130, 136
Kelsall, Derek, 39
Knox-Johnston, Robin C.B.E., 44
knuckle, 59
Koala III, 44
Kumulai, Alfred, 33

Lady of Fleet, 172
leeboards, 84
lee shore, 84, 116, 166, 177
leeway, 81, 82, 105, 106, 155, 156, 162, 163
Lewis, David, 47, 48, 167, 171, 172
lifejackets, stowing of, 137, 142, 150, 152
liferaft, self inflating, 130, 136, 137, 140, 148, 150, 152
lift, 59–62, 182
lightning, damage by, 161
look out, importance of, 85
Louis XIV, 26

MacAlpine-Downie, Rod, 38, 62, 146
Mackenzie, John, 27
MacKinnan, P.V., 40
Macouillard, Louis, 54
mainsail, 93, 94, 98, 99
man overboard, 152–6
Manu Kai, 33, 34, 36
Manureva, 43, 50, 53, 60, 63, 74, 140, 143, 148, 168, 174–6, 178
Marsh, Rodney, 45
mast climbing, 116 20
masthead buoyancy, 140–2
masts, general, 70
Micronesian proa, 21, 22
Miller, Patrick, 27
Minnetaree, 53
Minter-Kemp, Martin, 170
Mirrorcat, 62, 131, 133
Misty Miller, 41
mizzen, 89, 92, 95, 170, 171, 176
mooring, leaving, 80
mooring, picking up, 114
Morning Cloud, 164
Morwood, Dr. John, 40
motion, 84, 181
moulded glass fibre construction, 70, 72, 74
Mudie, Colin, 47
multihull advantages and disadvantages, 49–52

navigation, 85
Newick, Richard C., 40, 56, 68
Newport Bermuda Race, 45
New York Yacht Club, 27, 29
Nicol, Hedley, 39, 126

O'Brien, Bill, 38

Observer Round Britain Race, 41, 53, 81, 100–3, 130, 137, 138, 146, 153, 157, 184–9, 192–5
Observer Singlehanded Trans-Atlantic Race (OSTAR), 39–45, 48, 54, 101, 117, 168, 170–2, 177, 184, 185, 190, 191, 196, 197
Olympic games, 45
outriggers, design of, 60–2, 175, 176

Paris, Admiral, 20
Patty Cat II, 183
Pelican, 131, 133
Pen Duick IV, 42, 63, 74, 168
Pepys, Samuel, 24
Pesty, Gerard, 54
Petty, Sir William, 24–6, 40
pilotage, 85
pitching, 46, 84
pitchpoling, 148, 162, 163, 176
Piver, Arthur, 37, 39
Polynesian Seafaring, 17
pooping, 162, 163, 176
preparation, 84, 85
Priestly, Mike, 133, 136
Privateer, 39
proa, Atlantic type, 43, 52
proa, flying or Pacific type, 18, 20–3, 52, 53
Prout, Roland and Francis, 35, 38, 47, 133

Quailo III, 81
quick release cleats, 144

Racing and Cruising Trimarans, 31
Ranger class, 47
reaching, 98
Read, Martin, 153–6
reefing, 98, 99
Rehu Moana, 41, 47, 48, 167, 171, 172
Reynolds number (IOMR), 182
rig, 85–93
rigging, 67–70
Robertson, Don, 38, 47, 53
Rongo, 46
Round the Island Race, 53
Royal Ocean Racing Club, 41
Royal Yachting Association, 40, 45
rudders, 65–7, 75, 80, 159, 177
running before heavy weather, 173, 174, 176–81
running under headsails, 98, 99

Sadrin, André, 36
safety, catamaran compared with
    trimaran, 54
safety harnesses, 130, 131, 133, 134,
    154
sailing differences, multihull com-
    pared to monohull, 78–85
sailing stern first, 80
sail shapes, 92–7
sail trimming, 97–9
Saint Michael the Archangel, 26
Sayle, Murray, 172
Schwartzenburg, Von, 38
sea anchor, use of, 166–8, 177, 181
Seabird, 53
seamanship definitions, 77
Sea Trail, 153
self steering, 122–4
Shearwater, 35
sheer, importance of, 60, 61
Simonds, David, 134
Simonds, Raymond, 133, 134, 136
single outrigger, 18, 20–3
skegs, 65
Smeetons, 148
Snow Goose, 38, 47, 53, 131, 133
Snowgoose class, 47, 65
Solaris class, 65
Southby-Tailyour, Ewen, 153
spars, 70
speed, 49, 53, 85, 100–3, 108, 160,
    162, 164, 165, 181
spinnaker poles, 70, 96, 97
spinnakers, 96, 97, 145, 146
spreaders, 68
stability, 50
stalling, dangers of, 146–8

Startled Fawn, 42
staysail, 93
Stern, Doctor Vic, 45, 182, 183
Stiletto, 133
Stokes, Anson, 30
storm jib, 93, 176, 181
structural damage, 159–61, 164
structure, 62–7
Suhaili, 44
Sunday Times, 44
surfing, 83, 159
surfing sideways in heavy weather,
    171–4
survival beacon, stowing of, 140,
    150, 152
Sydney Hobart Race, 45
symmetrical hulls, 57, 58, 59

Tabarly, Eric, 41–3
tacking, 79, 84
tacking a flying proa, 22, 23
tacking downwind, 101, 103
Tahitian war canoe, 18
Tahiti Bill, 44
Tangaroa, 46
Tarantella, 27
Tasman, Abel, 17
Tatibouet, Joseph, 31
Tchetchet, Victor, 31, 37, 40
Tetley, Nigel, 44, 175
Three Cheers, 40, 53, 60, 64, 80, 96,
    100–3, 106, 141, 148, 153–6, 164,
    165, 172–4, 177
Three Legs of Man, 53, 106, 130
tide, tactical use of, 106, 107
Tom Tom, 129, 130
Tongiaki, 19–21, 24

Toria, 39, 41, 42, 53
Tornado class, 45, 77, 94
Trans-Pacific Race, 45
Trifle, 53, 66, 68, 94, 131, 133
Trimar 52 class, 54
Triple Arrow, 53, 137–42, 151,
    157, 158
turning circles, 82
Tzu Hang, 148

ugliness, 51, 52
under deck handholds, 130, 135–7
unsinkability, 49, 162, 165

Vendredi Treize, 43
Victress, 44, 175, 176

warps, trailing in heavy weather,
    177, 178, 181
wave damage, 160, 164
wave interaction, 57
Webber, J., 19
weight, 56, 83, 84, 126, 128, 142,
    175, 181
Weld, Philip, 115, 141, 161
Wharram, James, 46, 47, 62
Whitbread Round the World Race
    1973, 43, 152
windage, 64, 75, 81, 142
windows, 75

Yachting Monthly, 138
Yaksha, 44, 63
Young, 38
Yvonne, 37